# Dear Joan

Love Letters from the Second World War

Tony Ross and Joan Charles

IMPERIAL WAR
MUSEUM

MAINSTREAM
PUBLISHING

EDINBURGH AND LONDON

First published in Great Britain in 2010 by
MAINSTREAM PUBLISHING COMPANY
(EDINBURGH) LTD
7 Albany Street
Edinburgh EH1 3UG

ISBN 9781845966249

This book is a work of non-fiction based on the life, experiences
and recollections of the author. In some cases, names of people have been
changed to protect the privacy of others. The author has stated to the
publishers that, except in such minor respects not affecting the substantial
accuracy of the work, the contents of this book are true

A catalogue record for this book is available
from the British Library

Typeset in Caslon and Requiem

Printed in Great Britain by
Clays Ltd, St Ives plc

1 3 5 7 9 10 8 6 4 2

# ❋ DEAR JOAN ❋

To Anne and Patrick,
with thanks for all their love and kindness.
And
to Christopher,
for all the help he has so willingly given me over many years.

❋

Fifty per cent of the author's royalties go to the charity
Leonard Cheshire Disability.

# ❊ CONTENTS ❊

# Introduction

Joan and I first met in August 1943. We were both 22 years old.

I was in the RAF, flying with Coastal Command from Squires Gate airfield in Blackpool. Joan was a civil servant who had been evacuated from London with her Ministry and lived with her family in nearby St Annes.

One evening, walking with a Czech pilot to our mess in St Annes, we passed two girls going in the same direction. The Czech, who was never shy, called out a casual greeting, and we walked along together.

Joan's parents welcomed members of the forces, and she invited us into her home for coffee.

We soon found we had many interests in common and began to go to the ballet, theatre, concerts and the cinema, always finishing back at her home for coffee. It soon became a warm friendship, but I was far too shy to kiss her!

So began a love affair that was to last 63 years.

A few weeks later I was posted away to Crosby-on-Eden in Cumbria to convert to Beaufighters for anti-shipping operations in the Mediterranean.

In November I managed to get 48 hours' leave and spent it all with Joan. In the taxi taking her home from the theatre on the last day I plucked up courage to kiss her for the first time. I had hoped to spend more time with her, but losses in the Mediterranean were heavy and I was posted to North Africa without any more leave.

We would not meet again for nearly three years.

A few hours before I took off from England, I wrote to Joan saying I loved her. Her reply took five weeks to reach me!

As soon as I arrived in North Africa, I began to write letters to Joan and numbered them so that we would know if any were lost. We exchanged 675 letters in nearly 3 years. There was, of course, no telephone or e-mail contact, and letters often took weeks to arrive.

The exchanges began warmly but were at first restricted to news of what we had been doing.

Although she was not strong, Joan was working a 48-hour week as a permanent civil servant. She was a volunteer Fire Guard Section Leader, patrolling the streets at night. At the weekend she chose to work in the land-army, digging potatoes by hand in deep mud and hand-weeding mangolds. She volunteered to help in a Red Cross canteen, sometimes on the night shift from 1 a.m. to 7 a.m.

Over the months we increasingly relaxed and wrote of more serious things.

Eventually Joan told me everything: when she was happy, when she was sad, when she was ill, when she was well. She wrote about her family and friends, her work, her problems with officious supervisors. She described her war work. We discussed the political situation in Europe, the war and every sort of social problem, even divorce! We wrote about the children we might have and how we would bring them up.

Above all, Joan wrote about her beliefs, her hopes and ambitions, her dreams and fears for the future, her worries, what she thought were her shortcomings and the things she loved: family and friends, countryside, sea, flowers, music, the arts. She was a very good descriptive writer, and her letters painted a vivid picture of life in England and of the changing seasons in the countryside we both loved.

Had we been together we might have been too shy to reveal our innermost thoughts. Thousands of miles apart we became closer and closer until there were no secrets between us. Whenever one of us was worried or depressed, the other was quick to offer sympathy and understanding. We were, of course, well aware that we might never see each other again.

Despite the stresses, dangers, fears and discomfort of war it was, strangely, a very happy time for me, looking forward to letters from Joan and feeling closer and closer to her as I read them again and again.

Her letters were the one thing that kept me in touch with reality in the strained and artificial world in which I then lived.

For my part, I wrote of the problems and unexpected beauty of life in the desert and of my dreams for our future. I could, of course, only tell her of operational activities if news had been officially released.

I visited many countries and cities in the Middle East and wrote graphic accounts of daily life in each of them. As I assumed more and more responsibilities, I shared all my experiences with Joan.

After hostilities had ceased, there was considerable anger over the pace of demobilisation and there were mutinies at several RAF stations in the Middle and Far East. Joan was very sympathetic to the men, who only wanted to go home, but, as I was at that time responsible for personnel and discipline throughout Iraq and Persia Command, I took a very different view.

Paradoxically, I myself was then held long beyond my official date for release, much to Joan's indignation. On this occasion I entirely agreed with her!

And so our long correspondence came to a happy end. We were married three weeks after my return. For both of us there was never anyone else.

Joan died on her birthday in 2006, soon after our Diamond Wedding anniversary.

Writing this, some 65 years after we first met, re-reading her letters brings back the same happiness, though this time mingled with great sadness and regret that I left unfulfilled many of the promises I made to her.

I hope these extracts from our letters will be a fitting memorial to her.

# I

# PARTING IS SUCH SWEET SORROW

### 12 SEPTEMBER 1943

Dear Joan,

This letter will surprise you, as by now you will have given up all hope of ever hearing from me again!

It would be terrible to leave without making coffee for you once more!!

I will write again as soon as possible.

Very best wishes,

Tony

### 19 SEPTEMBER 1943

Dear Tony,

I was pleased to hear from you.

Life in St Annes continues much as it ever was. One works, eats, sleeps and makes a weekly expedition to our super cinema.

This morning was beautifully sunny, and I walked and walked for the joy of it.

I do hope you can come down again before you go on operations, although they must urgently need every possible plane in Italy. The war does seem nearer a brighter conclusion than it did this month three years ago.

Won't it be wonderful when we can just think about lovely things again?

Joan

### 20 NOVEMBER 1943

Dear Joan,

I paid a flying visit to London and went to see Ivor Novello's *The Dancing Years*. It was lovely, but I kept wishing you were with me to enjoy it.

I hope you like the 'wings' I am sending by separate post.

My hopes of a long leave were shattered today by a telegram ordering me to report to Lyneham on Monday. Still, I am sure to get a few days before I finally leave the country and I shall certainly come and see you.

Tony

I had two days' leave and spent them with Joan at St Annes.

## 23 NOVEMBER 1943

Dear Tony,

Thank you for those two very happy days; I should have loved you to stay longer. I almost regretted not seeing you off on such a cheerless morning, but railway station goodbyes always seem so final to me. Let us never say goodbye on a station.

Some friends took me to a party in the evening. The Army and ATS officers at The Bedford were our hosts and hostesses. It was a lovely party; I wish you might have shared it.

The mess was very homely – oak-panelled walls, warm lights and big open fires. The ATS had added festivity with flowers and evergreen and holly. I ventured to suggest to one of our hosts that some fine woodcut etchings would be more fitting than the 'French' girls adorning the walls, but he disagreed with me on the grounds that it would not be the thing to invite young women to see their etchings. A suitable rebuke for being serious at a party! There was dancing and so much chatter and laughter.

There were two high spots in the evening. A young American found it impossible to resist jitterbugging, even on such a tiny, crowded floor. The General, very fat and generously red-tabbed, whether in hospitality or sheer delight no one could say, attempted to jitterbug too! Then the food took my breath away! I thought for an instant I had been whisked away back to 1939. It was a feast, from dainty sandwiches to chocolate layer cakes, beautifully iced and decorated. The secret lies with the ex-Café Royal cook of 'B' Mess.

There was an ARP practice at night. I wore stockings, socks and slacks, a shirt, two sweaters, a scarf and overcoat! Perhaps it was as well we only had to patrol – I could scarcely have moved fast! Friday

– the Ministry dance. We returned the Army's hospitality with tea and a stale bun!

Very best luck,

Joan

## 23 NOVEMBER 1943

Dear Joan,

I am very sorry that I could not see you before I left, but the RAF doesn't worry about personal feelings! We are just cogs in a machine.

Thank you very much indeed for the happy times we have had together.

Please try to send a photograph of yourself when you get my address.

Don't forget me altogether and remember I shall always be thinking of you.

Love,

Tony

## 25 NOVEMBER 1943

My dear Joan,

Just a note to let you know that I am still in England and this is the last chance I have of writing to you before I get to Africa.

I wish I could have told you in person, but, as I shall not have the opportunity, I must try to put it into writing.

Please don't be cross, but I love you very much – and thought I would like you to know in case anything happens.

I shall always be looking forward to the day when I shall see you again.

Love,

Tony

## 27 NOVEMBER 1943

Tony dear,

I have just received your letter from Plymouth. There seems a tiny chance you may be in England a few days more, and I should like you to have this letter before you go.

Of course I'm not cross, Tony. We have had wonderful times together, and I shall look forward to many more when you come home.

Goodbye for a little while.

Joan xx

# 2

# WAR AND MIRAGES IN THE DESERT

After a brief stay in Cairo, I was posted to 603 City of Edinburgh Squadron, based at Gambut in the Libyan desert. The entries in brackets are extracts from my flying logbook.

## 30 NOVEMBER 1943

My dear Tony,

I wonder and wonder where you are.

A little while ago, I was lazily watching the dreams in the fire and made one for us. I hope you like it.

It is early autumn 1944, one of the first cool days after an August heatwave, a breeze just rustling the treetops and the loveliness of birdsong in the stillness. And we two are alone in it, and so it all belongs to us – roaming (not climbing because the path winds effortlessly as Surrey hill paths do) to the summit of Leith Hill. It will be four o'clock, perhaps, when we reach the top, and we will rest, sitting on the soft turf until the sun goes down, and talk.

Then, in the dusk, we will run and skip and laugh at our foolishness, down into the village. We will find a darling 'tea shoppe', cosy with a big log fire, olde oak furniture, chintz curtains and gay tablecloths. There won't be many other customers, because it will be a weekday, this day of ours. Perhaps a serious hiker, bespectacled and wearing green corduroy shorts. Perhaps two old ladies gossiping over poached eggs on toast will glance at our light-heartedness disapprovingly and gossip about the shortness of my skirt. And a proud and indulgent papa who has left his stocks and shares to spend a day in the country with his wife and little daughter. And the little daughter is holding everyone's attention with her charming chatter.

What shall we have for tea? Home-made scones and country butter, fruit salad and cream (my favourite dish at any hour) and cream buns.

And two sleepy people will go home to supper Mother has ready for us. So we will leave us, curled up in the firelight, maybe talking a bit more, yawning and looking at the time and pretending not to notice and, at a guess, I should say, purring?

Now you make a day for us you would like best in all the world.

If you would like me to, I will try to write often, but there is so little news from this great metropolis, and maybe you aren't interested in daydreams? Tell me, please.

I would like to hear often. Remember your friends are less happy about your job than you are.

May there be many sunny days for you,

Joan xx

## HQ RAF MEDITERRANEAN AND MIDDLE EAST, 2 DECEMBER 1943

My dear Joan,

Our trip out was very interesting but uneventful.

We were out of touch with post offices, and I could not write to you. Please excuse the writing, but I am sitting in my tent and have only a hurricane lamp.

Please write soon as I am longing to hear from you.

Love,

Tony xx

## 7 DECEMBER 1943

My dear Joan,

Remembering how fond you were of your lost gold bracelet and knowing it would be very difficult to replace in England, I got one for you as a Christmas present. I do hope you like the design.

I miss you very much, Joan, but am grateful for those two happy days we spent before I left.

Living conditions are rather rough, but there is no real hardship. The chief nuisance is the number of mosquitoes.

There are so many things I want to say, but, when I try to write them down, it seems so difficult. If I could speak to you in person it would be so much easier.

With all my love,

Tony xx

## 10 DECEMBER 1943

My dear Tony,

This letter is to say thank you very much for my wings, which arrived yesterday. They are beautiful, and I shall be very proud to wear them.

You seem to have been away a long time already, Tony. I was disappointed that your leave was not longer.

When I've managed to summon a wee bit of energy (I am *so* impatient of feeling ill), I have been filling Christmas stockings, some for a nursery of little children who have lost parents in air raids and some for our Ministry party on Boxing Day.

I know it is useless to say 'Take care of yourself' to a flier, but I say it: 'Take care of yourself, Tony'.

A great and bright New Year for you.

Joan xx

## 12 DECEMBER 1943

My dear Joan,

I am now posted to 603 City of Edinburgh Squadron.

Living conditions are considerably worse, and we live in a continual cloud of sand. So far the sand has managed to penetrate all my kit, and I have long despaired of getting it out.

I have seen some really beautiful sunsets. Last night there was a rather dull grey sky, with roll after roll of brilliant orange and gold clouds towards the setting sun. As the sun sank, they gradually changed to a very soft shell-pink and then gradually faded in the darkness.

Don't worry about me, Joan. I am doing quite well and always looking forward to the day when I shall see you again.

With all my love,

Tony xx

*(16 DECEMBER 1943. OFFENSIVE SWEEP COS, LEROS.)*

## 18 DECEMBER 1943

My dear Tony,
One week to Christmas and, apart from the muddle of presents and wrappings everywhere, we don't feel very Christmassy. We have no puddings or cakes made yet because they go bad made with wartime flour, if they are kept. We have been lucky to get icing sugar so we can have a *real* Christmas cake.

The children's choir came to sing carols. They sang 'Silent Night' for me. I think that it is my favourite of all songs. I gave the children lumps of sugar, because we hadn't any sweets.

I do hope someone gives you a nice Christmas – tho' you sound to be miles from civilisation.

Your writing by the light of a hurricane lamp reminds me of air-raid shelter days – I used to sit up writing by candlelight, and Daddy always worried lest I fell asleep and caught fire!

I spent your coupons yesterday. I bought a hyacinth-blue silk dress to wear at the children's parties. It was very naughty of me, because I should have bought a woolly jacket – the days are freezing now.

Love,
Joan xxx

## 19 DECEMBER 1943

My dear Joan,
Did you have an enjoyable Christmas? I can imagine you sitting beside the fire – purring!!

With all my love,
Tony xxx

*(20 DECEMBER 1943. FIGHTER COVER – LARGE CONVOY – 36 VESSELS.)*

## 24 DECEMBER 1943

My dear Tony,
The dawn was so lovely this morning, I thought I must tell you about it. There were grey clouds, housetops and wheeling gulls silhouetted against a creamy gold sunrise, and high up a new moon and the morning star hung in a blue sky. It seemed like a picture of Bethlehem.

I have been running up and down ladders, fastening holly and mistletoe and cotton-wool 'snowflakes'. The tree is hung with silver balls, fairy lights and gaily packed gifts, and the puddings and cakes are made. I wish there might be as bright a Christmas for all the peoples of Europe.

My love,

Joan xxx

(24 DECEMBER 1943. OFFENSIVE SWEEP. LIGHT FLAK OVER MONEMVASIA HARBOUR.)

(30 DECEMBER 1943. OFFENSIVE SWEEP. HEAVY FLAK RHODES HARBOUR. LIGHT FLAK SYMI.)

## 31 DECEMBER 1943

My dear Tony,

I was so pleased and excited to get your first real letter from 'over there'.

These mornings I walk towards the wonder of the sunrise, and the day seems good.

There has been quite a lot of excitement, with three weddings recently and another next week. The big affair was an American one at St Thomas. We have had a letter from the bride recommending American husbands, but she seemed rather lost in a country home in a tiny village in Oxfordshire with only a pump from which to draw water!

It already seems a long while since you made coffee for us, Tony. We had a lot of fun, didn't we?

The old year is nearly done – may all its hopes and promises be fulfilled for everyone.

I wonder how you will be seeing in the New Year – surely among Scots it will be gaily.

Now, Big Ben: one, two, three, four, five, six, seven, eight, nine, ten, eleven, twelve.

A Happy and a Wonderful New Year to you.

My love,

Joan xxx

## 2 JANUARY 1944

My dear Joan,

I feel happier today than I have felt since I left St Annes and
saw you last. This afternoon I received an air letter from you
– the first letter I have had since leaving England five weeks
ago!!! Your letter, Joan, was posted on the 20th and only took 13
days to get here.

I stopped writing for a few minutes to listen to the wireless. I am
writing this in my tent but heard someone singing Weber's 'Invitation
to the Waltz' and went outside to hear it more clearly. Desert life
certainly helps you to appreciate lovely things far more. Perhaps that
is why I think about you so much now, Joan. You are seldom long
away from my thoughts.

I am so pleased to hear that you have used my coupons on a lovely
dress – I know how much you like beautiful things. At the moment
I am trying to picture you in it, but I love you, and will always love
you, no matter what you wear, for yourself alone.

You would have enjoyed it here yesterday, Joan. There was a lovely
cool breeze to temper the warmth, and the inevitable sandstorm
had not materialised as we had had a heavy rainstorm in the night.
It reminded me of those walks along the shore with the wind
ruffling your hair and teasing you, although I liked you even more
like that because it always made you laugh and you seemed so
carefree and happy.

The nights, too, are wonderful. It gets very cold, but it is so clear
the sky seems like velvet and the stars are so bright.

We are not too badly off, Joan. I feel far more sorry for the ground
crews. They are here for much longer periods of time and have very
little to relieve their monotony. We at least always have plenty of
excitement and adventure.

We had quite an enjoyable Christmas. We managed to get a few
luxuries flown down, and it made a wonderful difference. Someone
had bagpipes and, as became a Scottish squadron, we had the
Christmas pudding piped in. The effect was rather spoilt as the

tent was so low that the pipes kept catching in the canvas, but no one minded very much.

I hope to be back in England next Christmas – able to spend it with you. I think it very possible; the war seems to be going so well.

With all my love, dearest,

Tony xxxx

## 10 JANUARY 1944

My dear Tony,

Your second airgraph arrived on Friday. So far I have received a cable, two airgraphs and one air letter. It is great to know that more are already on the way. You are surely becoming a model correspondent!

Thank you, thank you for the sweet bracelet, Tony. It arrived this morning as I was leaving for the office. Of course, I stopped to unpack it. Such excitement; it was Christmas morning over again!

I look forward always to our next meeting.

With my love,

Joan xxxx

## 12 JANUARY 1944

Dear Tony,

The girls around me (it is teatime at the office) are discussing the possibility of our getting the ration of lemons which is promised. How we cling to custom in a world of strife!

I will write again very soon. This is just to say thank you for all your thoughts for me.

My love,

Joan xxxx

## 13 JANUARY 1944

My dear Joan,

Your description of that lovely dawn made me long to be back with you in England, wandering along the shore, happy in the enjoyment of the beauties of life and not living merely for the war. Still, these things will be even more precious to us now that we have had to fight to retain them, and we shall appreciate being together more after the unhappiness of parting.

Your last letter only took a fortnight to arrive, Joan, and it makes you seem very near to me. It is the second I have received so far, and I carry both of them on me always, even on operations – although I am really not supposed to.

When I close my eyes I can see you walking along the shore, well wrapped up with your hood and muff – with the wind ruffling a stray curl – and the grey sea with the waves breaking in clouds of white spray and the stormy sky we used to watch. I think England is so great because of the hold she keeps over you, even when you are far away, and, although other lands may seem pleasant for a time, England always has first place in your heart.

I suppose I ought to get some sleep as I am flying early tomorrow. Do you remember how I kept you up when you had to go to work in the morning?

Still, I can think of you even when I am asleep – it is wonderful how comforting it is to have someone you can hold in your mind out here, so far from everyday life.

Good night, Joan dear, and God keep you safe.

With all my love,

Tony xxxxx

*(14 January 1944. Offensive sweep Central Aegean. Small fire on aircraft extinguished.)*

## 15 January 1944

My dear Tony,

I am so glad my letters are at last reaching you.

My friends seem all at once to have written for news of me. They seem to be living most excitingly in London these days. There is news of weddings, broken romances and many a 'foreign affair' jumbled up in every letter I receive. There must be something in the London air!

Here the most thrilling thing was the sunset last night. I strolled home along the front fully to admire its loveliness. I stopped a while down by the pierhead, and the wind blew refreshingly through my hair as I watched the sun go down and listened to the mysterious roar of the faraway sea.

It was so good to be in the fresh air after the long, stuffy office day that I lingered, humming to myself in the quietness until it was quite dark.

We must go together to the ballet on your next leave, Tony. Your next leave – that sounds lovely, doesn't it? Please spend a lot of it with me.

It is nice to make plans, isn't it? It seems so much *nearer*.

My blessings and my love,

Joan xxxxx

*(16 JANUARY 1944. STRIKE ON KHIOS HARBOUR. WAREHOUSES AND SHIPPING DAMAGED. ONE BEAUFIGHTER SHOT DOWN.)*

## 19 JANUARY 1944

Dearest Joan,

603 has always been a fighter squadron and played a big part in the Battle of Britain. I cannot tell you much of its activities since it came overseas, but it has been and still is very successful.

It was very sweet of you to write to me as the old year ended and the new one began. I thought of you too, Joan, and hoped with all my heart that the coming year would bring us together again.

Please don't worry about not having exciting things to write to me. I love your letters just as they are – telling me what you are doing and about the sunrises and little details of life in England. We are rather lonely out here, and these small things seem to bring you so much nearer.

Since I have been out here I have completely revised all my opinions about a well-behaved desert. For weeks it was dry, and we had continual sandstorms, and we were all longing for some rain. The Fates were evidently in an obliging mood, for we got our rain – days of it – and now we are living in a gigantic sea of mud! Fortunately, we can escape both dust and rain by flying.

Sometimes, when we fly early in the morning very low over the desert, we disturb flocks of birds – gulls, wild geese, plovers and herons. It seems like a Peter Scott scene come to life.

All the birds are not so stately, Joan. There are a lot of amusing wagtails. I watched one the other day. It had been raining heavily, and there were large pools of water. I think these were rather a novelty to him, for he was cautiously edging up to them and then fluttering away again. Eventually, however, he decided to go really close and was soon splashing away and chuckling excitedly to himself. I stood there for a long time before he finally flew away.

Peace will seem very unreal for a while, but we shall certainly appreciate it after so long a war. There will be a lot to do, though, to rebuild our England – but we must make certain that in future people will be able to enjoy to the full the beauty and peacefulness of the countryside without fear of any danger of aggression. If we can do this, the sacrifice will be worthwhile.

Take good care of yourself, Joan dear. We shall have a lot of celebrating to do when I get back, and I want to see you well and happy – I do miss your contented purr.

I heard the *Wizard of Oz* song on the radio the other day, and it made me think of those evening strolls when we laughed from sheer happiness and enjoyment of life.

With all my love,

Tony xxxxx

## 21 JANUARY 1944

Dear Joan,

Yesterday was another eventful day for me. I received your airgraph photograph and Christmas airgraph.

The photograph is lovely, Joan, and I was delighted to get it. I am having a frame fitted in my aircraft so that I can see it when I am flying.

With all my love,

Tony xxxxx

## 23 JANUARY 1944

Tony dear,

It is evening now. The curtains are drawn against the rainy world outside, and I am curled in a chair close to the glowing fire. There is dreamy music on the radio. I wish you were here – that we might talk and laugh together again.

There is nothing I write especially to say, only to talk to you, Tony, and this is the only way.

Thank you, dear, for saying you love everything of me and not

*'I love her for her smile – her look – her way*
*Of speaking gently, – for a trick of thought*
*That falls in well with mine, and certes brought*
*A sense of pleasant ease on such a day' –*
*For these things in themselves, Beloved, may*
*Be changed or change for thee, – and love, so wrought*
*May be unwrought so.*

*But love me for love's sake, that evermore*
*Thou mayst love on, through love's eternity.*

I wonder where you are just this moment. I wonder if you fly at night. I have so many 'wonders', don't I? And the biggest wonder of all: when will you be home again?

One of the girls in my office is expecting her boyfriend home next month after 18 months' parting. It isn't to be the great day they once planned, because their letters have spoilt everything. Letters are so much more difficult to understand than people.

Your letters are very like you, Tony. They could not be anybody else's! But I wonder if my letters sound like me because often I cannot write as I would wish. I suppose if we could all do that we should all be great authors!

Don't let us ever grieve over some mischosen phrase, imagining we ourselves have changed.

Good night, Tony.

My love,

Joan xxxxx

(24 JANUARY 1944. OFFENSIVE SWEEP. SUPPLY VESSEL DESTROYED. FIRST OPERATIONAL USE OF ROCKETS USING ASV (AIR-TO-SURFACE VESSEL).)

## 26 JANUARY 1944

Dearest Joan,

I don't know what I should have done if I had not met you before I came out here. Being in the desert without someone dear at home to write to would make life almost unbearable.

On Monday morning I went for a stroll across the desert, as

it seemed quite pleasant after the rain. Suddenly, I came across a little dried-up watercourse leading down to the sea. It was fairly sheltered from the wind, and the rain had worked miracles. The whole valley was carpeted with fresh green grass, and at the bottom were masses of flowers. There were all shades – from exotic purple blossoms to little yellow and white daisies. It seemed like a corner of England. It was the more welcome as it was so unexpected after the everlasting waste of sand and rock.

Your photograph has not arrived yet, but the airgraph copy is doing excellent work. I arrange it so that I can see it just before I go to sleep at night and as soon as I awake in the morning. It also accompanies me whenever I fly. It is certainly travelling about a lot!

The other day we were flying far out to sea very low, and we disturbed an oyster-catcher who was balancing on a wave. He was so startled that he fell off and vanished, spluttering. I expect he was most indignant!

Thank you again, Joan, for your letters. Do take care of yourself and don't work too hard.

With all my love,

Tony xxxxx

*(27 JANUARY 1944. OFFENSIVE SWEEP. THREE JU 52S WITH ESCORT OF FOUR ARADO FIGHTERS DESTROYED. ONE BEAUFIGHTER SHOT DOWN.)*

*(28 JANUARY 1944. AIR-SEA RESCUE SEARCH FOR BEAUFIGHTER. UNSUCCESSFUL.)*

## 29 JANUARY 1944

My dear Joan,

Leave is drawing nearer and nearer. In a few days' time I shall be in Cairo – about to commence my grand shopping expedition!

I was lucky enough to 'break my duck' the other day. I certainly hope I can keep up the good work.

All my love,

Tony xxxxx

## 29 JANUARY 1944

Tony dear,

I grow so impatient now for the war to be done. After the wave of optimism about Christmas-time, American opinion that the Japanese war may be an even more bitter struggle than the German war makes me realise it may yet be a long, long while. Forgive me. I have been thinking so much of the atrocities that are being committed. I have seen films of Russian women going mad in their grief, Chinese children starving and our own fliers being murdered by the Japanese this week.

Enough of this war talk.

Do not worry, dear, that I fret too much. I am mostly happy and gay and confident. I only wish everyone might have so much to be happy about.

Forgive me for writing of sad things to you.

When I returned from the cinema last evening, the American lad who spent Christmas with us was here. He has the most amusing present from his girlfriend: a book of coupons exchangeable for kisses! These are printed in 'official' language and purchasable at a 'ten-cent' store!

My love,

Joan xxxxx

## 30 JANUARY 1944

My dear Tony,

There are a thousand and one miracles of mending and sewing to be wrought that I never dreamed of before coupons came to town. I never had much money to waste, because Daddy brought me up on the theory that everyone should be financially independent, but I confess I did little mending and would have been horrified at the thought of going out in mended stockings, because I had so many pretty clothes before the war.

I listen now to beautiful prose on the radio: *The Postscript* by Ian Findlay.

Good night, dear one, and bless you always.

My love,

Joan xxxxxxx (coupon free)

*(30 January 1944. Strike on shipping Melos. Eliminating flak for torpedo Beaufighters. One Beaufighter ditched, three crash-landed.)*

## 3 February 1944

Dearest Joan

Yesterday I started my leave. I came down to Cairo by air, for which I was very grateful, as the journey across the desert by road is long and very uncomfortable.

I went to Shepheard's Hotel, which was crowded. Another sorrow: there is practically no hot water, and the one thing I was looking forward to was a hot bath. Still, I shall only be in Cairo until Sunday and will be going on to Alexandria.

In the afternoon I went to a club called 'Music For All'. It is a very pleasant place where you can have tea and cakes and listen to some good music. A quartet plays every afternoon, and in the evening they have gramophone recitals.

I had dinner in a little French restaurant called 'Au Petit Coin de France'. It is a quiet place, and the food is very good.

Cairo is a crowded city and very dirty. The amusements it provides are for those who like life at high pressure – there are plenty of cabarets and nightclubs. The Arabs are always pushing things in your face, trying to persuade you to buy them, and there are more pickpockets than, I should think, in any other city in the world. Yesterday I had my fountain pen stolen but fortunately saw it in the thief's hand and managed to catch him.

Strange though it may seem, I prefer the desert, at least at the moment when the rain is fairly frequent and we are free from dust storms. The air seems so much fresher out there than in these cities.

We lived up to our fighter reputation the other day and had some fine hunting. I, myself, was quite successful, and I am feeling very pleased about it.

I went along to Weinberg's – *the* photographer in Cairo – and actually had my photograph taken!!!

I had tea at 'Music For All', but I'm afraid that I did not listen to the music. I began by wishing that you were with me, and then began thinking of you and wondering what you were doing and making plans for us in the future and realised with a start that two hours had gone by! But they were two very pleasant hours, Joan.

I think of you more and more each day, dear. You have become the one really important thing in my life, and everything I plan or do is influenced by my wondering how you would like it or what you would think about it. Above all I want to make you happy, and it is wonderful to have such a lovely objective always to strive for.

With all my love, darling,
Tony xxxxxxx

## 5 FEBRUARY 1944

Tony dear,

I am glad to hear you found a particular interest of yours in the desert; the birds flying up into the sunset sounds so beautiful.

So at last I have achieved my ambition to fly with Fighter Command – in my image at least!

I always wear your wings, Tony, so now feel almost like a real pilot!

There was a Fire Guard lecture about explosive incendiaries and butterfly bombs, but the lecturer couldn't tell us how to tackle them!

I went to the Ministry dance for a little while on Thursday, and then decided to walk home alone – it was such a beautiful moonlit night. It reminded me very much of your last leave in England, Tony. Remember how I wanted to ride on and on in the taxi coming home? It was such a lovely time I wanted to hold it for always. But, of course, we will have wonderful times again when you come home. I dream of it, do you?

I awoke on Thursday night in a *hailstorm*! The wind was blowing the rain and hail through my bedroom window. Today has been wonderful, though, from a glorious sunrise through a frosty sunny day. For the first time for a long while, I wore a pretty hat and light shoes. The florists are bright with spring flowers: tulips, jonquils, snowdrops and sweet violets. How lovely it will be to see them blooming in our garden again!

My love, dear,

Joan xxxxxxx

## 7 FEBRUARY 1944

My dear Tony,

Kathleen and I may spend our holidays together in Derbyshire. Of course, if the Second Front begins before June, we shall be unable to travel, but how gladly we will forgo holidays to see more clearly the end of the war.

How I dream of peace in our land and in all the world: a time when there may be no hunger or evil or strife among men. It seems a frighteningly enormous task, and yet we must believe in it undaunted and with all our hearts. I wonder what *our* part will be, Tony? Probably to live quietly at home as well as we can, trying to make this England a happy and worthwhile example to the troubled countries of Europe. Do you ever think what your destiny is? Mine, I believe, is not to be a great one. I haven't the courage and self-sacrifice to devote my life, as many people will do, to the future of some foreign land. I think it the most wonderful thing to do to give one's heart to serving people in desperate need of help, so much more wonderful even than other great things like science and exploring.

My thoughts are straying, I am afraid. But I think so much about all this, as we all do. Sometimes I envy a little the ones who have been called to a clear duty for the future of the world. You will have done so much, and I, so little. I believe you will understand my thoughts and wonderings.

It is time I shut my sleepy eyes. Dad has brought me some coffee with an 'isn't-it-about-time-you-went-to-bed' look!

I have volunteered to help with a new Red Cross canteen at Lytham. It is to be for Americans – there are few of our men stationed here now – and called 'The Donut Dugout'! I certainly should be qualified to make coffee!!

God bless you, dear.

My love,

Joan xxxxxx

## 12 FEBRUARY 1944

Dearest Joan

At the moment I am on detachment at a fairly well-established aerodrome. The quarters are solid buildings, and the food is excellent.

There are bathrooms, and we have Italian batmen. It certainly is a change from the desert.

When I left there was a sandstorm, and it was impossible to see more than about five yards. Breathing was very difficult, and we gave up trying to eat – the food was coated with sand as soon as it was uncovered. We drove to a neighbouring aerodrome about 60 miles away for dinner and drove back that night. There was a full moon, and the desert seemed so beautiful. The effect of the deep shadows and contrasting silver moonlight on the sand was wonderful.

In your letter you say that you just chatter as your thoughts flit. I think that is why I love your letters so much – it makes you seem so much nearer than a more orderly letter. Please just continue writing as you do, Joan darling.

With all my love,

Tony xxxxxx

## 12 FEBRUARY 1944

Tony dear,

There were two lovely days this week. The sun was quite warm on Thursday afternoon, and I walked back to work along the front. As I passed the pierhead, a lovely sheepdog rushed up to me, barking, and led me down on to the sands. The tide was up, and the sea and sky were blue. I wanted to stay walking along the shore, throwing stones for the old doggie forever.

Instead I arrived at the office breathless, with sandy shoes and untidy hair. I shall never be glamorous!

I am sending some more magazines, which I have begged from the stationer's. Won't it be wonderful when the shopkeeper's reign ends and one has no longer to prefix every request with 'Could you possibly let me have . . . ?' I hoped to get *Country Life*, but so far it is hopeless. Today I found a new magazine: *Transatlantic*. If you find this at all interesting, I can get it every month.

We have another job now: knitting vests to go to Europe for the children of the liberated countries. And I have a distressing number of letters which may not be left unanswered. How great it will be when we are all on the telephone again!

May it be soon, my dear.

My love,

Joan xxxxxx

## 16 February 1944

Tony dear,

Thank you for your wonderful long letter. It was very interesting and a lovely surprise. You do succeed, Tony, in making me very happy.

I hope that you found Alexandria a pleasanter and more restful place to spend the remainder of your leave. It seems a terrible pity the wonderful places of the earth could not have been preserved in their true beauty. Often I have thought that, if ever I travel abroad, I should like to explore my own ways, to get to know the real people and their lands and not to see only the tourist's 'show places'.

I am very proud of your achievements. How many adventures you will have to relate when you come home!

'Coming home' is a lovely sound. We *will* plan your next leave. What plans did you make during that afternoon in the music club? Days in the country and evenings at the theatre sound great to me. Perhaps we could stay part of the time with friends in London? And to mark the occasion we'll go out to dine . . . But you can decide: I think you have the nicest of ideas, and it *is* rather nice to be looked after – these independent days have their disadvantages!

I have been to 'Donut Dugout' to learn the mysteries of 'donut' making and to have a preview of the premises. It is a very smart canteen, decorated in eggshell blue with light oak furniture and with fine writing and games rooms. How thoroughly the Americans look after their men – there is even a needlework outfit in the information desk for sewing on stripes and loose buttons! The American Red Cross woman in charge is very gay and charming.

I am home now, Tony, and the fire is too cosy to leave, so I will go right on writing another air letter. Until we meet again on the next page, then,

My love, dear Tony.

Hello again!

I wonder what you are doing this moment? Perhaps you will be sitting in your tent dreaming or planning or maybe writing to me! Thank you for writing often, Tony. I love to get your letters. The long one from Cairo was a particularly nice surprise.

I am afraid you will get tired of my letters if you read them so often, Tony. I still cannot help wishing I had more to write about. Perhaps when you tell me those plans you have been making I will have many observations to make!

My love and thoughts,

Joan xxxxxx

## 17 FEBRUARY 1944

Dearest Joan,

I started wondering why life seemed empty these last few days and realised that it was because, since I have been away on detachment, I have not had any letters from you to look forward to.

I love to think of you with your hood pulled tight, snuggling in your muff and laughing at the wind. Even out here it makes me feel some of the sheer happiness I always felt when I was with you. I think that is one of the most wonderful things about being in love: that, even under the conditions out here and with the distance between us, the mere thought of you makes me so happy, and everything seems worthwhile if it is bringing us nearer.

Goodbye for the moment, dearest.

With all my love,

Tony xxxxx

## 21 FEBRUARY 1944

Dearest Joan,

You would have been very amused could you have seen me this morning.

While we have been away our tent got into a very sorry state – we found over six inches of sand over everything when we returned. So, this morning, I shifted all our belongings outside preparatory to cleaning up! Unfortunately, there was a high wind blowing, and everything had to be anchored down with weights or else it blew away. Eventually, the tent was clear, and I shovelled the sand out and ended off sweeping the remaining dust away. By then, however, everything outside was coated with sand, and I had to shake every individual item vigorously before returning it to its position.

At last everything was in its proper place again, and I turned my attention to the tent itself. Several of the tent pegs had come out, and I replaced these. Others were loose and required tightening. Three of the ropes had frayed through and broken, and I mended these.

The canvas itself had ripped in two places, but fortunately I had a large sail needle, and I set to work with a ball of string, sewing it up again. The wind was very playful and insisted on flapping the canvas as I tried to sew – I fear the final result is not very artistic, but it is quite strong!!

You must give me some lessons in sewing when I get back home again, Joan. It is a most useful accomplishment – personally, I required quite a lot of first aid after my monumental task! I stitched more of my hands than the tent!

This evening, though, the dust has stopped, although the wind is still strong. It is a clear, cold night, and the stars are glittering brilliantly against the soft, velvet sky. I like to think that the same stars are looking down on you in England and that perhaps you are watching them – it makes the distance dividing us seem so much shorter.

This letter is being written under rather adverse conditions: an emergency lighting system provides power, but while we were away our bulb got broken and we are now reduced to one of only 15 watts. This is supplemented by a small hurricane lamp, and I am balancing on a case, writing so as to get as close to the light as possible.

Good night, darling, sleep well – I shall be dreaming of you.

With all my love,

Tony xxxx

*(22 February 1944. Strike on large motor vessel and two corvettes covered by Me 109s, Ju 88s and Arado 196s. MV Livenza sunk. Corvettes damaged. Heavy flak. Three Beaufighters shot down.)*

## 23 February 1944

Tony dear,

I dream so much of your next leave. And after the war, Tony, when we go to London, you know what I would like? For you to give me flowers. Pale Parma violets and the dark sweet-smelling ones and beautiful red rosebuds from the flower girls at Piccadilly. How carefree we shall be then and how happy!

London is being raided again, and the barrage is terrific. Mother is writing to invite her sisters to stay with us for a rest if the raids continue, so we may have a house full again!

I was at a Fire Guard lecture on Monday. It was given by a fireman, and he explained the organisation of the NFS and our duties in cooperating with them in a raid.

I wonder if you receive any of the ordinary letters I send you? How strange you have only recently received that letter I wrote in September.

It is three months since you left England, and yet it seems so long. I miss you so much, although you were near only a little while. Come home soon, soon, soon, Tony.

My love and thoughts and prayers for you.

Joan xxxxx

## 25 FEBRUARY 1944

Joan dear,

In one of your long letters you sent me a lovely poem by Laurence Binyon. It made me long for the time when we shall be able to live merely to appreciate and keep alive the beautiful things of life, instead of existing merely for war.

I have long despaired of being able to tell you adequately how I feel about you but thought that in poetry it might be a little easier, so I wrote a few lines, which I'm afraid are very poor poetry but do seem to express my thoughts. The words and metre are terrible, but I know you will forgive them.

> *Would that I had the treasures of earth*
> *To lay them all at your feet.*
> *The power to fulfil your slightest wish,*
> *Ne'er were there task so sweet.*

> *Would that I had the power to create*
> *A world of unfading beauty,*
> *Fit setting for your presence dear,*
> *Your happiness my duty.*

> *Humble, alas, are the things I can give,*
> *But with them I gladly part*

*A pledge of love, quenchless, undying,*
*An ever-loving heart.*

I'm afraid that they seem even worse now, but I really do mean all they try to say.

I try to see beauty in everything now, so that I shall be able to tell you about it – I know that you love beautiful things so much.

One striking thing I have noticed out here is the wonderful range of hues that the sea assumes. Sometimes it is a hard, steely grey with crests of tossing foam; at other times it is a beautiful soft blue with merely a few lazy ripples. The other day it was a most beautiful turquoise – the more lovely because it was transparent and the colour seemed to spring from the heart of the sea. Great white gulls wheeling against a clear sky completed the picture, and the result was almost breathtaking.

You would love the Mediterranean, Joan, especially around the Greek islands. We must come out after the war. It is impossible to describe the loveliness of it all; you must see it for yourself.

I am writing of some of my plans in my long letter and do hope you will like them. At the moment they form a misty pageant which I pray some day, very soon, will come to life.

I, too, love to plan, Joan. It makes parting so much easier to endure.

Please keep happy, dearest, and still write to me about your dreams and hopes – it brings you so close to me.

With all my love,

Tony xxxxxx

(25 FEBRUARY 1944. OFFENSIVE SWEEP. SUPPLY VESSEL DESTROYED SANTORINI. LIGHTER SUNK NIOS.)

The squadron was now suffering a number of casualties (we lost 22 in a few months, out of a flying establishment of 42), and I thought I should write a letter to be given to Joan in the event of my death. I sealed it with sealing wax and left the necessary instructions. It remained sealed for many years after the war, until Joan found it and insisted on reading it.

My sweet and very dear Joan,

By the time you receive this you will already have been notified by Air Ministry that I have been unlucky. I want you to have this letter so that you will not grieve over me but realise that it is all worthwhile in the end and a very small penalty I had to pay.

I completed a tour of operations, Joan, and was lucky enough to do more for the war effort than I had ever dared hope. I expect always to return safely but think it wisest to make all preparations.

I am grateful that I have had so many letters from you. They were dear messages of love and hope on which I could always rely, and my greatest happiness was to know that you cared for me as I truly loved you.

I loved you very dearly, Joan, and to my sorrow did not realise how deep that love was until I had said goodbye to you after that visit which was destined to be our last meeting.

Thank you again for those two happy days, Joan; they gave me a picture that I have always cherished and made everything since then worthwhile.

There is an old and very true saying: 'whom the gods love die young'. I shall be spared all the worries and troubles of the post-war world, although it would have been a finer thing to help rebuild than to destroy. But I am sure that our sacrifices will not have been in vain and that a new and better world will arise out of the ashes of the old. It is a very small thing to die to ensure that other lovers will not have to be separated and know the uncertainties and sorrows of parting as we have done.

And Death is not really so terrible; I have faced him too often to be really afraid. There is the uncertainty, but that is all.

I hope you will find someone else to love, Joan, and know you will be happy. You could not possibly be otherwise – you love the beautiful things of life too much: the lovely sunsets we used to watch, the countryside and all the things that go to make our England.

Yet I am selfish enough to hope that you will think of me sometimes and know that somewhere I am still with you, for I cannot believe that Death will end my love.

Peace is near at hand now, Joan, and the whole world can return to quiet and tranquillity – doubly precious, as is anything we fight and make sacrifices for.

Darling Joan, please be happy so that this sacrifice is not in vain. I would have sacrificed everything for your sake, and I would only have you as I have always known you: happy merely with the joy of being alive and able to see and love everything beautiful.

Goodbye, sweetheart; my thoughts were always with you.

With all my love,

Tony xxxxxxxxx

## 25 FEBRUARY 1944

Tony dear,

Thank you very much for sending some tinned fruit to Mother. We all love it, particularly me. I almost lived on oranges and apples and fruit sundaes before the war! But there has been very little recently. There are some oranges coming from Spain now, and I certainly enjoyed my ration of one and three-quarters!

We are very busy at the office, but today I had a 'rest', collecting for the Red Cross Penny-a-Week Fund. I confess I rather like this job. I have so many pleasant chats on my rounds, except for one or two crosspatchy people who act as though I were asking for a personal gift of 100 pounds! A very new wisp of hair is tickling my nose. It is time I brushed it back and left for dreamland.

Good night, my dear. God keep you.

Joan xxxxxx

PS I think you are the nicest person in the world xxx

## 28 FEBRUARY 1944

Dearest Joan

The weather has taken a turn for the better, and we are basking in warm sunshine. Today the warmth was tempered by a cool breeze, and the result was lovely. Unfortunately the insect world also approves of the change and is increasing and multiplying alarmingly. I believe most of them are quite harmless, but they will insist on climbing up the inside of my tent and dropping on my bed.

Yesterday we drove down to the beach – the weather was so tempting, and we were not flying.

We stopped at the top of the sandhills and walked down to the beach. There was no path, so we were free to wander whichever way we liked. The sea sand is very different from that of the desert. It is a beautiful silver colour and consists of large grains, not the dust we have inland. The hills were covered with small gorse bushes and were like an English seaside scene on railway posters!

As we topped the first rise, we passed into an enchanted land. The desert lay behind, and we went forward, down into a little valley carpeted with beautiful, fresh thick grass and covered with masses of bright-yellow sunflowers. The valley was sheltered from the breeze and was very warm, and there were large bumblebees droning lazily about from flower to flower.

We lingered for a while and then went on, over the next hill and into another garden. This time the carpet was of pleasant blue flowers – rather like cornflowers – and there were scattered marigolds. The industrious bees shared this paradise with great yellow butterflies, and there were also giant dragonflies hovering overhead, with their rainbow wings shimmering in the sunshine.

At last: the lovely blue expanse of sea rippling gently on the sloping silver beach.

The water was very cold at first, but we splashed about and swam lazily and then dried and sat in the sunshine on the beach until it was time to come back.

Yet more surprises were in store for us. We passed an Arab encampment and a herd of grazing cattle. These were not the usual woebegotten, angular native cattle but sleek, well-fed Jersey cows. We felt we were really dreaming! And there were graceful swallows swooping playfully along the ground: sheer poetry in motion. No doubt they were preparing to return to England after a winter abroad. They, too, followed the sun; I wish I could return with them.

More glimpses of England: shy skylarks, startled by our noisy progress, and a great kestrel hawk sweeping across the sky searching for prey.

And so to bed in the evening, tired but happy and grateful to the enigmatic desert for these fleeting glimpses of home.

We took our wireless to pieces today and found that it was nearly full of sand. Now that this has been removed, reception is much better. This is a good thing as there are often excellent programmes of music, and they do help to keep us in touch with the really worthwhile things in life.

It is getting late now, Joan, so I will bid you good night and happy dreams. I will continue tomorrow. Until then, God keep you safe.

Hello, Joan. It is now the first of March!! I was unable to write yesterday as I promised – we were flying. It is now evening again. Today has been terrible; the sand has been blowing all day, and it was almost impossible to breathe. Still, it has stopped now, and we have cleared most of it out of our tent, and all is well again.

It is getting late once more, and I am drowsing – slipping off once more into dreamland.

The quiet country lane with its green hedges and wild flowers is leading us on in its own calm, unhurried way. We have long since fallen in with its mood and ramble on contentedly, pausing here to look at some shy flower hidden among the brambles and there to fondle the velvet nose of an inquisitive roan mare with a white patch on her forehead and appealing liquid-brown eyes. The fields are already assuming a golden tinge, and the kindly sun is playing on them from a clear blue sky, across which a few fleecy little cloudlets are floating gracefully.

A sudden turn, and we are in the diminutive high street of a tiny village.

There is the inn with its cobbled courtyard and ancient mounting block. The snowy swan on its signboard inclines its neck in graceful greeting and mine host calls a cheery 'Good day' as we pass.

Now the little church with its grey Norman tower and quiet churchyard. The neat path and well-trimmed grass are tribute to the loving care of the old sexton whose pride they are.

On through the village, but we must stop and wonder at the tiny general store with its quaint old bow window and square leaded panes of twisted glass.

Lovely cottages with spotless whitewashed walls and neat thatches beckon us on. We stop outside one where a discreet notice announces 'Teas' and push open the little gate. The path leads under a fragrant arch of glorious roses, and our smiling hostess comes forward to greet us.

We are soon settled at a little table on the grass just under the shade of the twisted and friendly apple tree. The snow-white cloth is soon laden with fresh country scones and butter and fruit and cream: fit feast for the gods.

We linger in the pleasant garden, lulled by the drowsy hum of the bees and the fluttering of the gay butterflies among the flowers.

The rustle of the leaves above grows louder and louder and falls into a measured cadence: the remorseless rise and fall of the sea.

The headland on which we stand juts out a little, and we brave the full force of the wind – grateful for our warm clothes. The sky is growing stormy, and the dark clouds are massing far off.

The sea is a deep grey-green, and the proud breakers are tossing their manes and charging down on the steadfast rocks below. The attack breaks into flying spray, which reaches us even here, and over all the thunder of battle. Formation after formation sweeps down, and the relentless struggle goes on.

The creamy foam is forming lovely patterns of delicate lacework, and even as we gaze, a picture forms.

But the creamy colour is the mellowness of age, of strong stone weathering the ages.

The massive buttresses spring forth from the soft green lawn, impressive in their strength, only to dissolve into the wonder of the Gothic flying tracery.

The great twin towers with their delicate pinnacles dominate all, yet their impression is not of might but of marvellous grace and beauty.

And below them: the noble doors with their ornate carving and tracery, the massive oak and its wrought iron. We pass through and marvel at the lofty nave with its sweeping arches towering up to the carved roof.

Now the transept and the glory of the great rose window. A shaft of sunlight strikes through and casts a glowing pool of rich colour at our feet.

We linger in the quiet cloisters and then out into the peace of ancient sanctuary in the cathedral precincts. The smooth lawns. The serene old houses clustered in the protecting shadow of the noble church. The peace of the ages and of England.

We are gay as we drive up the broad drive to the brilliantly lit house beyond. The ball has been long awaited, and now all is excitement.

Our friends greet us warmly, and then we move on, into the ballroom. I realise, with reluctance, that I cannot in politeness dance with you all the evening (probably to your relief – I am a very poor dancer!) but insist on as many as I dare.

I drift around disconsolately for an eternity, and then we are together again. We float around to a dreamy waltz for a while, and then an open window tempts us and we skip out onto the terrace.

We are not the only ones who have yielded to temptation, and there are several others around. So we wander down the steps into the garden, hand in hand, and along the winding path. The music grows fainter and fainter, and soon all is silent. On and on in the soft warm darkness until we chance on a rustic seat under an ancient oak, gazing out over the rolling Downs.

Your dainty shoes were not made for walking; we had better pause a while. We nestle close together on the seat in the silence of complete happiness that needs no words to express it. The calm stars and wise old moon gaze down from the velvet arch of the sky and cast a faint light transforming everything into a magic world of silver. From time to time we whisper sweet absurdities and laugh happily at our own folly.

As far as the eye can see, the pleasant countryside stretches, resting quietly after a busy day. Here and there cheerful lights twinkle from little cottage windows, often alone but sometimes clustered into friendly little groups.

A sudden sound breaks the stillness. The silvery chime of a far-off church clock recalls the passage of time to two reluctant people. We laughingly protest, but then, why should we care? All life and all time are before us, and our happiness increases with the passing of each day.

We start up, you gather up your dress and we run and stumble light-heartedly along the path and up onto the terrace. Suppressing our merriment, we stroll, seemingly unconcerned, back into the ballroom, feeling like guilty children in case anyone has missed us. All is well, and soon the time comes to bid our hosts farewell and go home again.

In the car two drowsy, happy people purr contentedly, curled up close to one another and dreaming of the treasures the new day has in store.

Dream on, dearest, it will not be long before we awake to a reality far happier even than these passing dreams.

Until then don't worry about me, darling. Nothing can hurt me – I have too much to come back for.

With all my love and hopes,

Tony xxxxx

## I MARCH 1944

Tony dear,

I went to an NFS lecture on Monday to learn how to break into burning buildings! Actually I am scared of fire, but no doubt I should forget my fear in the excitement, if the occasion ever came for me to shoulder my stirrup pump and go into action!

The crocuses have been blooming for a while now, and I hear primroses are out in Sussex hedgerows. Best of all I love bluebells – they make the glades on the commons at home so very beautiful.

I guess you are back in the desert now and missing the comparative civilisation of the well-built aerodrome. I think if I were you I should spend hours each day in a bathroom when I returned home! Our coal is rationed to five hundredweight a month, providing the coalman has it to deliver, so our hot-water supply isn't terrific.

My love, dear,

Joan xxxxx

Good morning! It is a white March – a very-hard-to-get-up-in-the-morning March! But once one is out it is lovely. I walked along the prom on the soft snow; the sun was winking through the clouds and white horses racing in over the sea.

## I MARCH 1944

Dear Joan,

You tell me not to think of you when I am flying. But I do, and it is wonderful how the thought of you helps me. The other day we had a rather risky flight to make, and as we neared our objective I began to feel rather nervous, so I looked at your photograph and determined to remain calm, and we went on and did very well. Having someone always before you for whom you can fight is a very great help, and every time I go out I feel I am fighting for you – there is so little else I can do for you out here.

We shall have wonderful times together when I get back; fate owes us so much happiness after this long parting.

It is nice to know that you can wear pretty hats and shoes once more. I love you always, but nice clothes set you off as a beautiful frame does a lovely picture.

The desert has a solemn grandeur – awe-inspiring, especially at night when the silver moonlight casts deep shadows on the sand and forms a wonderful subtle harmony of tones.

Living out here with so little apparent beauty makes one strive to find the best in everything. There is a canvas water container outside my tent, and the water is slowly leaking out into a tin beneath. The silence is broken by the lovely, clear, bell-like sound of the drops of water and conjures up many pictures of far happier days.

I have made very many plans, Joan. I hope you like them. They form a long, bright pageant, spread over many days and countries, but after the war all time will be ours to devote to our quest for happiness.

We are wandering hand in hand along the bank of a little laughing stream that is chattering its way through quiet autumn woods. A breeze is stirring the treetops and rustling the gorgeous carpet of russet and gold leaves. The stream is deep and clear just here, and the proud fairy fleets of graceful leaves are drifting lazily along. Now they begin to stir and draw together faster, faster until, around a bend in the stream, we come upon a little waterfall where the stream seems to pause before leaping over the brink and dissolving into a shimmering cascade of sparkling diamonds. We wander dreamily on until the music of the little stream is lost in a new and wonderful melody: the paean of praise of the birds bidding farewell to the day.

Suddenly the little stream breaks from the woods to the glory of the setting sun, the blaze of orange and gold on the far horizon fading imperceptibly into delicate, creamy-pink, fleecy clouds. And even as we gaze into the sunset we see the dawn of another scene.

The sun is barely up and sparkles on the bright early-morning dew in the fresh grass. The velvet lawn is sprayed with golden buttercups, and the spring flowers are rioting under the stately trees.

In the lake at the front of the lawn two snowy, dignified swans are floating lazily over, ready to accept, condescendingly, whatever we have to offer. Their less haughty cousins are already scolding excitedly in the trees, ready to explore the wonders of a new day.

The sun gleams on the latticed windows of the house beyond, on its mellow bricks and dark timbers. Through the open French windows – opening on to the terrace – we can catch a glimpse of a cheerful room with bright curtains and crystal and silver neatly arranged on the dark sheen of the oak table. An excited barking! A lovely golden retriever, begging us to finish breakfast and take him for a walk: who could resist such a gentle tyrant? And we hasten to obey!

We must be sleepy still for, as we enter the room, we realise we are far away, not in a quiet Tudor manor but in a small restaurant in London. The head waiter shows us smilingly to our table – for is it not peacetime again? – and places the menu before us. Even as we choose, the soft music of a dreamy waltz calls us away onto the dance floor. Time passes quickly; we start and tear away from the soft lights and enchanting music, or we shall be late at the theatre.

The play is a new one by Ivor Novello, and we let ourselves be carried away in the lovely melodies and pleasing harmony of colours to a land where everyone is carefree and gay and all life is a song.

And afterwards, two sleepy, happy people curl up drowsily in a taxi speeding home.

We awake with a start and realise that the warm sun had lulled us to sleep on the smooth lawn in front of the old Greek temple we had so eagerly explored. We gaze over the calm blue waters in an age-old silence broken now by the soft cooing of pigeons amid the stately ruins.

The sun is sinking in a blaze of glory to the west, and the sea catches and reflects its wonder until we seem to be looking at a lake of gold. The last lovely rose-tinged clouds fade; then the soft warm darkness, with the deep satin sky pierced with its myriad glittering stars, and we slowly wend our way down the little hill path to the friendly lights of the tiny town below.

The scene is slowly dissolving, and through it we catch glimpses of many more happy scenes spreading on in unbroken sequence across the arches of the years.

May all our dreams come true, Joan. I will strive with all my heart to make them so.

I love to hear of your plans and hopes, Joan. I think we are born too dreamy and impractical to do great things, but it is a wonderful formula for happiness.

You say that you will never be glamorous. I must gently, but *very* firmly, disagree with you, although I agree insofar as I dislike the word glamorous – it reminds me too much of highly made-up film starlets. I think 'lovely' suits you more than anything else, and I refuse to let you contradict me!!

Goodbye for the present, darling. I will write again soon. In the meantime you are always in my thoughts.

With all my love,

Tony xxxxxx

## 4 MARCH 1944

Dearest Joan,

We obtained a wonderful new treasure the other day, a Nissen hut: one of those tubular corrugated-iron huts that you often see in England. It had been used by a previous squadron to store torpedoes. The three tents comprising our mess were in a very bad way and were no protection against sand or rain. Consequently, when we got this hut, our joy knew no bounds. It has been painted and generally cleaned out, and we moved in this evening. It even has a concrete floor!! We intend to have a house-warming party in the near future.

Goodbye for a little while, dear.

With all my love,

Tony xxxxxx

(*6 MARCH 1944. NIGHT INTRUDER PATROL.*)

# 8 MARCH 1944

Tony dear,

I am so very pleased with the portrait and the poem you wrote for me.

Although I feel so sorry, I could not help being amused at your spring-cleaning the tent on your return to your squadron. The sand must be terribly exasperating – I imagine you will not be able to bear the sight of even an egg timer full after the war!

Oh but, Tony, how lovely the islands sound! I think it would be wonderful to visit them and sail around on the still blue water. If only it were tomorrow our dreams come true.

I am going to a meeting on post-war reconstruction in the Civil Service tonight. The Association has done so much for our working conditions etc., and it is well to keep it alive in wartime, but I shall be glad to hand over my interest in it to the men when they come back. I believe in equality in things like respect and freedom, but I think men are best suited for men's jobs and women for their quite equally important ones. Perhaps I am not ambitious – I just don't want to be head of a department! Lots of girls do, though. No, I just want time and sunshine, flowers and trees and maybe pretty clothes – and very, very much to see you again.

There are many things I should like to do. One is to see Switzerland when the snow melts on the mountain slopes and the wonderful little flowers blossom from the newly warmed earth. But I don't need an awful lot to make me happy.

I am very *glad* of you, Tony – glad of your kindness and thoughtfulness, that I believe are your nature and not for me alone because you love me. They are such important qualities, particularly now when the whole world is suffering from selfishness and cruelty. (These words are poorly chosen. Please read instead: you are very dear to me.)

Your poem is very sweet to me, Tony, and I will read it over and over when I miss you very much.

Goodbye until tomorrow, then.

My thoughts and love speed to you.

Joan xxxxxx

*(8 March 1944. Single aircraft on offensive night patrol. German destroyer Crispi sunk by rockets; second destroyer damaged by cannon fire.)*

## 9 March 1944

Tony dear,

I said a 'piece' at the Civil Service meeting, but gained little support or sympathy because the other members were mostly higher-grade folk who were more interested in furthering their own interests than bothering with the 'youngster's' pleas.

One worthwhile proposal was made: that there should be a Factory Act for offices, so that office workers shall have good accommodation. This is badly needed, particularly in those dreary city streets. One of our departments was housed in an old warehouse, with great rats running around! Other proposals were the removal of the marriage ban in the Service and a lower pensionable age.

I wish so much for the time when we may be together – there will be so much for us to do and talk about.

My love and prayers for you.

Good night, dear.

Joan xxxxxx

## 9 March 1944

Dearest Joan,

The quotation in your letter was very apt, dearest. I *do* love everything about you – not merely your smile or your beauty, but you yourself. Nothing shall destroy that love, Joan, I promise you. I was so very happy merely to be near you, and even now your letters help me to recapture that happiness. And so it will be again, dear. I shall come back safely, and soon. Nothing can happen to me; I have so much to live for now.

We went swimming again a few days ago and had to drive through several herds of haughty camels. They refused to give way but looked disdainfully at mere human beings. I think they are the most supercilious creatures I have ever met. They curl their lips and sneer every time they see you!

On the way back we saw tomatoes growing in a little oasis and stopped to get some. The Arab who owned them was a wonderful old man. He had baggy white trousers and a white tunic with a red sash. A handkerchief to match was wound round his head, pirate fashion. He looked like Long John Silver come to life! He was very dignified, too, and refused to name a price, saying that it did not matter. However, we gave him some money, and he bade us a grave farewell as we drove off. How very different from the Arabs of the cities!

Here is another poem I wrote for you, Joan dear. I have tried to polish it up, without much success I fear, but have so little time these days.

> *Dearer, sweeter far thou art,*
> *Than honour, wealth or fame.*
> *I love thee more than life itself*
> *My deeds do thee proclaim.*
>
> *And if perchance I hesitate,*
> *Or waver in the fray,*
> *'Tis thought of you that strengthens*
> *And guides my faltering way.*
>
> *Oh, thy sweet face my guiding star,*
> *Thy presence, dear, my shield;*
> *With you there to inspire me*
> *Then shall I never yield.*
>
> *When noise of raging battle fades,*
> *And Peace again supreme,*
> *I pray God make me worthy*
> *Of you – my dearest dream.*

It is morning once more, Joan, as I resume this letter. We fly at all sorts of odd times, and I have to keep breaking off and starting all over again. That is why my letters are so patchy. Please forgive them.

I seem to have known you such a long time, dear, although it is really a very short while.

But your letters bring you very close to me, and it is lovely to dream and plan ahead.

Even as I write I am dreaming.

The day is beautifully warm and sunny, and the deep-blue sky is flecked with fleecy white clouds. It is warm work even strolling slowly along the velvety grass at the top of the cliffs, so we decide to find a shady retreat. There is a deep inlet just ahead with a little path winding steeply down to the cool sea. Forgetting the sun, we rush and stumble in among the rocks and finish off breathlessly laughing at the bottom. The startled seagulls rise steeply, shrieking and scolding us for disturbing their tranquillity.

We find a smooth stretch of silver sand in the shade and sink gratefully down.

The little ripples are splashing musically against the beach in a lazy network of creamy foam. The sea is a beautiful, deep greeny-blue with only an occasional white crest breaking its serenity.

The seagulls have stopped chattering now and are wheeling slowly round in graceful circles in an effortless ease that fills us with lazy admiration. Even in our shady nook it is very warm, and we sit, letting the sand trickle through our fingers in a drowsy contentment.

There is a peaceful hush broken only by the murmur of the sea, and we have no need of words to express our happiness.

The shadows lengthen, and we reluctantly stir. A cool evening breeze is springing up and ruffles your curls as we wander up the path again, stopping to admire flowers hidden in nooks that we missed in our headlong descent.

Once more at the summit, we gaze back into our little inlet and then tear ourselves away with a sigh to the bustling, cheerful world once more.

Arm in arm along the cliffs – thinking perhaps of days when we were far apart – and keeping even closer to one another, and so to the close of another wonderful day.

Things are looking very bright now, and I feel sure it will not be long before we are together again.

With all my love and God bless,

Tony xxxxxx

(10 MARCH 1944. FIGHTER COVER TO DESTROYERS.)

(11 MARCH 1944. FIGHTER PATROL CASTELROSSO.)

## 13 MARCH 1944

Tony dear,

I was pleased with my mail today.

Your plans are so lovely; I shall think and dream of nothing but the happy time of their coming true. Your great love and the beauty of your plans for me make me very humble, Tony. It seems that God so guides the ways of men and women that two people with the same dreams and hopes and understanding are destined to meet, that their lives may be more beautiful together. And we will try to show others the way to happiness in thanksgiving for our own.

Thank you, dear one, for showing me these things.

Tony, how did you know I wanted a golden retriever? I know I chatter a lot but don't remember telling you that.

Why do you say we are impractical because we dream? I don't think so! If we were, we would not strive or fight for the things we want. Impractical people, surely, just wait discontentedly for their desires to fall into their laps? Sometimes I am not even patient. I long to do something to bring your homecoming and peace nearer.

There is so much in your letter to answer, and yet there is not, because your plans seem too perfect for comment. And if we are granted less than your dreams, then I shall be happy so long as you care for my happiness, Tony.

I have little more room, so must say good night, dear Tony. Thank you again and again and again for the lovely letter. I cannot think of any plans for which I should care more than yours.

My love, dear,

Joan xxxxxx

(14 MARCH 1944. ANTI-SHIPPING SWEEP AND NIGHT INTRUDER PATROL OVER MALEME AIRFIELD. VIOLENT STORMS.)

## 16 MARCH 1944

My dear Tony,

I read your letter again today and saw so clearly the beauty of England's woods and streams, the exciting 'feel' of the theatre and the gracious house and garden you describe. When do you dream these lovely dreams, Tony? I imagine you sometimes in all that vastness of desert under the stars, your dreams and plans seeming so very clear in the great stillness. And you seem so very *sure*, Tony.

A vase of golden daffodils looks so gay and beautiful on the table. Flowers are so rare now, and I miss the lovely garden posies, long-stemmed roses and delicate pink blossom that used to bring such joy and sweetness into the house.

And everywhere and always I, too, wish you could be with me, Tony.

With my love, dear,

Joan xxxxxx

## (17 MARCH 1944. OFFENSIVE SWEEP, CENTRAL AEGEAN.)

## 18 MARCH 1944

Joan dearest,

I promised you a character sketch of myself but have found it rather more difficult than I thought. I have tried to make it as impartial and complete as I can.

I have always been very shy and, before I joined the Air Force, did not go out very much but generally preferred to be on my own. I believe I am quite clever but am at the same time very lazy. Fortunately, I have always been able to succeed very easily in anything I have attempted. If I am interested in anything, I can work extremely hard at it and enjoy doing it. I like tidiness but fear that I am often very untidy myself. From time to time I have a furious outburst of energy and arrange everything exactly as it should be. Alas, things soon get disorganised again! I am very fond of comfort and often read rather than do something more energetic. On the other hand I am quite fond of games: fencing, tennis, squash, swimming, golf and riding.

I think it is far nicer to give things to people than to receive them. Also I like people to have a good opinion of me.

Now for my tastes, which I think you know fairly well already. I like classical and indeed almost any music. I am fond of poetry and art. In the field of literature my tastes are very wide, although I prefer historical novels and autobiographies. I love animals and flowers and all wildlife. As you know, I am fond of sunshine – although now I begin to think it is better in moderation! – but on the other hand love wild and stormy scenes, mountainous green seas crashing in a wild spray on the rocks and great dark clouds racing overhead.

I have left the most important thing to the last, and I think you will guess. I love you so very, very much that I despair of ever being able to tell you on paper how I feel. The mere thought of you helps me to forget the discomforts and annoyances of life out here, and I have tried to express my thoughts in another poem.

> *From the heat and the dust of the desert,*
> *A vision of sweetness I see,*
> *Of the beauty and grace of my darling,*
> *Of the one who is dearest to me.*
>
> *Oh sound of her rippling laughter*
> *Is borne to me over the miles,*
> *And the memory I cherish most deeply*
> *Is the glorious warmth of her smiles.*
>
> *Oh the sweet, yet short time I have known her*
> *I'd exchange not for Eternity,*
> *For I gladly declare to my loved one*
> *Her fair presence forever won me.*
>
> *And so now I would pay my devotion,*
> *Lay my heart at the feet of my Queen,*
> *And my life and my every possession,*
> *And all that I am or will be.*

Here are some more dreams, Joan dear, dreamed while reading through your letters.

The snow is crisp and firm underfoot as we follow the little path winding upwards through the pine forest. The stately trees are groaning under the weight of their mantles, and from time to time we hear a sigh of faint relief as some overburdened monarch lets his cloak fall from his weary shoulders.

Shafts of bright sunlight penetrate the leafy glades and are flung back by countless glittering diamonds until the whole forest is glowing with brilliant light.

On we go, grateful for the protection of our warm clothes and feeling the glow of health and physical well-being that one does in cold, pure air.

The broad avenue grows yet wider, and the trees begin to spread out until we break once more into the vastness bounded only by sky and mountains. On and on, up and up, for the challenge of the heights has caught us up, and we could hardly refuse it if we tried.

Over there are still nobler crests – Jungfrau, Eiger, Wetterhorn, Mont Blanc – tinged with the faint blue of great distance and towering so remote as to form part of another and greater world.

Far below us is the forest and the little town nestling in the valley, and above, the summit of our own little peak.

We toil on and breast the final rise, and there is our goal: the massive mountain log cabin with its broad veranda and heavy roof.

A wisp of blue smoke curling lazily upward gives promise of a blazing fire and cheerful company, and we forget our weariness and race light-heartedly across the few remaining yards to collapse laughing breathlessly on the steps.

And afterwards in the glowing flames we see another picture, cast – who knows? – by some imprisoned ray of sunshine at last breaking free.


Emeralds in a wonderful sapphire setting: lovely green islands floating in a sea of incredible blue. Quiet inlets with silvery beaches and a faint creamy border of foam. And rising beyond: the terraced hills and the tiny villages nestling among them with their snow-white houses and little churches.

A great gull dips inquisitively to see this strange creature gliding so slowly across the sea and, apparently satisfied, soars and wheels away. We watch him dreamily until he merges into the little fleecy clouds floating over the island.

Nearer and nearer, the houses, which seemed like a part of some age-old tapestry, spring to a sudden and startling reality as our tiny yacht floats up to the little jetty.

But in all my dreams there is only one important thing: that you are with me. With you I could be perfectly happy anywhere; without you everything would be empty.

I love you and miss you so very, very much.

Goodbye, darling.

With all my prayers and love,

Tony xxxxxx

## 20 MARCH 1944

Tony dear,

Your plans are wonderful – if only we could talk about them together through the long, lovely hours.

I was on night duty at the 'Dugout' yesterday. It necessitated my leaving home at 1.15 a.m., and I didn't get home until after 7 o'clock, so it is a really hard day's work!

Unfortunately, some of the girls consider themselves more suited to conversation than cooking, so I spent three hours deep in washing-up and frying doughnuts. I rather like the cooking, but the kitchen gets so hot it reminds me of pictures I have seen of stokeholds in ships! I wonder rather wistfully if Americans eat doughnuts in summer but fear their capacity is unaffected by anything! It is a source of unending wonder to me that anyone can eat six of these stodgy, fatty, uninteresting lumps!

Apart from the war, the Irish question is causing no end of controversy. It is hard luck on the many Irishmen in our forces, and the Northern Irish people to be unable to go home on leave, but I understand the precaution is absolutely necessary. A friend of mine, whose home is in Ireland, tells me that there was a disgraceful leakage of information through technicians and munitions workers holidaying in Eire, drinking and subsequently boasting about their work. Increasing numbers of Free State girls have been crossing the border to fill in the jobs vacated by northerners, and it is the feeling in N. Ireland that de

Valera hopes in this way to gain votes in the Belfast government, thus eventually putting in a government favouring a united Ireland.

Sometimes I feel a bit lonely, Tony. It is silly, I guess, because there are plenty of folk around to talk to and plenty to do, but I miss my friends who have returned home to London and miss you more and more, dear. I could be so content in your company all the hours, Tony. We are lucky as can be, you know, to want the same things as well as one another. Even if every dream doesn't come true, since we shall share the disappointment, each will be able to sympathise so sincerely with the other.

A lighter item: men must be satisfied with short socks until Germany is conquered.

I shall think of you, Tony, as I watch the swallows flying home, and I watch always for your return.

My love, dear,

Joan xxxxxx

(*21 MARCH 1944. HUNT FOR U-BOAT OFF TOBRUK.*)

(*22 MARCH 1944. OFFENSIVE SWEEP. TWO SUPPLY VESSELS DESTROYED.*)

## 30 MARCH 1944

Dear Tony,

I went for a long walk yesterday evening to blow away the weariness of staying indoors all these lovely spring days. There was a bright new moon up by the time I reached home. I wished so much you might be here. We could enjoy so greatly wandering together in the spring sunshine and the clear starry nights.

Everywhere in England people are discussing equal pay. I have been listening to a radio debate on the subject this evening after a discussion at our office teatime parliament! Opinion is widely divided, as is evidenced by the vote in the House over teachers' pay.

A poem for you, with my love. God keep you safe and send you home soon, soon, dear,

Joan xxxxxx

*Once, in another lifetime*
*I lay clasped by the scent of roses in a shaded walk,*
*And heard slow bells singing across warm fields*
*From the dry brown village, and the faint babble*
*Of children laughing in a blossomed lane.*
*All movement in the placid air was tiny,*
*Bees in pink honeysuckle, butterflies on laurel leaves,*
*Gnats swaying in an intricate gavotte.*
*The sky was bland and innocent; the Sun smiled,*
*And all my being was in harmony with time and peace*
*And with all loveliness.*

*In that same setting you will always be*
*When I remember you, so that inside me*
*There is perpetual sunlight,*
*For every hour I speak to you*
*Across the months and miles between us,*
*The breath of freshness, always new, strikes to my soul.*
*Each time I see you, perfection in my memory;*
*Lithe youth is in your walk*
*And raven's wing upon your head,*
*And in your eyes the love is clear,*
*Comforting me, and I know rest again,*
*Safe in my haven from the storm of war.*

*Govan Lord*

(30 MARCH 1944. NIGHT INTRUDER. ROCKET ATTACK ON
MALEME AIRFIELD.)

31 MARCH 1944

Dearest Joan,
You say you like my dreams and plans so much that you cannot
add anything to them; I feel the same way about yours. They
seem so perfect that any comment seems impossible. I am so
very, very glad that our hopes and wishes are so exactly alike. It
seems wonderful how so much happiness and love should come
from a chance meeting.

I mentioned that my tent had blown down – we had our usual

gale and sand, and after several hours the tent gave up the ghost. Unfortunately the great collapse coincided with a torrential downpour, and most of my kit was soaked. I managed to re-erect it and slept amid the wreckage that night. You will be pleased to hear that the tent is now perfectly serviceable once more, and I am convinced that nothing can move it.

Among other duties I am now Messing Officer!! I am responsible for all the supplies, for the preparing of menus, the upkeep of the kitchens, staff welfare, etc., etc. My spare time is now filled with wonders about whether the flour will last, the price of eggs, fruit, sugar and whether we can replace our broken cups!!! I never realised before how much a woman has to do in the house! I shall be able to cook as well as make coffee when I return!!!

Goodbye and God bless, darling,

Tony xxxxxx

## 1 APRIL 1944

Tony darling,

The reflection of the setting sun has just faded from my room, and the gulls, which until a moment ago were circling and alighting on the rooftops, have flown away to their nests.

I wrote you a long letter last night – mostly about my characteristics – in return for your self-analysis! Although really, Tony, I feel we know each other well – as well as people might who have always been together. Perhaps that is because we care for the same things and so understand one another.

I feel dreamy and contented, snuggled in bed, but this is not a help in getting my letter written! My thoughts are wispy and mixed up. I feel just like lying gazing at the slowly darkening sky and imagining myself sailing with you in a calm blue bay, far away in a lovely future.

Oh, Tony dear, if only the future could be as fair for all peoples, for the starving children of European countries and the heartbroken ones, then there would be such great happiness for all of us.

Do not worry that I fret too much, dear. It is impossible not to think and care deeply for this terrible suffering, but we can each do only our little share of improving the world, and I believe it right to be happy in the happiness granted to us.

Forgive me for writing sadly. I was thinking of a document I read this afternoon about conditions in Europe.

With all my love, dear,

Joan xxxxxx

## 3 April 1944

Tony dear,

This is a truly April month. I got wet walking home through the gardens, but it was quite warm and I was gazing at the delicate new leaves on trees and bushes and the opening chestnut buds and so did not mind the rain very much.

Spring is an unfailing wonder and joy to me. I remember how I always gathered 'sticky' buds from the horse chestnut trees when I was very young and watched them unfolding day by day. Oh, Tony, there are sweet peas and violets, anemones and yellow jasmine adding their beauty to the early spring flowers in florists' windows. And we actually have a blue, blue hyacinth in our front garden.

Your faith in a lovely future strengthens mine, dear heart, when just waiting seems wearisome to me. I so often wish I was doing some brave thing like the AA girls and nurses to bring it nearer.

You must think me grown very discontented, always wishing I might be someone else, when really being me is rather nice. I wear the things you send me and feel so pleased when people remark about their prettiness. There are all the things I love in this world and no reason why they should not someday be mine, and I have someone I care for to share them with.

I am dreaming again!

God guide you, dear, and grant your dearest wishes for the future. My love and thoughts are with you,

Joan xxxxxx

## 5 April 1944

Tony dear,

I like your poems very much and read them over and over. You must spend so much time in writing to me, dear. Although I love your letters, please do not write when you should be sleeping – you must get very tired when you are flying so much.

The old Arab you describe in your long letter seemed a wonderful character. I would love to see photographs of these people and the places you visit.

Joan xxxxxx

*(5 APRIL 1944. NIGHT INTRUDER. ROCKET ATTACK ON MALEME AIRFIELD. MOST INTENSE FLAK.)*

# 7 APRIL 1944

Tony dear,

I do like your long letters very much, Tony.

Your character sketch is very true, as I know you, except that I never imagined you to be untidy! I like everything to be particularly clean and tidy, too, but find tidiness rather difficult because I *spread* things. I become so absorbed in whatever I am doing that I just forget to put things down in their proper places! The result is a great deal of unnecessary tidying up! So far my efforts to improve in this respect have not been very successful.

You *are* shy, but somehow I cannot understand why you are, after gathering so much knowledge and spending years in the RAF – you must have met so many people on your travels? Then, to be less shy of older people is strange to me, because, until I know them well, they make me terribly nervous.

I am really very shy of meeting people and particularly nervous of crowds. People laughingly protest that I am not, because nervousness makes me noisy and excited, and so I do not appear shy. But with most people, as soon as I know them a little, I am not the least shy and like to be friendly with everyone; although I make only a few lasting friends.

Anything very beautiful moves and pleases me, whether it is nature, paintings, words or music, architecture or sailing ships. I learn from these things and from conversation better than from books. I am not studious, you see. But I do like to read, particularly books which help me to imagine other lands and times and lives than my own.

My knowledge of music is not great, but I love to listen to it, particularly to beautiful singing, whether it is opera with its solemn richness or gay light-hearted tunes from *The Vagabond King* or *Bitter*

*Sweet*. And particularly I like to listen to a young boys' choir. One of my ambitions is to hear the Choristers of the Wooden Cross at Baux, in the south of France.

I like to draw. I like cooking, too, and often think I might bake wonderful things.

I am eager and enthusiastic and want very much to live a full and a worthwhile life.

That is all I know about me, except that I *am* logical!!!!!!!!

Thank you for sending me all your wonderful dreams, dear. It will all seem so carefree without the anxieties of war.

I think of you constantly, dear one. If I can make you happier then please tell me.

Joan xxxxx

(*9 APRIL 1944. NIGHT INTRUDER AND ANTI-SHIPPING PATROL. MALEME AIRFIELD ATTACKED.*)

## 11 APRIL 1944

Tony darling,

We were very busy at the canteen, and we had to get a taxi to speed back to St Annes for the Easter service. I arrived breathless, just as the choir was filing in! The church was crowded to hear the children's 'Adorning of the Cross', and so I had to go right down the aisle to the front pew, where I continually caught the children's eyes and made them smile! Some of the children sang beautifully. Several of the girls in the choir are from Barnardo's homes, but they are so nicely dressed and brought up, no one could know they have no parents to look after them.

What a wonderful improvement has been made in these institutions. If only something great could be done about our slums, we might be a fitting example for the European countries to build on after the war.

Somehow when I write to you I forget that you are not here, and I sit chattering to you. And so my words seem such a jumble written down.

Remember the evenings when you and I pulled the world apart and put it together again? What a lot of things we shall have to talk about when you come home, my dear. It is a fine thing to have so many interests in common, because I think then we can never be out of sympathy with one another.

My love, dear one,

Joan xxxxxxxxx

## 11 April 1944

Tony dear,

It is such wonderful weather it is hard to think of anything but how good it is and how much I would like to be in the country. It would be so green and fresh in the little woods and on the Downs at home.

I agree with you, dear, that little things contribute so much to our happiness. For me the smell of April violets rising in the steam of my bath and clean, rough towels. Walking very early on a summer morning. Finding an unexpected glade of bluebells. Running, laughing and breathless, with a puppy. A table laid for tea with a snowy cloth and fine china and flowers in a shallow bowl.

I have written two letters to you today. It is really a funny thing to do, because I haven't anything special to say. I should like so very much for you to be here and look forward with all my heart to your coming home. I hope my letters cheer you up a little when you feel weary, although I know I get a bit solemn and 'put the world right' once in a while! We will spend lovely lazy days when you come home.

My love, dear Tony,

Joan xxxxx

## 12 April 1944

Tony darling,

Thank you, thank you, thank you for sending more parcels to me. I love to look forward to such things – I am like a donkey with a carrot dangling before its nose.

The blue silk sounds lovely, Tony, and very glamorous.

My love to you; may all be well with you,

Joan xxxxxx

(12 April 1944. Anti-shipping patrol. Jumped by three Me 109s. One Beaufighter shot down.)

## 13 APRIL 1944

Tony dear,

You seem so patient with all the trials of the desert. I fear I should be reduced to tempestuous tears if I returned weary from flying to find my home and belongings collapsed in such a mess!

Beaufighters were in the news this week on convoy protection and sweeps against enemy shipping off the Adriatic coast. I listened most intently.

God bless you, dear, and send you home soon.

My love,

Joan xxxxxx

## 14 APRIL 1944

Tony dear,

I wish you were here today; it would be lovely to go out together. The sky is blue, scattered with fluffy white clouds, the sea rippling gently up the beach and the sands golden in the sunlight. There has never been such wonderful weather since I came to St Annes.

Thank you very much for the fruit and honey, Tony. I want to tell you how much we enjoyed the peaches – looking a long time before we ate them to impress the beautiful sight in our memories! We are keeping the second tin to set in jelly for a special (as yet undecided upon) occasion.

All my love and thoughts to you,

Joan xxxxxx

## 14 APRIL 1944

Joan dearest,

Please forgive me for keeping you waiting so long for this letter. I started it over a week ago. Unfortunately we have been very, very busy lately and even the evenings – my usual letter-writing time – have not been free.

Your description of the lovely, yellow, sticky horse chestnut buds and the sweet peas, violets and all the other lovely English spring flowers makes me long to be back in England again, Joan, although if you were with me it would not matter where we were.

I have been wondering about a lot of things lately, dear, and I fear they have mostly been idle thoughts – I have been too lazy to direct them.

I wonder if I have changed very much since I have been out here? I think I have, although I am not sure if the change will be lasting. I used to be fairly ambitious but lately have thought that I ask nothing more than to be with you, living in the peace and beauty of the English countryside. Does that seem very selfish of me, Joan?

At times I feel that it is all only a dream and that I shall wake up to find myself at home.

Alas, I have soon been brought back to reality. A large sheet of corrugated iron just sailed over my tent, caught by the wind. Fortunately it did not hit it. The wind here is amazing; 40-gallon oil drums weighing about 200 pounds are driven past at about 20 mph – if I had not seen it I should have thought it was impossible. Still, now I can believe almost anything of the desert!!

At night, though, everything seems so peaceful. It is generally cold and clear. The sky seems as soft and deep as velvet, and the stars are so bright. They seem so tranquil and serene as they look down on this troubled old earth, and I realise with a start how insignificant events are. The same timeless and unchanging stars will be there when this present conflict is but another chapter in the history books of some future generation of school children and the sorrows and worries and partings are all forgotten. Still, perhaps they will be grateful to those whose sacrifice made their peaceful and trouble-free world possible.

But enough of these idle thoughts, Joan. Our own future stretches bright before us, and we have our own dreams and plans to bring true!

Next spring, let us wander through the quiet woods where peace is yet disturbed by that indescribable stir and awakening that is spring. The buds are bursting forth on the trees, and the lovely bluebells are rippling in the cool, shady grass. The birds are rejoicing, and the first early migrants are already back. A feeling of joy and hope is in the air, and we are caught up in it and yield laughingly to the temptation to run hand in hand chattering absurdities and rejoicing in youth and love. It is so wonderful to be in love – everything seems so much finer, and it is so lovely to be able to share the beautiful things of life with someone you care for.

There is so much beauty in the world for those who seek it. Let us make our life a quest of loveliness, Joan dearest, and let us help others to find it also.

There is a lovely country, Joan, which I will leave nameless, almost as beautiful, I think, as England. I long to take you there someday.

Its fields are pleasant and well kept, and the peasants are kindly folk who love their land. The villages are neat with white buildings and tidy streets. The roads wind happily along, not like the great unfriendly German highways but as the spirit leads them; down little valleys with tiny streams of crystal-clear water and shady tree-lined banks; across the gentle hills with little windmills perched on their brows; now wandering towards the sea and running along rocky ledges with the waves rippling quietly just below; and inland again, past pleasant vineyards and grassy meadows with peaceful grazing cattle.

Soon we begin to see a different aspect: higher ridges and yet higher. The road winds on, and as we reach the summit we burst on to a scene of almost unbelievable beauty.

The slope falls away before us across a lovely green and fertile plain to a little range of mountains on the far side. In this clear air we can see every detail: the mountain paths and sturdy trees and torrents cascading down towards the valley. Around the crests of the range are little fleecy clouds so thin as to be almost transparent and forming a delicate veil. And beyond our little range rise the true monarchs, towering up into the blue sky, bewildering in their immensity. Their lower slopes are tree-clad, but beyond lies the eternal cloak of dazzling white snow. Yet at this vast distance the cloak assumes a gentler hue. It is the deep, rich, creamy colour of old ivory and softens and beautifies the stern countenance of the rocks.

And on the left is the sea: a beautiful deep blue with dancing wavelets sparkling in the pleasant sunshine. Little fishing boats with snowy sails are gliding peacefully across the waters, with their attendant gulls scolding and screaming.

Above all, the feeling of serenity and peace make it a dream-like world – a world from some old, half-forgotten legend where old dreams and hopes might come true.

It is growing dark once more, Joan, and I have been watching the sunset. The sky over there to the right is a mass of gold and orange with little pink clouds. On the other side it blends smoothly and yet so suddenly into a tawny yellow. Nearer are the great storm clouds, grim and menacing: a steely blue-grey with dark hearts, yet tinged with an ivory hue which gives them a beauty all of their own. And behind them a lovely, delicate, creamy-blue sky – lovelier perhaps by contrast – with two stars, startlingly bright.

Why do stars seem so much friendlier at twilight and dawn, Joan? At night they are lovely but so cold and remote, yet their coldness melts against a sky still light with the glory of the setting sun. Then, too, at night they are in brilliant constellations, but in the early evening they are few – and perhaps seem lonely?

The thought of the night and the wonder of dawn gave me the idea for this poem, Joan, and how glorious it will be when we are together again.

*Grieve not my sweet that the far miles divide us,*
*Fate owes us much and her debt will repay,*
*Dark though the night of our sorrow and parting*
*Bright dawns the hope of a wondrous new day.*

*For the Sun of our love will dispel all the dark clouds,*
*And we'll be together happy and free.*
*What matters rain or the tempest's dark fury?*
*All will be heaven when you are with me.*

*Till then, dearest Joan, all my thoughts are but of you,*
*My life and my actions are only for thee.*
*And my love brighter glows 'cross the long miles dividing,*
*And brighter will glow until Eternity.*

It is just a little lonely here, dearest, and my thoughts go wandering forward to a happier evening.

It is so restful sitting like this in the firelight; the dancing flames are so friendly and sympathetic. The clock is ticking solemnly on, but who worries about time on an evening like this? You are so lovely,

Joan, and so dear. Life itself would not be too great a price to pay for just this one heavenly moment with you in my arms so close to me and with your cheek so soft against mine. I feel so humble and so grateful and so unbelievably happy.

Do you remember – was it a thousand years ago? – when we were so far apart? But we are together again now, and nothing shall part us.

The fire burns on, and the pictures in it come and go. An eternity passes, and we sit, dreamily watching the glowing embers and building lovely castles – the more lovely since we know that they will not fade with morning but remain strong and beautiful since we have each other and a lifetime of joy and happiness before us.

The long and weary parting was well worthwhile, darling, since it makes this moment so much more precious.

Sleep peacefully, Joan dearest. My life and every thought are always yours.

With all my love,
Tony xxxxxxxx

## 14 APRIL 1944

Dearest Joan,

Thank you so much, dear, for writing so often. Your letters make me happier than I can possibly say. There are times when things seem so grim and you are so far away, and then I hear from you and all is well again.

I have a fine collection of operational pictures which, although they are secret now, will be very interesting to look back at after the war. Already the incidents in most of them have taken on a dream-like quality of distance. How quickly we forget!

But there is one thing which I shall never forget, and that is how much you mean to me and how dear you are, even more so now that I am out here. I cannot bear to think what life out here would be like without you and . . . but I can never write to you as I would like. I grow so incoherent and muddled, but I know you will sympathise. What I really mean is that you are the dearest thing I have in the world, and it seems so wonderful that you should care for me.

I do so long to see you again and to be able to tell you my thoughts
instead of trying to write them.

With all my love and thoughts always, dearest,

Tony xxxxxx

*(16 April 1944. Shipping strike, Nios. Supply vessel sunk.
Intense light flak. Aircraft hit, fortunately behind
armoured protection!!)*

## 19 April 1944

Tony darling,

Your air letter 40 arrived this morning. So you are messing officer as
well as censor and your other duties now! We shall have to put your
housekeeping to the test when you come home!! Only don't let the
camp get used to you running things too much, or they won't want
to part with you.

With all my love,

Joan xxxxxx

*(20 April 1944. Hunt for U-boat off Derna. Motor vessel
burning in Gulf of Bomba.)*

## 21 April 1944

Joan darling,

The weather here is getting really warm now, and we go swimming
more and more often. We found a little inlet on the coast with lovely
silver sand and a rocky shore. The water is so cool and clear, and
you can dive from the rocks instead of having to wade out from the
beach. Then, too, the rocks shield our retreat from the wind, and we
can sunbathe to our hearts' content.

The track is interesting, too. It winds across the desert and then
down a rocky escarpment, twisting and turning as it goes; on and
into a level valley with a charming oasis with feathery palms and
cool, green grass; now running along a ledge beside a stretch of water
that has found its way in and which we have named 'The Lake'! It
seems so lovely after the dry desert. There are little green shrubs by
the water's edge and silvery thorn bushes. It is almost England.

The days are going by very rapidly now, Joan, and I am happy because each one is bringing me nearer to you. Such happiness as will be ours is well worth waiting for, because we have known what it is to be apart, and it will be so much more precious when we can really make our dreams come true.

Goodbye and God bless.

With all my love, dearest,

Tony xxxxxx

*(23 APRIL 1944. FIGHTER COVER, LARGE CONVOY OF 35 VESSELS.)*

## 24 APRIL 1944

Tony dear,

I had a busy day yesterday taking seven children for a picnic on the beach! The weather wasn't very promising at first, but fortunately it did not rain. We camped in a dip of the sandhills, out of the wind. We played hide-and-seek and deck tennis and just rushing around. Then the boys built a fire while I laid out the tea. I noticed too late that they had made the fire so that smoke blew towards the picnic, and everything had to be gathered hastily and removed from the smoke clouds!

I set sponge roll in little dishes of the jelly you sent and put a blob of strawberry mould on each – it was almost as good as ice cream. We had sandwiches and cakes and plenty of sand!

The children laughed all teatime and then bounded with renewed energy into grand tumbles on the sandhills. They slid down the slopes, jumped all over me, stuffed me with sand – the little girls, forgetting which side they were on, set on me too! It was great fun, but I don't think I should like a regular job – I should be reduced to dust in a week!!

I am sending a few more magazines. The new publication, *Transatlantic*, arouses my interest in America. How strange that we two English-speaking nations should know so little of each other, apart from the very distorted view shown in films. I have such a thirst for knowledge of other lands and people.

That is all my chatter – I have only my love yet to send.

Joan xxxxxxx

## 28 April 1944

Tony dear,

Come home soon, darling, so that we may talk and talk and do wonderful things together. And please tell me when you are coming, because, although surprises are lovely, I want to know the very first minute and meet you. Yes, and wear my prettiest dress, instead of being at work or washing my hair or something!

Oh yes, may it be soon, soon, soon.

Lovingly,

Joan xxxxxx

## 2 May 1944

Tony dear,

Your plans are beautiful, Tony, and your 'secret' land so lovely I long to begin the happy voyage. We will go to the country next spring and wander together all the days and dream evenings away until you forget your loneliness and this long while away from dear loved things.

I walked with a friend a long way through the lanes behind Lytham on Saturday. Everything was very green, and ditches were bright with golden-yellow kingcups. I passed one farm where dozens of ducks were waddling, fluffing out their feathers or sleeping under the trees in the garden. Then cows and growing calves were grazing contentedly. The rich, brown, new-ploughed earth was a lovely sight after the sandy gardens near the sea.

There is great talk of the 'Churchill' houses. They are made in steel sections for quick construction. I do not like the idea and think there should be finer houses for returning servicemen than these, which have the appearance of glorified holiday camp chalets. I am so afraid, too, that there will be forgetfulness in years to come and these temporary homes will not be replaced. Surely we must have no slums in this new world of ours?

Joan xxxxxx

## 3 May 1944

Joan dearest,

I have another occupation at the moment. In my spare time I have to audit all the squadron accounts – it is proving quite a job.

One of my purchases in 'Alex' was a volume of Martial's *Epigrams* and a Latin gradus – so I shall spend some interesting evenings translating them. You must have some occupation in the desert to stop you thinking about the loneliness and monotony!

The clouds have been so beautiful all day – towering, creamy masses in a lovely delicate-blue sky. I only wish I could capture the colour.

I miss you more and more each day, darling, although I keep reassuring myself that it will not be long before we are together again. And even now our dreams and plans are so lovely that it makes you seem so close to me.

Let us always plan to do lovely things together, Joan. Beauty is so much more real when you can share it with someone you love.

Goodbye and God bless.

With all my love, dear,

Tony xxxxxx

(5 MAY 1944. STRIKE ON RADAR STATIONS, PALIOKHORA)

(8 MAY 1944. ANTI-SHIPPING SWEEP. THREE SUPPLY SHIPS SUNK OFF SYROS. DESTROYER ATTACKED WITH ROCKETS. MOST INTENSE HEAVY AND LIGHT FLAK. HIT BY .303 BUT NO SERIOUS DAMAGE. FORCE LANDED EL ADEM.)

## 10 MAY 1944

Joan darling,

Your letters are lovely, Joan dearest; it seems as though you were talking to me – which Chesterfield says is the criterion of a good letter. I fear mine must be very dull. Once more I am tired. I have only had 10 hours' sleep in the last 72 hours, but I had a swim this afternoon, which greatly refreshed me.

Goodbye for a little while, dear.

With all my love,

Tony xxxxxxx

## 12 May 1944

Joan darling,

I'm glad you like my 'secret' land, Joan. I feel that my description did not do it full justice – it has to be seen to be believed. We will have such lovely times seeking the beautiful places of the world and enjoying them in each other's company. A pleasure shared with someone you love is so very much greater.

This afternoon we went swimming again and found a chameleon on the rocks. He was very tame and sat quite calmly in our hands and let us stroke him. Alas, he would not change colour, although we tried to persuade him to do so on several different backgrounds!

I have finished my auditing at last and am truly thankful. It is quite a lengthy procedure.

I have seen an unusual number of sunrises lately, each one seemingly more beautiful: lovely traces of rose with golden tinges fading into a lovely emerald green and then to blue, and graceful white herons soaring up from little valleys to greet the morning sun.

Yet I would exchange all the glorious colour for even a dull rainy day in England with you. I do so look forward to seeing you again, and the time passes so slowly.

Dearest, let us both wish hard, and perhaps our dreams will come true, even sooner than we dare hope.

With all my love,

Tony xxxxxx

(*14 May 1944. Strike on Paros airfield. Supply ship sunk, Tenos. Jumped by four Me 109s Paros. Two Beaufighters shot down, one damaged.*)

## 15 May 1944

Joan darling,

The temperature rises steadily, and I almost regret my journey in quest of the sun! But I am getting darker and darker and am assured that I shall soon be able to pass as an Arab. I must try to acquire a camel!

We continue to swim frequently, and I must admit that I am feeling very fit indeed. Life in the desert has one or two compensations.

Even if it was almost perfect, though, it would be no use since you are so far away. I am living and longing only for the day when I shall see you again.

    With all my love, dearest,

    Tony xxxxx

## 18 MAY 1944

Tony dear,

Is this awful?

    *May Month 1944*

    *Her sons and daughters*
    *Wherever they may be*
    *Shall, as clearly as they stood*
    *On windy downs or in a shady wood*
    *Behold this English scene.*

    *Kingcups and cowslips*
    *Brave in ditch and hedgerow,*
    *Dazzling daisies on a lawn*
    *Wood violets opening with the dawn,*
    *Blossoming English scene.*

    *Slow winding river*
    *From mountain stream flows down*
    *Past cottage, church and town.*
    *Orchards white with promised yields,*
    *Lazy cattle grazing the green fields,*
    *Peaceful English scene.*

My thoughts and love, dear one,

    Joan xxxxxx

## 18 MAY 1944

Joan darling,

We were out on our own the other night and encountered an enemy destroyer. We attacked it with rockets, and it caught fire, blew up and sank almost immediately. It was confirmed afterwards by ground sources. Needless to say we were very pleased about it. Intelligence say that it is all right to write about it without breaking security.

After a trip like that you feel that you are really doing something worthwhile. I have so many more adventures to tell you, but, alas, they have not been released by Air Ministry so I must wait for a happier day.

Please believe me, Joan, when I say that it is always the thought of you that helps me if I am nervous when there is a trip on which some little risk is to be faced. But I have nearly completed my 'tour' and will be going on a rest, so there is no more need for you to worry. Would that I could get back to England.

With all my love,

Tony xxxxxx

## 21 MAY 1944

Joan darling,

Yet another day is drawing to a close. I think that it has been the warmest we have had so far, with the temperature soaring well over 100 degrees F in the shade and a hot dry south wind – the 'khamsin' – blowing.

As is usual on these days, we vanished under a thick pall of sand and lost no time in driving away down to the beach, which is sheltered and where life seems quite bearable and the desert an unpleasant dream. I spent a lazy afternoon sunbathing until I felt too warm and then went swimming and splashing about in the cool, clear water. The water is quite deep beside the rocks, and I dived down to the bottom and swam along admiring the moss-like seaweed growing among the rocks. The water is so transparent that you can see things from an amazing distance.

At the moment I am feeling very fit. The sun, swimming and the simple existence we lead all contribute to this. On the other hand, though, we are all dulled mentally.

The heat tends to make one very lethargic, and although I try to keep alert by reading and playing chess, the indifference of the Orient very soon begins to prevail. Then, also, we live in a series of periods of intense excitement and nervous tension, and in the intervals between the instinctive reaction is to relax and live merely for the moment. A heartening thought is that this lethargy is merely local and momentary and will disappear with a change of environment and occupation.

The other evening we were flying rather late and decided to climb above the clouds. The sky overhead was growing dark and the moon and stars were already glittering brilliantly. Towards the west the horizon was a most beautifully clear green, deepening to orange and gold where the sun had just set. Below us were countless masses of fleecy white clouds with fantastic billows and pinnacles. Here and there deep chasms yawned, and we could catch glimpses of the sea through a faint blue haze. Home again, and a thrilling dive into a clear gap past the rolling cloud masses, now plunging through an almost transparent veil – and so to the prosaic earth once more. Flying above clouds is a most wonderful experience – one feels so detached and remote; it is an enchanted world on its own.

Things must be very difficult for you at home now; I expect very many restrictions and shortages exist. Still, anything is bearable that will bring peace nearer and help to bring us close again.

Good night, darling. I am living and longing only for that most happy day when I shall see you again. Goodbye and God bless.

With all my love,

Tony xxxxxx

## 25 May 1944

Tony dearest,

You seem weary, dear. I wish and wish you might have more rest. I thought so much of you when I was at Windermere. You would have loved to have wandered by the peaceful lake with its wonderful views of tree-clad hills and misty mountain tops. White gulls circled above the lapping water, and a yacht sailed slowly before the gentle breeze.

It was a fine sunny day, and the countryside looked perfect. There were carpets of bluebells beneath the great trees and yellow broom on sunny banks. Gardens were glorious with rhododendrons of every shade from pale yellow to deep, mauvey red.

We had lunch and tea at a quaint café, its walls hung with old pewter platters and its antique dresser laden with blue-and-white china.

I gathered more flowers than I could carry, and they remain a lovely reminder of my first day in the country for a long, long while.

It is dear of you to say I write good letters, because they are really dreadful, scribbly scrawls.

You are dear altogether, and I send you all my love and thoughts for always.

Joan xxxxxxx

## 26 MAY 1944

Joan darling,

Yes, we must smile through our tears and always look forward to the wonderful days when we shall be together again. In these troubled times it is lovely to have someone you can really love and long to see again. It is like a haven of safety from a stormy sea where all our values and standards are being destroyed. Human nature cannot be so bad when two people can care for each other so much and our love prove so much stronger than all other feelings despite the unhappiness of separation.

Dearest Joan, it seems so long since I saw you. I would give anything for even a little while with you. I must be patient though. We have such a long time before us, and this parting will seem very short in happier days when we look back. May those days come very soon.

In the meantime the news is good, and our hopes are running high.

Goodbye for a little while, darling.

With all my love,

Tony xxxxxx

*(2 JUNE 1944. INTRUDER AND ANTI-SHIPPING. ATTACKED AIRFIELD MALEME.)*

## 7 JUNE 1944

Tony dear,

I wanted to write to you yesterday, the 'D-Day' for which we have waited so long, but I was so excited and my thoughts and emotions so mixed up that I could not express them.

I wondered what you were doing, thinking, feeling yesterday? I listened intently to all the news bulletins, the King's speech. As much as anything (is it strange?) I was impressed by Uncle Mac's fine voice speaking to the children of the world just before the *Six O'Clock News*.

Can you guess how much it meant to me to have a letter from you yesterday, to have heard almost every day lately? I had impressed upon myself that I must not worry if I did not hear from you once the battle began; perhaps I shall still have need to remind myself of this, but so far I have been so fortunate.

I wanted to write to wish you a happy birthday, but I do not know the date?? So I will post this letter now and hope it will be in good time.

Bless you, dear. I, too, am confident that we shall see each other soon.

With my love,
Joan xxxxxx

## 8 JUNE 1944

Joan darling,
The landings seemed to have gone so well. I do wish I could be transferred to France – there is so much opportunity for aerial warfare there. Still, I may get a chance later on.

With all my love,
Tony xxxxxx

## 8 JUNE 1944

Tony dear,
I am pleased with my newly arranged room. The curtains are daintily colourful with sprigs of flowers, and the light streams through them in the morning on to my own favourite possessions beside my bed: a leather studded box which came a long way from someone very dear and which I will keep as long as my teddy bear, the last of my 'couldn't-do-without' things.

People laugh at my teddy, at his bald patches and lost eyes, and at me for keeping him still. But I shall defend him till the end, when his last bit of stuffing comes out. He has been my dearest friend, sharing my childhood fear of the dark, my joys and sorrows for 23 years. And so, my darling, it is a condition that, wherever we go across the world, Bear goes too!

God bless you,

Joan xxxxxx

Sixty-five years later, Bear lies beside her still.

## 9 JUNE 1944

Joan darling,

I am so sorry to hear that you are feeling lonely. I pray that it will not be very long before we are together again. Won't it be wonderful when we can make all our dreams and hopes come true? I am sure that they will be far lovelier than I can ever hope to put into words. I sympathise with you very deeply, though. I know how terribly trying it must be to stay at work in a dull office and not see any results of the things you do. I think it requires far more moral courage than any of the things we have to do.

We live in the excitement of the minute and can see tangible results, which make any slight risk we take worthwhile. Our task is to fight for the life of England, and unless that life can continue normally through the painstaking efforts of the patient people at home, our task is pointless. Yours is the more difficult part – imposing a continuous strain. We can build up reserves of energy during rests between sorties.

England is the heart, and if it were possible for the enemy to interrupt the beating of that heart, we who are fighting would fail, for the true strength of England is the people who carry on so well, amid all the anxiety and hardships, with their quiet tasks, without praise or glamour or hope of reward.

Do please forgive me, dearest, if this is dull, but I do most sincerely believe that you are playing a most vital part in preserving the England that we love so well.

With all my love, dear heart,

Tony xxxxxx

(*10 JUNE 1944. STRIKE ON CONVOY OFF ATHENS.*)

## 16 JUNE 1944

Joan darling,

Since we are parted your letters bring you so close and make me very happy indeed. They are very good letters; someone, I think it was Chesterfield, once said that a good letter was one in which you could imagine the writer speaking to you, and when I read your letters you seem so, so close, and I can look at your photograph and pretend that you are really here, chattering to me. It makes our parting so much easier to bear.

I am hoping soon to be able to start another tour – perhaps in France; there seems so much that I could do. Still, I suppose I must be patient, although it is so very difficult at times.

In the meantime, please stay well and happy, Joan, and know that my thoughts are always of you.

With all my love, dear one,

Tony xxxxxx

## 19 JUNE 1944

Dearest Tony,

I am a little sad that you are eager to join the French battle. I understand, of course, that if you wish and can, then you must go. But sometimes I am a tiny bit afraid you will get too tired, dear one. You are not the few any more, Tony. You haven't got to win the war all by yourself; there are many, many planes and men for all jobs to be done now. I am sorry; I have no right to influence you and do not seek to, because I understand so well how you feel.

I want to see you again so much.

God bless you, dear.

My love,

Joan xxxxxx

## 20 JUNE 1944

Joan darling,

Today has been one of the worst days, so far as weather goes, that I have yet experienced. We started with a thunderstorm – normally very welcome – but unfortunately there was a sandstorm at the same time, and it literally rained mud. When the rain stopped, the sand thickened, and visibility was less than two yards! I was driving and could not see the surface of the road in front of me – there was a solid wall of sand. We all abandoned the desert and went swimming!!

Fortunately, on our return the weather was clear again; the temperature, though, was over 110 degrees. Still, the bad weather makes the swimming even more welcome.

I long for the day when I shall be back in England with you, no matter what the weather. May that day come soon, soon.

With all my love, dearest,

Tony xxxxxx

## 21 JUNE 1944

Dearest Tony,

Your air letter arrived today. Thank you for curbing my impatience to be away doing a real job towards ending the war. I guess, really, we are all most useful in the work for which we are trained.

I have a new job, too: Fire Guard Section Leader! I am now entitled to wear a white helmet (to indicate the target to the enemy?!) and a red armband. My duties involve issuing notices of lectures and practices and keeping records of attendances, assembling stirrup pump parties and, of course, accumulating knowledge about incendiaries etc. (Since we frequently get new and sometimes entirely opposing orders, I have decided to stick to common sense. In the event of a raid I should be too scared to tell one bomb from t'other anyway!)

The raids on London again are saddening everyone, but it is hoped it will not be for long. Thank you, dear one, for your kindness always. I look always for your coming home.

I believe it will be lovely anywhere with you, because it seems you want to make me happy so much that I could not help but be happy.

That is a topsy-turvy sentence, but I know you will not mind.

I send you my love, and hope with all my heart to see you soon.

Joan xxxxxx

## 22 JUNE 1944

Joan dearest,

I have just been watching the lovely new moon riding peacefully among the clouds, and I made a wish that it may be, oh, so very soon that we shall be watching it together in the quiet of an English evening. It seems so very, very long since I saw you, but the memory of that last meeting is still as fresh and dear as ever.

Goodbye for a little while, darling.

With all my love,

Tony xxxxxx

## 23 JUNE 1944

Joan darling,

I am still hoping to be able to get to Cyprus on leave. Lately, the only times we have been able to get away have been on duty, and we have had only a few hours free. As I have only had one week's leave and a 48-hour pass since leaving England, I am entitled to some and hope it will not be delayed much longer. If it would help bring me closer to you, I would gladly do without leave. It all seems so empty going out and planning things without you.

May it be very soon that we can plan a holiday together.

With all my love, dearest,

Tony xxxxxx

## 28 JUNE 1944

Joan darling

As I promised, here is the continuation of our travels.

Let us leave modern Cairo, make our way through narrow streets to the Mousky: the native bazaar.

It is very crowded here, Joan, and not too clean. Perhaps it would be better if we walked in the middle of the street – if one can call this space between two rows of buildings a street!

Turn left here, down this narrow passage and see the silver workers. Here we are: mind your head; the doorway is very low. In a minute or two your eyes will get accustomed to the gloom, and in the meantime here is the owner. He begs us to sit down and rest and offers to show us over the entire workshop whenever we like. 'Workshop' is a grand name for this narrow room, perhaps 40 ft long and 15 ft wide!

First, he shows us the spools of thin silver wire, which go to make up the delicate filigree work. This wire is drawn out from solid blocks of silver here in the shop. The first stage is to cut the wire into tiny pieces the right length, and this – as is all the work – is done by little children of about seven. They sit around in circles on the floor, cutting away and dropping the pieces into a wooden bowl.

The bowl is full, and one of the children takes it along to the next group. They are busy bending it with delicate touch into the required shape. Here, there are different bowls for the different pieces, and these are being filled at amazing speed. More children are collecting the shaped lengths and heating them to weld them together. Slowly, brooches, bracelets, chains and a multitude of tiny trinkets take shape before our eyes. Yet one more stage: it is dropped into a clear solution, which will clean away any trace of tarnish and give it that finished shiny appearance.

We come back to our chairs again, and the owner claps his hands. A native appears, bringing tiny cups of Turkish coffee and glasses of water and places them before us. The coffee is dark, thick and slightly sweetened and is very pleasant.

Now commences the real business. We are shown countless silver trinkets, and the proprietor goes into rhapsodies over them. How very precise his English is, and how strange it sounds!

This brooch: nowhere else in Cairo could we find anything half so lovely, and how cheap it is!

If you prefer plain silver, it is here. If you like it with gaily coloured enamels, it is here also. He lowers his voice confidentially: he likes us and will let us have anything we like at specially reduced prices.

That bracelet is rather nice; would you like it? He names a price; we laugh; he is only joking. He assures us he is a poor man – things are so difficult now, the price of silver, the children's food – but he will take two-thirds of what he originally asked. We offer him one-third, and now it is his turn to laugh: we are English; we are rich. It is a very funny joke. No! He cannot sell it at less than half. We agree, and he, smiling, puts it on one side for us, and the bargaining goes on.

When, at length, we leave, he comes to the door with us and thanks us for the honour we have done him. We must come again, and he will have many more even lovelier things to show us.

❖ ❖ ❖

The time has come to say farewell to Egypt and we set off along the coast road across North Africa. We must choose a comfortable car for this journey, Joan, for the way is long and often rough.

The first part of our journey is along an even, straight road with frequent clusters of palms and native dwellings. Soon these are left behind, and we come to the desert proper. All the while, however, the road follows the coast only a few miles from the sea, but to the south stretch hundreds of miles of even yet uncharted desert.

Past El Alamein, with traces of the great battles in the form of wrecked tanks and lorries, and on to Bardia and Tobruk.

Although the desert is so barren, the hills, or rather ridges, along the shore are full of interest.

Generally three or four ridges run parallel to the shores with the wadis, or dry valleys, cut into them at right angles. It is in these wadis that most of the cultivation takes place. Small patches, cleared, ploughed, sown and reaped – all by hand. Often at the end of the wadi is an oasis, with a shady group of feathery palms. Here is the real activity.

The organisation is immense for a nomad race. Each tribe is allowed a certain space of time at the oasis, and this time is strictly adhered to.

Let us leave the road for a little while and drive down this track and watch.

At the moment a herd of camels is crowding the narrow floor of the valley. The camel is the most independent of desert animals and shows it in his supercilious bearing. Among the drab sandy colour of the herd is a sudden contrast: a snow-white camel – quite an unusual sight. As we watch, the Bedouin herdsmen begin to drive them along with shrill cries, and the reluctant beasts move away and up the hill. Even as they start, a flock of sheep is drifting in from the other side. The sheep are not the sleek, snowy creatures of England but are a dusky hue and look far thinner: the sparse desert grass offers but poor grazing. As the flock approaches, we see that it is very plentifully interspersed with goats, which are seldom seen in separate herds. The hungry flock is soon happily engaged in cropping this more luxuriant grass, and over the hill a herd of cattle appears and stands, patiently awaiting their turn.

So the endless cycle goes on – inevitable in a land where water is so scarce.

While we are here let us look more closely at the landscape. The ground is rocky with a thin layer of sand and is covered with hardy vegetation. Cactuses of every shape and size abound beside other more attractive plants. Here is one with tiny silver leaves and bright red flowers and another with blue blossom like a forget-me-not.

This plant has no flowers, but its silvery twigs look very attractive. The wind seems to be ruffling some of them – but it is almost perfectly calm? We look closer and see that among the twigs are beautifully camouflaged insects, exact images of the branches on which they live.

A thin, black line crosses our path, and we stop to investigate: a long column of ants divided into two files – one going one way, and the other, the other. We follow one way and find that it splits up and covers perhaps 20 square yards, each ant returning with a minute twig or leaf. We retrace our steps, curious to see where they are going. On and on – we must have covered over 100 yards – and eventually finishing at a little hole in the ground. Down the hole pour the ants with their treasures, and, simultaneously, empty-handed workers are emerging to hurry off along the line: an amazing example of insect industry and organisation.

Let us stroll up to the top of the ridge and look at the sea. Surely no sea could be such a brilliant blue? Bluer even than the Mediterranean of travel posters! On roll the waves, crashing on to little submerged rocks in a dazzling expanse of snowy surf and into the shore, where they slowly dissolve into a wonderful translucent green. It is a most marvellous sight and one which could never be forgotten.

A sudden sound as of needles clicking: we start! It fades and then returns, yet nothing is visible. We strain our eyes again and again, and at last we are rewarded by the sight of a snow-white insect which is flying rapidly with its wings clattering away like knitting needles! Certainly this is a land of strange things.

We retrace our way back to the car and start off once more. As the sound of the engine breaks the silence, there is a flash of colour, and a little brown fox, which had been sleeping close by, leaps to startled life. He is very similar to his English counterpart, although his brush is not so fine.

The car moves slowly back along the track, disturbing little lizards and chameleons who doubtless wonder what this noisy intruder can be. Now a small, furry creature darts almost under the wheels; its fur blends perfectly into the surrounding countryside – necessary precaution, for the eyes of the fox are keen. It is a desert rat which ekes out a precarious living by hunting the elusive lizards. His enemies are not only on the ground – as a flash of sudden wings reminds us – for there are fierce hawks also and, at night, an occasional owl.

An Arab astride a little donkey raises his hand in stately salutation as we pass and continues on his way to that little cluster of square, low tents that you can just see over to the right. He looks old, but people age quickly out here in their battle to force a livelihood from the relentless desert.

At last, the road, and we speed on our way westwards through the waste that looks so empty but which we have seen to be so very full of struggling life.

On winds the road past Tobruk, Derna and Benghazi: mere shells scarred by remorseless war.

Dearest, this seems a suitable place to bring this letter to a close. I do so long for the day when these will be dreams no longer but a lovely reality.

May that day be very, very soon, dearest. I miss you so very much. Until then, if these dreams and plans make you happy and help pass away some of the wearisome time that divides us, I shall be more than happy.

With all my love and thoughts, dearest Joan,

Tony xxxxxxxx

## 29 JUNE 1944

Joan darling,

About the fighting in France: wishing to be in it is, I think, partly a longing to get into action and finish the war more quickly and partly curiosity to see conditions on another battle front and try out tactics gained in experience out here. As you say, though, they have so very many planes and men already.

Please forgive me for writing about this again, but I must take the plunge!! Would you please accept the material as a present? Money is of little use to us out here, except for buying presents, and I really do love to be able to send you things you cannot get in England. If I were in England I should be able to take you out to the theatre and cinema and to dinner and dancing, but, since I have to be away, please accept these 'carrots' instead. And please, am I forgiven?

I, too, am like you in that I like to have a 'carrot' to look forward to or something to strive after, and now I have a most wonderful 'carrot'. It is to make you as happy as I possibly can. I can always work far better with an object in view, and now your happiness is the one thing about which I really care. If there is anything at all, dearest Joan, in which I can make you happier, please let me know, and no matter what it means, I will do it. Please don't hesitate, because doing anything for you makes me so happy that it is really quite a selfish thing to ask of you.

With all my love, darling,

Tony xxxxxxx

## GRASMERE, 30 JUNE 1944

Dearest Tony,

I have been just two hours in Grasmere and feel I might contentedly settle here for life. I am sitting in the cottage garden, bathing in the beautifully warm sunshine. The cottage nestles on a hillside surrounded by trees, and through these I can see the lake and beyond the great hills. They are 'patched' with sunlight and shadow from the big white clouds riding overhead.

Immediately below, cows are grazing a field, and farmsteads and cottages peep from the trees.

I have already wandered into the village and visited the dear old church. Its beamed ceiling has held the roof for hundreds of years, and the altar is very simple, decorated with sprays of syringa, looking so beautifully white in the dim church. I should like to be married in a country church.

This is a sparklingly clean cottage, and my first meal was very pleasant. It was beautifully laid with a bowl of wonderful red roses on the table.

I wish you were here with me; you would like it so much, I know.

I have just had tea brought me. It is so long since I last had tea in a garden.

This is going to be a lovely holiday. I wish again you might share it.

All my love, dear,

Joan xxxxxx

## 5 JULY 1944

Joan darling,

We have discovered a new and crazy pastime for the beach. Four or five of us swim down to a large rock in deep water and sit around in a circle, anchored to the rock and looking solemnly at each other. Usually the strain is too great and we burst out laughing and come breathlessly to the surface. I think we must all be a little mad!!

Goodbye, dearest.

With all my love and thoughts,

Tony xxxxx

## 9 JULY 1944

Joan darling,

I would willingly exchange all my leave for an hour with you in the Lake District. It sounds so lovely and so very peaceful. I am so longing to get back to England again and see you. I fear, though, that it may be some time yet.

The idea of getting married in a country church is a lovely one, Joan. It would be so quiet and tranquil and far from the hurrying and rushing of the town.

With all my love and thoughts,

Tony xxxxxx

## 11 JULY 1944

Dearest Tony,

Thank you very, very much, dear.

Your long letters are like adventure stories with you and me as hero and heroine. The war over, I hope there will be no villain in our story – no fiercer, anyway, than Baron de Income Tax!

In haste to get the post lest you should be worried at not hearing from me, I send you all my love and thoughts.

Joan xxxxxx

## 12 JULY 1944

Telegram
To Joan Charles. Awarded DFC. Address same at present. Love,
Tony.

## 12 JULY 1944

Dearest Tony,

You ask if I like your letters; of course I do, every one, Tony. I missed
your frequent messages so much when I was away.

I am more than glad, my Knight, that we are not living our lives in
the thirteenth century, for then when you rode away to war I should
have had no sweet messages to console me for your long absence.

We went for some lovely walks around Grasmere but did not
climb very much because of the continuous mist and rain. One of the
finest afternoons, we crossed between Grasmere and Rydal Water
and climbed over the hills to Loughrigg Tarn. After tea at a pleasant
inn we continued to Elterwater and so back across the hills and lake
once more to Grasmere. The road winds along by a beautiful river
with a waterfall; across fields where the grass was cut and turning
golden; over Skelwith Bridge, beneath which the river dances and sings
and the trees, hanging low, are mirrored in its surface. One glimpses
whitewashed cottages and slate-grey ones smothered with roses and
snowy cloths laid for tea through open doorways.

We listened to the news outside a cottage on the hillside. It was
Tuesday, and Churchill's grave speech about the doodlebugs seemed
so strange and a world removed from the quiet beauty of the hills and
countryside around us. And yet it is not possible to keep one's thoughts
from the rest of the world, from the war, even in so remote a place. I
wondered about the people who live in peaceful villages. I think they,
too, fail to live apart, for almost every home must have some loved one
at the battlefront, and the radio must penetrate every hamlet now.

There is more excitement in St Annes, with evacuees coming from
London. It is difficult to find billets for them all, because housewives
have their hands full with their own families, homes and shopping now.
I do hope it will not be necessary to put the children into the boarding
houses, because they will be so unhappy if they are not wanted. The
landladies are not likely to welcome them warmly as it will mean the

loss of their livelihoods if the children take their rooms. Four little children were found on Saturday walking home to London. How sad everything about war is! I would rather like an evacuee but, of course, have not the time to look after it, and Mother is not strong enough to do any more.

Please do come soon to roam and talk and laugh with me.

My love to you, Tony,

Joan xxxxxx

## 18 JULY 1944

Tony darling,

I went up to Dalton's farm to pick peas yesterday, straight from the office, at six o'clock. It was lovely to spend a few hours in the fields after the close atmosphere of the office. Two friends and I gathered 120 pounds of peas, and I brought some home. I am going again this evening and hope to earn my little blue badge.

Some friends who returned to London only a few months ago had their home damaged by blast last week, and so we are hoping to make room for them to stay with us a little later on. It seems we shall have a very busy home until the flying bomb is mastered. It means more work, but it is really fun to have people staying. I am a little disappointed, though, that I may not have a little evacuee.

I haven't much news today, so with my love and thoughts I will say goodbye for a little while.

Joan xxxxxx

## 18 JULY 1944

Joan dearest,

I had a very nice letter yesterday from the Air Officer Commanding-in-Chief, congratulating me on the award. I must get it framed when I get back to England!!

Another highlight of recent days was a party given by the squadron in my honour – but for which I had to pay! I managed to slip away early but it went on until about three o'clock in the morning.

God keep you safe, dearest.

With all my love,

Tony xxxxxx

## 20 JULY 1944

Dearest Tony,

The evacuees are the main subject of conversation in St Annes. This is a great problem, which, it seems, the government optimistically hoped would solve itself. Hundreds and hundreds of mothers and children have been brought out of London, as indeed they should be, but accommodation was not prepared and so, weary and irritable, they are lodged in church halls while billets are found for them.

Many are slum families who are as unwilling to go into nice homes as the residents are to have them. They ask to go to working-class homes and yet demand that their families shall not be split up – impossible because working-class houses are small and cannot accommodate an extra family. The big boarding houses, which have room, are unwilling to give up their holiday business and, if forced, will give an icy welcome to the evacuees. Perhaps British good humour will save the situation, but how much more sensible it would have been to have taken over some hotels or Butlin's camp and converted them into hostels when this new blitz on London threatened last December.

No wonder you are amused at my efforts to run the country!

I offered more practical help at the church and talked with some of the evacuees and their children. They were all so tired and dirty and disgruntled.

Do not worry about my working too hard. It is very pleasant to go from the office to the fields; I am feeling well and am told I look bonny these days.

Your love makes me very happy.

God bless you, dear one,

Joan xxxxxx

## 23 JULY 1944

Tony darling,

Thank you for your cable. It is wonderful news; I am very pleased and proud for you. If there are accounts of your award in the papers and you have copies, will you send one to me? It is so difficult to get copies of the papers here.

I have had such a busy week; there has scarce been time to breathe. I spent two evenings farming and one at a Fire Guard officers' meeting.

We had a celebration supper for my parents' 30th wedding anniversary and your DFC in the evening.

I chatted with the farmer's wife on my farming expeditions. She was very kind, inviting us into her kitchen to wash and drink tea, and she told me that I must just go in and make tea for myself whenever I go to the farm straight from work. I met the ever-increasing family of kittens and the farmer's little daughter, who worries constantly for a pony and was trying to bribe her father by offering to pick peas every night for a week if he promised her one!

One of the men promised I might drive the horse and wagon back to the farm, but the girls fiercely opposed the suggestion lest the horse had different ideas of the direction from mine! Next time I shall drive, and if they do not choose to ride with me, they will have to walk back!

We had the big tin of peaches you sent me set in jelly, with real cream (made from butter at home), at supper last night. A friend gave me roses from her garden for the table, and it looked quite festive. I wish you might have been with us. I wish you might have celebrated your award in England, but rather would I look forward to peace when you will come home for good, and there will be so much cause for celebrations.

Thank you, thank you, for all your letters and thoughts for me.

My love, dear,

Joan xxxxxx

# 3

# A Time of Uncertainty

At the end of offensive flying operations, I was posted to Shallufa, a training station near Suez in Egypt.

## 4 August 1944

Joan darling,

I think you are the dearest person in the world.

How wonderful that two people who love the same things so much should meet in such a lucky manner. I shall always be very grateful that Laddie was with me that evening; I should never have plucked up courage to speak to you on my own!!!

I feel very sorry for the evacuees, especially the children. How sad it must be for them to have to leave their homes and come to a strange place where so few people are really interested in them. I wonder what will happen to the children of the wartime generation? It will be very different from the last war when there were no such wholesale evacuations. Somehow I feel that everything will turn out all right in the end. The greatness of the British character lies in its ability to recover quickly from setbacks and in accepting everything with a sense of humour.

I, too, would love to be back with you, holding you in my arms and chattering happily away, although I fear I would not be able to discuss anything serious – I would be able to think only of you.

Goodbye and God bless you, darling.

Tony xxxxxx

## 4 August 1944

Dearest Tony,

Weeding mangolds was rather back-breaking work, but it was pleasant to be out in the fields after a hot day in the office.

I had wonderful fun with a shepherd dog pup. He was so friendly and full of joy. I was upset at the sight of a bull chained close to the stable wall. Apparently there is no field to spare for him, but at least, I thought, he might be free in the stall. The creature looked in such ill condition compared with the cattle in the field.

Of course, I have earned my badge now and hope that I may have helped to bring the war a little closer its end. If it affected the duration one second, the work would be well worthwhile.

My love,

Joan xxxxxx

## 7 AUGUST 1944

Tony darling,

This fine weather will allow more air support to be given our forces in Europe and in destroying flying bombs.

I wonder if you are in Turkey with the new force? I 'wonder' you to so many places, don't I?! If wishing would bring you, dear, you would be home.

Poor Kath has lost all the glass in her flat, but fortunately she is uninjured.

With all my love and wishes for you,

Joan xxxxx

## 9 AUGUST 1944

Joan darling,

Your farm sounds very charming, and I should love to see you driving a horse and cart! The fresh air will do you good after long hours in the office.

I like to think of you sitting alone, quietly writing to me. It is so easy for me to pretend I am watching you and smiling as you puzzle over what to say! You say you think your letters are dreamy; I love them, for I am really a very dreamy person myself.

I was very sorry to hear in your last letter that you are feeling unhappy. I do so long for the day when I shall be with you again and we can laugh and be really carefree. Shall we do the *Wizard of Oz* skip along the promenade? It would be lovely but, I feel, very undignified!! Best of all, I think, would be romping breathlessly among the peaceful fields and hills. Goodbye, dearest, and be

happy. We shall not have long to wait.
    With all my love,
    Tony xxxxxx

## 15 AUGUST 1944

Dearest Joan,
I agree that, in spite of all the sad things, life is well worth living.
We are so much luckier than many people, in that we have each
other and so many happy times to look forward to.

    You seem to be part of everything I do now. When I read a book
I wonder what you would think about it, and if I hear music on
the wireless I wonder if you are listening to it. At times I wish you
were here so that we could watch the lovely things together – the
beautiful sunrises and sunsets, and the colour of the sea – and then
when things are not so nice, I am glad you are in lovely England,
for to me you are inseparable from loveliness and beauty. It makes
it so much easier to bear our parting, for we can still share all our
thoughts and dreams.

    Peace on earth. It is for so many, many years that we have been
hearing of wars. Please, God, this is truly the war to end wars.

    God bless you, darling.

    My love,

    Tony xxxxxx

## 16 AUGUST 1944

Dearest Joan,
At the moment I am feeling rather stiff. The Group Captain is a
keen fencer, and he asked me to help him with some fencing classes
he is holding. I did not fence, but merely demonstrated, but fear I
am sadly out of practice. I must be getting old!!

    I have just been thinking how one can adapt oneself to one's
surroundings so easily. Before I came out here I hated insects and
could hardly bear to touch them; I still detest them as much as ever,
but now if I find a beetle or something on me I brush it off without
thinking about it. Yesterday, as I was writing to you, a large cockroach
started slowly climbing up the wall in front of me. I continued to the
end of the sentence before dealing with it, although I would have
shuddered to think of meeting the creature in England!

Joan! (I was going to try to be severe but thought of you and realised you would only laugh at me!) You say you are not working too hard, but weeding mangolds seems very strenuous. Also you say you haven't been out anywhere. I fear that all my protests will be in vain, so must wait until I return, when I shall take you out very gently but very firmly and insist that you enjoy yourself and rest!!

I must reform, though, and let you go to bed early at night, otherwise your mother and father will think it would have been better had I stayed overseas!

Joan, darling, I am sure it will not be long before we can enjoy the happy times we plan together, but until then all my thoughts and love are with you.

Goodbye and God bless, dearest,

Tony xxxxxx

## 16 AUGUST 1944

Dearest Tony,

I am looking forward so much to your return. We have so many wonderful things to do. I should love to go to the investiture with you.

I visited Liverpool on Monday for the first time. I was not at all successful with my shopping as all but utility goods are exorbitant prices. A good dress costs at least 15–20 guineas! My own wardrobe rose greatly in my estimation, although I added nothing to it!

Otherwise, I enjoyed the day very much, visiting the still incomplete cathedral, which so fortunately escaped the devastation all round.

The docks, too, were a fine sight, full with the ships unloading. Thrilling to think how they cross the Atlantic almost unmolested now. The sun sparkled on the water, and the ferry-boats chugged back and forth across the river; tiny tugs fussed round the big ships, and men with the sea in their eyes leaned on the pier rails, watching and dreaming. I always think of the women in a dock town who wait so patiently, not only in wartime, but always, for their menfolk.

The countryside looks lovely now, patched with the fields of golden corn, but I miss the bright poppies of the southern harvest time.

You are seeing so many interesting places; it will be lovely to spend winter evenings sitting by the fire as you tell me all about them.

God keep you, dear.

I send my love,

Joan xxxxxx

## 18 AUGUST 1944

My dearest Tony,

How wonderful, wonderful is the news? I still think we shall be lighting candles on the same Christmas tree.

I may go to Grasmere for a few days while the family are there next week, if they can find somewhere for me to stay. That will still leave a week's holiday for your return and, if the war is over, maybe I can get special leave in addition so that we can have a really lovely holiday! Bless you, dear. Come home soon, soon, soon.

My love,

Joan xxxxxx

## 20 AUGUST 1944

Joan darling,

Hearing from you is like suddenly coming across a lovely, fresh oasis in the heat of the desert. It heartens me so greatly, and I feel refreshed and happy once more. It is the same each time. I never lose the feeling of wonder and gratitude that you should care for me.

With all my love, dearest,

Tony xxxxxx

## 21 AUGUST 1944

Joan darling,

I have tried to think of all sorts of nice things to say to you on your birthday, but it is no use; nothing I can think of seems right. So I just say from my heart, I love you.

And a very, very happy birthday to you, dearest,

Tony xxxxxx

## 22 AUGUST 1944

Joan darling,

Very, very many happy returns of the day. I wish I could be with you to give you all my love, but since that cannot be I will try to express all my best wishes in a letter.

It is just under a year since first we met, and what a wonderful and eventful year that has been, despite the unhappiness of parting. I feel that through your lovely letters I know you almost as well as if we had been together all the time. How wonderful it will be when we can rediscover all the things we have written about and share our hopes and joys together instead of merely planning them.

Perhaps it is a good thing that we have learnt about each other's tastes and likes and dislikes while we are apart, because now we can be certain that our love is very real and not merely a passing mood. I know I have said it before, but please forgive me if I say again how wonderful it is that we both love the same things and understand each other's dreams so well.

If I have been able to do well, it is only because of you. Your letters have brought the loveliness of England so clearly before me across the weary miles dividing us and shown me so plainly what we are really fighting for. Your ideals and dreams have been ever in my mind and have encouraged me if ever my task seemed difficult.

Joan dear, I have written a poem for your birthday and hope you will like it.

*Born from the earliest dawn of time,*
*The flame of love unending,*
*Undimmed 'cross changing Age and Clime,*
*All other thoughts transcending.*

*Fairer than loveliest flower thou art,*
*Than brightest star e'er gleaming,*
*Without thy love to glad my heart*
*All life were empty seeming.*

*Dearer than all the joys of earth,*
*Foretaste of heaven above,*
*All sorrow changes into mirth,*
*Through, dearest heart, our Love.*

Dearest, I hope you will have a very lovely birthday and that all your wishes and dreams will very soon come true.

With all my love,

Tony xxxxx

## Grasmere, 23 August 1944

Dearest Tony,

I am sitting alone in the lounge of this happy cottage. The scent of red roses on the table is very sweet. The sky grows darker over the hills, and everything is very still. A big pendulum clock ticks away the minutes, and the church clock in the village sounds the quarter-hours.

It is as if Peace dwelt in this valley, guarded by the hills.

It is cosy, too, in this little room. I wish you were sitting in the armchair talking or reading or just quietly thinking; I believe you would be happy so.

Sleepy from the journey and walking, I am going to bed now.

Good night, dear,

Joan xxx

Thursday, 24 August

We walked to Ambleside this morning along by Grasmere and Rydal. We searched for cards, but views of this district are out of stock; in their places are scenes from Blackpool, St Annes and, stranger still, Buenos Aires and Jerusalem! I wonder how these came to tiny English village shops.

The sun came through the clouds this afternoon, dispelling the mountain mists and making us very warm on our climb up Sour Milk Ghyll. This is a lovely waterfall splashing down from Easdale Tarn. We intended reaching the tarn but wearied of the long stony climb at the top of the falls. We felt so very, very thirsty! So we rested and washed in the stream then wandered down, seeking wild raspberries (but others had found most of the canes before us).

How much we enjoyed our tea! Then we read, between yawns, the visitors' book and wondered if we could find enough energy to go out again and decided not!

Friday, 25 August
We walked around Rydal and Grasmere this morning. This afternoon we wandered through the village, filled our pockets with tiny apples at a wee shop and sat by the lake, too tired even to row far out on the placid water.

With renewed energy, we rowed after dinner, watching the strangely beautiful sunset as we drifted on the lake. The mountains change colour from dark, rich green in the sunlight to smoky blues as the twilight falls. I hope you may soon know this wonder and deep peace.

Writing later
Saturday was the happiest day of all. After wandering around Ambleside, through the hamlet of Clappersgate (another spot I would love to stay – it is just a cluster of cottages set in lovely rolling green countryside), we spent the afternoon on Windermere. The sun was really warm and I felt so *contented*. I *am* a puss for warmth, aren't I? We rowed across the lake to inspect some seaplanes based there. It was a real pullback to catch the bus in time for supper; there is quite a swell on Windermere!

All this joy I wish you and much, much more.

My love to you,

Joan xxxxxx

## 23 AUGUST 1944

Joan darling,
It is a lovely idea to carry air-letter cards about with you and write when you get an opportunity; it makes me feel as though I were with you on your walks and shopping expeditions.

Goodbye and God bless, dearest.

With all my love,

Tony xxxxx

## 27 August 1944

Dearest Joan,

Perhaps, after all, we have been fortunate, dearest. We can build our plans and dreams so that the very thought of them is breathtakingly beautiful, and yet they are nearly all concerned with the simple things of life and not the highly artificial pleasures of modern civilisation. Then, too, we have the joy of knowing that our dreams will actually come true and will be even more lovely since we shall always be discovering fresh beauties and living only for each other's happiness.

How wonderful it will be when we are together again at last. I must never lose you again, darling, for so long.

It is becoming far easier to bear the parting now, since the news is so wonderful and the belief everywhere that our hard-earned victory will soon be here.

How shall we celebrate the peace, Joan? I see from the paper that many English places are already making plans.

But, whatever happens, my thoughts are and always will be with you, and for me you will always be the dearest person in the world.

With all my love, dear heart,

Tony xxxxxx

## 31 August 1944

Dearest Tony,

After all, I have found a little while to write you again. Thank you, thank you, dear, for the beautiful things you sent for my birthday and most of all for your love. I could not resist opening the parcel as soon as it arrived today, but it is very close to my birthday so you will forgive me.

Oh, all the things you sent were so nice I cannot tell which I like best – perhaps the compact because it is so unusual. And I love all the initials, Tony. It makes the things seem as though they were meant specially for me even before you decided to buy them and that you bought them just because you knew that.

The husband of a girl in my department died a few days after his return to England, after escaping from occupied territory. He was not wounded but suffered from exposure. It was so very sad, because his son was born just the day before he died. The baby is beautiful, though, and makes up a lot to Vera for her loneliness.

How is your fencing class progressing, Tony? I think you should ask the Group Captain to organise some dancing classes, too, so that you can take me to a lovely dance on your next leave! I think you should be a good dancer but expect you have been much too busy to learn, since the war has taken up most of your 'dancing years'. Will you teach me to ride when you come home, Tony? There are so many things we have to do together, but my fondest thought is to sit in the light of the lanterns on a Christmas tree, by a glowing fire, and listen to all the things you have stored up to tell me. I wonder and wonder if that will be possible.

So I have chattered to the end. I send my love and hope you will be home very, very soon.

Joan xxxxxxxx

## 1 SEPTEMBER 1944

Joan darling,

A very happy new month to you.

The weather is still as hot as ever, and I have quite forgotten what it is like to be cold. I shall soon remember when I get back home again. Do you remember those walks in the St Annes gales last November? How long ago that seems, Joan dear.

With all my love,

Tony xxxxxx

## 3 SEPTEMBER 1944

My dearest Joan,

Today is your birthday, and since I first woke up this morning I have been thinking of you and wondering how you were spending it. Probably it will be fairly quietly.

In the morning you will stroll lazily along the front looking at the sea and trying, not very successfully, to be cross with the wind for ruffling your hair. I do hope that the day will be fine and the sun sparkling on the waves. Perhaps there will be little fluffy clouds chasing each other across the sky and the seagulls wheeling and scolding as though they could catch them. Then, in the afternoon, you may go for a long walk towards Lytham or, if the day is very sunny, perhaps just curl up in a deckchair in the garden.

I love just sitting quietly and thinking about you and trying to picture what you are doing at the same time in faraway England. If, for no reason in particular, I am not feeling very happy, it makes everything seem right again, and the only thing in the world that matters is seeing you again.

Do you ever have moods like that, Joan, when all the world seems wrong and you feel really unhappy? I do, but as soon as I try to decide what it was that made me miserable it all fades away and I am left feeling cheerful but bewildered, wondering why I was so silly.

For me, dearest, you have always been linked with happiness. No matter how bad things seem I have only to think of you to become as wonderfully happy as if I were actually with you. It is a beautiful thing that love should be so strong as to overcome all other emotions so easily. Sometimes the thought that you really love me makes me catch my breath, and I can only feel wonder that I should feel so far, far happier than I had ever thought it was possible to be.

Darling, we shall always be happy with each other, and as long as we are together, nothing else will matter.

With all my love,

Tony xxxxxx

## 5 September 1944

Tony darling,

Each time I write the date on a letter now, I think about the same date next year. That there will be peace in Europe and you will be home.

How tranquil we shall feel when peace is established after, of course, the excitement of victory celebrations. I wish you could be home, and I wish I might be in London, but I shall not be there in time for the first wild joy. I wonder if London will be the same as in France and Belgium, or are we too sober to go crazy even on such a wonderful occasion?

My love and thoughts for you,

Joan xxxxxx

## 6 SEPTEMBER 1944

Joan darling,

Dearest, it was a beautiful picture that you painted of Christmas together. We shall be able to smile about our parting and look on it as merely an adventurous interlude or journey in quest of the sun! At the moment I would gladly exchange all our sunshine for a cold wintry day with you in England, sitting in front of a blazing fire, dreamily watching the pictures in it flicker and change.

The fencing is continuing as usual, and I am merely awaiting a suitable opportunity for suggesting dancing classes! Seriously, though, I intend to take some lessons next time I am in 'Alex' – I have seen an 'English Dancing Academy' advertised.

Goodbye and God bless, dearest.

With all my love,

Tony xxxxxx

## 7 SEPTEMBER 1944

Dearest Tony,

Thank you again for your letters, all 106 of them!

I am your 'blue girl' today, dressed in my dark-blue frock and baby-blue woolly. Yes, and untidy curls tumbling in my eyes and being tossed back and tumbling down again. I shall have to groom this 'seaside' head of mine before I return to London and lovely evening dresses. There are lots of little readjustments we shall have to make to peacetime life, some nice and some dreadful. One of the dreadful ones I hope will not return are social functions like card parties and entertaining because one is entertained and needing to wear new dresses because everyone has seen the old one. No, I like the friendly, more sincere spirit which prevails in wartime. But that is the only thing I like about war, and I hope with all my heart mankind will really care and work to live in peace.

Already at home we are benefiting from the approaching victory: blackout is to be relaxed; Fire Guards are released and Home Guard is no longer compulsory; one may travel anywhere in Britain; and summer fruit – plums and apples – is plentiful. We are glad of these things, but our thoughts are with the men who fight on to make real peace and happiness possible.

I do not agree with you that childhood is happier than 'grown-upness'. I am happier now than ever before, not just because circumstances are more favourable for my happiness, I think, but because I feel I have more 'power' to live life. Oh, it is so hard to explain. I mean that as one learns about disillusionment and makes friends with pain and sorrow, and I believe everyone has his share of these, one is given more strength to face them and so loses the fears of childhood – of the unknown, really. I feel I shall not be frightened any more, and it gives me confidence that I shall be able to take all life brings and live it fully and joyfully.

That is all a bit muddly, and of course I do not always feel happy and confident, but I do feel I understand life better than when I was young, and that makes it easier to live.

That is a lot to write about me! And I have come to the end of my letter.

Never mind, you will soon be home and finding out what a funny person I really am!

My love and eager, happy thoughts,

Joan xxxxxx

## 9 September 1944

Joan darling,

As I was writing the address on this airgraph I heard some music coming from the wireless in the mess. It was a selection from *Orpheus in the Underworld*, and I drifted off into a daydream, remembering the time I heard it with you at the Opera House. For a moment I felt a little sad, but then I thought how near even happier times are and how much more precious they will seem since we have waited so long and so patiently for them. It will be a true storybook romance, with meeting, parting and adventures, and then 'they both lived happily ever after'.

With all my love, dear heroine,

Tony xxxxxx

## 10 September 1944

Dearest Joan,

Welcome to Shallufa.

The road has been long and the journey hot. It lay across sandy wastes with the outlines of grim hills rising to the south.

An Arab hastens to open the great barbed-wire gate; a brief word to the khaki-clad service policeman and we pass on.

On the left is the guardroom: a wooden building with the sloping roof coming down to cover the veranda. A little further on, and on the opposite side of the road, is Station Headquarters: a long, low building with a few valiant creepers trying to climb rope networks at intervals along the front. It, too, has a covered veranda running the entire length.

Most of the buildings in this part of the world are bungalows with grey corrugated asbestos roofing. There are, though, one or two exceptions, which I must show you.

Shall we drive on? Past the tall, white flagstaff with the RAF ensign and the CO's pennant flying, and on to the Church Army canteen.

This is one of the exceptions I mentioned and is built of greyish stone. The bricks are a quaint irregular shape, and the effect is that of crazy paving stood on end.

Next door, in friendly rivalry, is the NAAFI. This is rather more orthodox in style, being built of white oblong bricks. It is also rather larger.

The third of the stone buildings is the church, which is creamy, while the lower parts of the walls are a rosy sandstone. This again has a crazy-paving effect, but it merely enhances its charm. The windows are pointed and even boast some 'stained' glass, which, although only improvised, is very pleasing. Inside, it is whitewashed a light cream, with a grey tiled floor. A small 'belfry' and porch complete the picture.

We are now approaching the officers' quarters, the lines of long bungalows divided up into rooms. Would you like to see mine?

The first thing that would probably strike you would be the untidiness! There is a table with a pile of books on one side which the Italian batman conscientiously tidies each morning. It remains so until the afternoon, when I return, and then chaos prevails once more. On the left is a bookcase which contains the books I am not actually referring to at the moment and is consequently more orderly. On one side is an ordinary door and double window and, opposite, French windows open onto another veranda. How grand it sounds!

Perhaps I should explain that the verandas are merely cement floors extending out on either side and covered by the roof. My bed is enveloped in a mosquito net, and the window is also gauze covered. The remaining space is occupied by a wardrobe and a chest of drawers with a mirror. All the furniture is dark stained wood, except the camp chair on which I am sitting as I write. The defects of the table are covered by a blanket!

The main mess building is only a few yards away. It is T-shaped, more or less, and is of wooden construction.

We enter through a narrow passage with a row of hat pegs on either side and come into the 'junction' of the rooms, rather reminiscent of the booking hall at a busy station. If you want to find anyone, the easiest thing to do is to wait here; he is bound to appear fairly soon. On the walls around are the various noticeboards and, most eagerly watched of all, the letter rack.

Turning to the right we find ourselves in the small anteroom which, at the moment, is being whitewashed a light green – if I can make such an Irish remark. The wicker chairs are all crowded together in the centre of the floor and look as lonely and disconsolate as chairs do on these occasions.

The bar opens from the left of this room. The actual bar is semicircular with an awe-inspiring array of bottles on shelves behind it. The rafters are oak stained, and the roof itself is covered with the names of the officers who have passed through Shallufa.

Retracing our steps through the 'junction' once more, we reach the main anteroom: a long room with an oblong of leatherette armchairs in the centre, so that wherever you sit you are gazing at someone else. This terrible effect has been overcome to a certain extent by placing tables in the middle with piles of magazines – rather reminiscent, this time, of a consulting room! On the left is a large glass-fronted bookcase, containing the Mess Library, and beside this is a small hatch opening into the office. It is from this hatch that we draw our letter cards!!

As a temporary measure, the wireless is in here, exiled from the smaller anteroom. It has a companion in the upright piano on the other side. A green-painted double door at the far end leads into the dining room. The separate tables are arranged in the form of a 'U'. At the end is the Group Captain's table, and he sits looking benignly down the tables on either side. From time to time staff officers are summoned to dine with him and sit on either side basking in the reflected glory!

From the roof of this, as in all main rooms, are suspended large, black electric fans, which click their way around throughout the day. One grows very used to the sound and is apt to be startled if for some reason or other the 'click' is brought to one's conscious attention. How very true of many things which we see or hear every day without 'realising' them!

But there is much more to see yet. We may as well drive; the camp is quite extensive.

Past the church and the NAAFI once more, we turn right, and the centre of Shallufa is before us: the cinema! This is yet another brick building and towers above everything else. Its proud name is 'The Green Lane Cinema', although apart from the gallant vines there is nothing green on the station!

The seats are wickerwork, and the tiers slope down to the screen. Class distinction is provided by low cement walls which assemble the sergeants at the back, the officers in the centre and the airmen in front. The charge is proportional!

The films are normally fairly good, though old, but the annoying thing is the cutting. This is done to increase the number of films that can be shown and is, I am sure, done by a non-English-speaking Arab.

The other day we had a stirring battle scene with the horses and their gallant riders waiting for the charge to be sounded. Their leader galloped to their head, reined his horse and faced the eager band. A sudden silence, then he spoke: 'Today is the 1st of June . . .' A pause, and then the battle was over, and we saw the victors reform. I shall always wonder what he said!

On the other side of the road are the airmen's tennis courts. The officers', I forgot to mention, are by the mess. They are reddish asphalt and, if rolled frequently, are quite good.

The rest of the camp is, I fear, strictly service, and as such we cannot venture into it, but I will let you peep at my office. It is a very imposing stone building, and we pass through an outer office to the inner sanctum!

My desk is at the end with its improvised trays: 'In', 'Action',

'Filing' and 'Out'. Fortunately work is not heavy, and they remain fairly tidy.

On the right is a stone bookcase – tables and shelves are built in – and this is, like the other one, full, this time with service publications. Charts covering the walls and a telephone add to the impressive sight. Let it be whispered, though: I can usually find time to write letters!

This, then, is Shallufa, some distance from civilisation but quite self-contained.

We have table-tennis tournaments, sports of all kinds, classes in the evening for airmen wishing to take 'matric' and last, but not least, a camp newspaper. This is a weekly affair, and I am contributing a series of articles on political and social re-education after the war. I wonder if anyone reads them!

Goodbye, dearest, and please come to visit me again.

With all my love and impatient thoughts, darling.

Goodbye and God bless,

Tony xxxxxx

## 11 September 1944

My very dear Tony,

It is a wonderful morning: a morning when the sunshine, a child's smile, the white clouds make one's heart sing for joy.

These are the fine, frosty autumn days and so welcome after the rainstorms of last week. Days we might be so happy walking across the Downs with a scampering puppy.

You should be home soon, I think, now that leave has been reinstated for the home-based forces. I am so impatient for you to come home. I reckon you would be just as well instructing in England – if only I ran the RAF!

Girls from the office are rushing off on leave unexpectedly as their husbands or boyfriends get leave, and those of us whose loved ones are abroad seem sadly out of this excitement.

You seem a little sad, too. Are you, dear? I will write another letter to cheer you.

Joan xxxxxx

## 12 SEPTEMBER 1944

Dearest Tony,

Thank you for wanting to see me so very much. You seem so sure, Tony, that I am all the lovely things you mention. Sometimes I wonder, dear, if you will discover my faults disappoint you. Perhaps it is my silly nature that I am a little afraid to count on things. It must be fine to feel so certain of the things one wants, to feel confident of their attainment.

I hope I shall have you home soon. I feel your nearness would reassure me about everything in the world.

That is a puzzling, puzzled way to begin a letter. I write ever as my thoughts run, for they reach much further than my life. Thought is a wonderful thing. In it one may know another's joy or sorrow, travel the world or to the stars. How small life would be without it.

Sometimes, reading your letters, I think how I have felt as you do, that I have seen and loved a place that you describe. I think sharing a glimpse of thought like that is one of the loveliest experiences in the world.

I think we must be in love, my dear, to understand so perfectly.

Evacuees are rushing back to London now the flying bombs have ceased. It is considered unwise lest the V-2s are launched, but I understand their eagerness to return home. Mother begins to think definitely about getting a house in Surrey and wonders if there will be any chance of getting a new one built when the war is over. I should like a bungalow on a hill but guess folk will be fortunate to get any house anywhere near London after so much property has been damaged. I have not seen a prefabricated house yet, but that plan appears to me like the beginning of slum areas. I am very interested in houses and buildings. Had I the skill, I should have loved to have been an architect.

So I have chattered to the end of another letter. I hope soon, soon, soon you will be here to talk with me.

My love and thoughts, dear,

Joan xxxxxx

## 12 September 1944

Joan darling,

I, too, hope that polite society 'at homes' and similar functions will not return after the war. They are not even friendly but often merely an excuse for gossip.

I am so glad that the blackout has been lifted and that a few austerities have been relaxed.

I think you are probably right about happiness. Childhood happiness is spontaneous, while grown-up happiness is the happiness of achievement. It is greater because we have had to strive for it and so appreciate it more. Consequently, it is deeper than that of childhood.

It will be really lovely when we can sit together in front of a fire and chatter away about all the strange things we write about. Oh, there are so, so many things I long to do, and the time is passing all too slowly.

With all my love,
Tony xxxxxxx

## 14 September 1944

Tony dearest,

The announcement that men may be transferred from their present overseas stations, without home leave, to the Far East worries me a wee bit. Tony dear, do you think it will apply to you? The possibility has affected my optimism just a little. I felt so sure that you who have been so long in service would return as soon as the European war was concluded. England has such need of her young men to rebuild her life, and there seem so many more men training both here and in America who are eager to take over the fighting.

Perhaps I am fretting without cause and must certainly continue to write more cheerfully.

Mother has just stripped down the blackout edging around the windows, and the room seems wonderfully lighter. She could not bear to wait the few more days until blackout is officially discontinued! The street lighting in St Annes was tried last night and was quite bright. How many torches will be laid away on Sunday! London is not to know this joy yet, but how wonderful it will be to see the bright lights in the West End again.

One of my war jobs is dissolved – Fire Guard duty – for which I am very grateful. It is very good, I think, that compulsory measures are being removed as soon as possible.

Oh, Tony, you should see Mother beamingly collecting and burning the blackout. It is a great sight.

I expect soon to be busy helping with a Red Cross aid-to-China fair at the Ministry. We organised one last year. We had great fun dressing as Chinese girls in some wonderful tunics. Mine was a gorgeous creation of cerise and black.

Joan xxxxxx

## 15 SEPTEMBER 1944

Tony darling,

There is little more to tell you since I wrote last night. Oh, yes there is! How lovely the lighted street lamp outside our house looked last night, its white beams sparkling on the wet bushes and pavement. Remember, we had never seen it properly lit before.

I was offered a transfer to London today, but, you will be surprised, I did not accept it. Our London office is terribly busy, and I would have to travel long hours, and Mummy would fret about me, because it seems that more raids are expected. I feel rather sad at missing the opportunity but am letting my head rule my heart in this decision. Do you think I am wise? I console myself with the fact that I shall probably be able to get transferred later and, if I wanted, could go home, transfer or none!

Yes, I feel miserable sometimes but soon cheer up, unless my misery is caused as it often is by tiredness, and then only a long, deep sleep will brighten me. Now, don't start worrying I work too hard again! I always use up all my energy enthusiastically and need a lot of sleep to replace it. Being alone a lot depresses me, though (forgive me, I forgot what I intended to write in the middle of a sentence! I feel most terribly dreamy).

Do come home soon. I feel so full of enthusiasm for a lovely holiday and shopping and going out and feeling gay. Tell me some of the things you want to do on your most wonderful leave, Tony. I keep wondering how long it will be and when, when, when. Goodbye for a little while.

Your scribbly, scrawly, most impatient Joan.
With love xxxxxxx

## 18 SEPTEMBER 1944

Joan, my darling,
Thank you for two of the nicest letters I have ever received. As you
had noticed, I was not feeling very cheerful, and then, as always,
you swept all the dark clouds away and everything is wonderful
again. Can you wonder that I love you so very, very much?

You are always so very natural in your letters that I feel you are
really just beside me, chattering as I read.

Your new clothes sound lovely, and I do hope I shall be home again
to take you out, feeling so proud and happy to be seen with you.

Darling, you say you wonder if your faults will disappoint me.
Joan, I love you as you are and would not change you for anyone
else on earth. There are so very, very many things about you that
I love: your wonderings and thoughts, your plans, your loveliness,
your cheerfulness and courage, your liking of beautiful things, your
love and, above all, you yourself for everything you mean to me
and for which I am so very grateful, but fear I can never express
in words. Oh, Joan, you are so very much a part of my life that
without you nothing would seem worthwhile and I should be lost
and bewildered. My only fear is that you should be disappointed
in me; I have so many faults. All I can say is that your happiness
means more than anything else in the world to me, and I would
sacrifice everything rather than cause you a minute's grief. Perhaps
this will help in my favour.

I have always loved you, but at first it was impossible to explain,
except that I felt happier when I was with you than I had ever
felt before. Now, since we have been parted, I have found how we
share the same hopes and joys, love the same things, have so many
interests in common that I feel sure that it was always destined
we should meet. My love is no greater, it could not possibly be,
but it is even more unquenchable now that I understand a little
why it should be. Oh, Joan, spontaneous love might have dulled
a little, but love based on such a perfect understanding of each
other can never die. We have known the sorrows and uncertainty
of parting, but they are nearly over, and we shall be together again.

My constant prayer is that I should prove worthy of your love; it makes me feel so very humble.

Good night, my darling. God keep you always.

My love and every thought,

Tony xxxxxx

## 26 SEPTEMBER 1944

My dearest Tony,

Thank you for your sweet, reassuring letter. I hope with all my heart that the dreams we dare to dream really do come true.

Yes, dear, I know we shall want to be alone on your next leave. We shall have a whole year to catch up on and then maybe memories to make for time to come, if you go away again.

I think of the long ago at home, when Kath and Margaret and I would lie in the grass on the common, gazing up at the sky, and pour out our thoughts for consideration and criticism by three very different outlooks. We each had such different interests, different friends and yet had much in common and a great interest and affection for each other's ideas.

They were great evenings when you and I talked for long hours.

You will have guessed I feel very lonely sometimes. I have nice friends here, but they do not think as I do, or perhaps I do not know them well enough.

The leaves are falling again, dear, and on fine evenings the sunsets are beautiful.

Good night, Tony dear. I wish that you were really here with me.

My love always,

Joan xxxxxx

## 2 OCTOBER 1944

My dearest Tony,

Last week was such a busy one. I very much enjoyed Thursday evening. We had a lovely dinner at the casino and went on to a dance at the Spanish Hall. I missed you most coming home in the taxi, dear. I wished so much I might lay my head on your shoulder and go driving on and on through the quiet dark streets.

I long for the time when I can give you more than scribbles, Tony – laughter and joy and companionship and love. Surely, surely it will not be long.

Joan xxxxxx

## 4 OCTOBER 1944

Joan darling,

I have been out sailing all the afternoon and had a grand time. The boat is a 27-ft whaler and sails very nicely, and then afterwards I swam lazily about. I thought longingly of the day when perhaps we would be sailing together on the peaceful Thames with nothing to disturb our happiness. Oh, how impatient I get for those lovely days to come!

Goodbye and God bless, my darling,

Tony xxxxxx

## 8 OCTOBER 1944

Joan darling,

Your day out sounded lovely, Joan, and I do so wish I could have been with you. I, too, would love to go driving on in a taxi with you close to me, curled up in my arms. Oh why do we have to be so far apart? The time seems to pass so quickly, and yet at the same instant it drags so slowly – it is a strange paradox.

As the summer draws to a close, we get lovelier and lovelier sunsets. This evening the clouds were rather stormy and stretching in billows across the sky. As the sun sank, it lit the crest of each cloud with a beautiful orange-gold tint, which formed a perfect contrast to the dark and sullen grey.

Thank you again, darling, for all your loving thoughts.

With all my love,

Tony xxxxxx

## 10 OCTOBER 1944

Dearest Tony,

I fear I have been feeling sad and a little frightened about the war. Sometimes it seems so overwhelmingly terrible, Tony. It seems wrong somehow to play and enjoy life light-heartedly while there is so much suffering, and yet one cannot help but be gay and happy when one's own life is pleasant. Life is sometimes very puzzling, *so* hard to understand. I am longing more and more to see you; the time is passing so very slowly for me too.

My love, dear, and constant thoughts.

Joan xxxxxx

## 13 OCTOBER 1944

Joan darling,

How time flies! I happened to glance at the date today and realised it will be exactly 11 months tomorrow since last I saw you. Your letters, though, have brought you very near, and we seem to have had many cosy chats, and I have a lasting record of them that I shall always treasure.

Goodbye and God bless, dear heart,

Tony xxxxxx

## 14 OCTOBER 1944

Tony darling,

Do go on feeling strongly about humanity forever, darling, and tell me always about your hopes and plans and dreams. I want to understand and walk very firmly beside you, if my way is truly beside yours. I hope with all my heart that it may be, that soon, soon we may be together to store up a lot more happiness to keep in our hearts if we are parted again. Or to go on being happy forever and ever like fairy-story people.

My happiest thoughts; good night, dear,

Joan xxxxxx

## 15 OCTOBER 1944

Dearest Joan,

Thank you, thank you for your lovely letter. How beautiful the countryside must have been. Your description was so wonderful that I could close my eyes and imagine myself sitting beside you and watching the lovely sunset on the lake.

We must go back there together very soon. I believe that the Lake District is even more enchanting, if possible, in a white winter.

Oh, I am so impatient of the long hours I spend away from you.

Goodbye and God bless, my darling,

Tony xxxxxx

## 16 October 1944

My dearest Tony,

Your sailing boat sounds lovely. Where did you meet her, and what is her name?

While I worked I made 'make-believe' – will you think me very stupid? – that you were sitting in the big armchair by the fire, reading a little and talking to me. We discussed, in my imagination, so many things: music, my worrying that I am losing touch with things – losing a little the ability to find words to express myself (I will explain this feeling later, Tony) – and the day's happenings to us and our friends. It does seem stupid to talk to someone so far away, but sometimes you don't seem far away, because I feel you will understand and help me with my thoughts and my problems. And, partly, the habit of childhood – of being so long an only child and making believe companions – remains with me. There, Tony, I would not tell anyone else about my childishness, but I have so much faith in your understanding, your love for me.

My love, darling,

Joan xxxxxx

## 16 October 1944

Joan darling,

As if you could ever be too frivolous! Happiness and laughter are more important than idealistic planning and rebuilding. In fact our plans are directed towards securing happiness to the world. It is only natural to feel happy when your life is pleasant. War is indeed terrible, and for that very reason being able to enjoy the lovely things of life seems even more wonderful by contrast. Our aim should be to help others to reach our high standard of happiness. Our own happiness is secured to us forever by our love, and oh, Joan, how glorious it will be when that happiness is not even faintly shadowed by parting!

Today might almost have happened in England, so sudden were the changes. The first part of the afternoon was still and hot, but towards evening it began to grow cloudy. Suddenly a gale swept across us, bringing in its train a sandstorm and then, wonder of wonders, rain! Alas, the rain was all too little, and our violent visitor departed, leaving clear, evening skies.

All my love and thoughts,

Tony xxxxxx

## 20 OCTOBER 1944

Dearest Tony,

Next week will be rather different; I am going farming for three days. Potato harvesting is not very exciting, but I am so much looking forward to days in the fresh air – oh, and away from the office!

I think often and often of your sailing, Tony. I wonder so much about your life at Shallufa, since your long letter telling me about it has not yet arrived. I wonder what work you are doing, the scenes you see each day, when you sail – yes, even the colour of the water, the colour of the sails on your boat . . . I loved to read about the oasis you found when you went swimming that day, the chameleon that would not change colour, the blue sea you flew over in the wonderful dawns. These pictures are in my mind as if I had seen them for myself.

Good night, dear.

God keep you and send you home soon, soon,

Joan xxxxxx

## 20 OCTOBER 1944

Joan darling,

There is a new moon riding in the sky, and everything seems so peaceful. I had been listening to Beethoven's 'Seventh Symphony' and *Egmont* overture and really enjoyed them. It is wonderful the tremendous effect music has on our feelings. A stirring march rouses all our patriotic emotions, and light music makes us gay and happy. Gilbert and Sullivan sum it up very well in the 'Wandering Minstrel' song. Dearest, how lovely it will be to be able to go to concerts and operas together once more.

With all my love,

Tony xxxxxx

## 21 October 1944

My very dear Joan,

It makes me feel very humble indeed when I realise how much you love me, and I hope and pray that I may be worthy of you. Our love is so much greater and true because our thoughts, loves, ideals and hopes are the same and not, as you once wrote, 'for a trick of thought' or 'a smile, a look, a way of speaking gently'. Oh, Joan, our ways must indeed be together to 'love's eternity' or else nothing is true or real in the world.

What high ideals, dearest, but I think that the pursuit of them will ensure our own happiness, for the highest happiness is the realisation that through us others are happy.

Help in this quest, darling, and let us live together happily ever after in a truly 'brave new world'.

With all my love and every thought,

Tony xxxxxx

## 23 October 1944

Joan darling,

Thank you for your air letter and more for your trust and confidence in me. I hope and hope that I may prove worthy of it.

Dearest, you are not being stupid, dreaming and 'making believe'. It does help to pass away the long hours of parting. I often pretend that we are together again in England, roaming along some quiet English lane, admiring the loveliness of the countryside and chattering gaily – happy merely to be together. All our dreams and 'make-believe' are really hopes and plans for the future and a longing for the day when they really will come true.

Don't worry that you are losing touch with things and unable to express your thoughts and words. Everything is so challenging and chaotic at the moment, and all our senses of values are changing so that there is very little left we can cling to as being real. Our age-old ideas of time and distance and monetary values, of the value of human life, of security are all swept away, and until they are replaced by new values, uncertainty must exist. It is only natural that this uncertainty will affect our whole lives and thoughts. I often try to write lovely things to you and tell you how much you mean to me and how much I love you, but my thoughts run away too fast, and I can never catch them and put them on paper.

It is wonderful of you to confide in me, dearest, and I shall always love and understand you.

The sailing boat, unfortunately, has no name and not even a number! She belongs to the RAF and comes under my control for instructional purposes in my capacity as Air-Sea Rescue Officer. She is very easy to handle in spite of her size. She is a 27-ft whaler, and she is as fast as any boat in the area, including one or two lovely Bermuda rig craft owned by local people.

Where shall we sail, Joan? Along the Thames, past Henley, Kingston, Teddington and Chertsey? How lovely it would be: a warm summer afternoon, a picnic lunch and a boat gliding gracefully along under snowy-white canvas. It is so much nicer than a launch. Launches scare the swans and ducks away, while a yacht seems to be almost one of them.

I have just been looking at the stars, and they seem so calm and wise; they have watched so many struggles on this earth, and all turns out well in the end. I wonder if you have clear skies overhead, Joan, or is it cloudy? No matter, the dawn will break, and it is often lovelier for the clouds its coming dispels. May we be together again very soon, dear heart.

Tony xxxxxx

## 30 OCTOBER 1944

My dearest Tony,

Sorry, dear, I have not written the last few days. Farming and canteen have made me rather weary, although I found much to enjoy.

Walking along the country lanes in the early morning was the happiest part of my farming days. Thursday dawned misty and grey and, except that it was not cold enough, might have been a December morning with the snow-laden sky. The countryside had a wonderful, softly mysterious charm.

Friday morning might have been reproduced from a gay modern painting, or rather from such a morning as modern artists paint their light-hearted pictures. On every side were the leafless trees forming quaint patterns, their branches silhouetted against the blue sky. Fluffy white clouds graced that blueness, and the sun streamed down on clusters of white and red farm buildings. I thought of Rowland Hilder's paintings. This morning had that same 'doll-like' quality.

The work was hard and muddy, but fortunately I did not stiffen or ache after the first day. Since I was the only one staying for lunch at the farm, I was invited into the big farm kitchen to eat my sandwiches and warm up by the fire.

Unfortunately, Saturday rather spoiled my experience of farming. Digging potatoes by hand in heavy rains, the land was bog in which one sank and squelched. The rain began at nine o'clock that morning and poured down, making us very wet and miserable. Feeling shivery, I packed up at 10.30, although braver and tougher spirits carried on. After a hot bath and wrapping up warmly I felt better but could not shake off my tiredness, so lazed by the fire all evening, listening to the radio. Altogether I enjoyed my days as a land girl and was glad of the opportunity to see how country people live and work. Although I envy them the fresh air and ever-changing loveliness of the countryside, I would not like the hardness of the life – the men so weathered and roughened and the women with little time or opportunity, I imagine, for graciousness in their lives.

Then again, I do not envy city dwellers.

We are lucky who have been brought up between the country and the town, learning the delights of each, yet suffering little from the disadvantages. I think it is as necessary that countrymen and townsmen should get to know and understand each other as for the nations to meet and exchange ideas.

I do not like to see children working for money, Tony. It teaches them only a false value of money, and the things they buy with it are often more harmful than good for them. I have been thinking about this because there were 35 children between 10 and 14 years old helping with the potato harvesting, working far too long because they were eager to earn the money. Several of them were smoking – one girl, seven cigarettes during the morning! – and their conversation was mostly of the pictures and how they dressed up to get into the adult films. Many of them, particularly the boys, had an insolent air. There is great concern in the country about young people spending so much time in 'pubs', the main reason given being lack of other places to go. That seems the likely reason in lonely country spots, but after seeing these children showing off so stupidly, and the very drunken kids in Blackpool where there is so much alternative amusement, I wonder if the greatest fault does not lie with the upbringing and education of children.

I wonder if most of these troubles were there before the war or whether they are evils of war. It is true that overworked parents and teachers have less time to watch and guide their children and pupils, so the children are old and independent beyond their years.

There is a tendency, too, I think, to neglect giving council schoolchildren sufficient opportunities to show off (a natural desire seemingly of everyone) in the healthy ways of sports. Do you think the American system of education better, Tony? Their aim is to develop a citizen rather than a scholar, I believe.

How I ramble on! Sorry, darling, but, though far from being terribly serious-minded, I long to discuss everything that interests me with you, and so vainly begin to do so in my letters. So many things do interest me.

The air smelt lovely this evening: a misty, fallen-leaves smell of autumn.

I feel a bit better this evening, but everyone has been telling me how awfully tired I look, and it is generally agreed that farming does not suit me at all! And I was so wishing I might look wonderfully well to prove Mother mistaken in saying I was not tough enough!

Your obstinate, stupid, loving Joan xxxxxx

## 30 OCTOBER 1944

Joan darling,

I have thought of another way of writing a long letter. I will start one and add to it day by day my thoughts and dreams. It should help to bring us even closer together and you will be able to watch my mood vary from day to day and realise how changeable I am!

I will sketch briefly the table at which I write (I mentioned it briefly in one of my long letters) so that you will be able to close your eyes and see me.

The table is of a dark stained wood with two drawers in front. A grey blanket with three light stripes and sundry iron marks covers the top and hides defects! On the left: more untidiness. The foundation is a sheet of brown paper, folded more or less neatly, then some of the magazines you sent me. Topping the pile are six books – on psychology, politics and economics – and my flying logbook.

This pile is flanked by sundry small items: a table-tennis ball, a bottle of ink, my sunglasses and a shoehorn. From time to time other objects make an appearance. The table is against a beige-coloured wall and, unfortunately, this gives me no inspiration! Slightly above is a switch for the rather hesitant light suspended by a suitcase strap above the table.

So you have a picture of my surroundings as I write, and it may help you to understand some of my odder thoughts, because sometimes something on the table catches my eye and I go wandering off in a maze of memories.

May it be very soon that we may be together again and able to share our thoughts and dreams and plan together.

With all my love, dear heart,

Tony xxxxxx

## 1 NOVEMBER 1944

Dearest Joan,

How many lovely memories of last year this month brings back. Those few, wonderful days were the happiest I have ever spent and the thought of them is one which will always be most precious to me.

It is in the future, though, that we shall find true and lasting happiness, and every day will see the fulfilment of our dreams and plans and link us ever closer together.

My thoughts and love are always with you, darling,

Tony xxxxxxx

## 3 NOVEMBER 1944

Joan darling,

Since I have started my long letter, writing my thoughts to you, I have realised that no matter what happens we can never be really separated. Our love, expressed in our thoughts and dreams, will always keep us linked close together, and I think that this lovely sharing is one of the most wonderful things about being in love.

No matter how much I console myself, though, I still long to see your dear face again and to be able to talk to you and hold you in my arms. Oh, Joan, I love you so very, very much. How weary the time of parting is! It will make our reunion so much lovelier, though, and surely after this disturbed preface the story of our romance will run on happily ever after.

With all my love and thoughts,
Tony xxxxxx

## 4 NOVEMBER 1944

Tony darling,

Mother is ill in bed, and so I am home, keeping house and being day nurse and night nurse as well! It is such a very big job for me that, after a week of rushing breathlessly around, I dissolved into a few silly tears this afternoon. I have everything under control again now and look much more confidently and happily towards next week's duties. The house has grown bigger and bigger as I've cleaned it; it always seems to be a mealtime, or time for Mother's medicine or doctor's visits. But these things have not proved too bad, and there have been nice spots in the week – Janie's visits, her willing help – only cleaning greasy pans and the cooker has been very hateful: somehow I cannot accustom myself to doing dirty, greasy jobs without a sickening sensation!

That does not seem much of a subject to write about, but I tell you all my impressions of life that you may really know me, and, unfortunately, that has been one of the deepest impressions of my week!

So, since last I wrote to you, I have been cooking, sweeping, cleaning, washing and ironing, mending, shopping and managing the family. Strangely, because my hours have been equally full, I have not felt so tired as I do when I am working at the office. My mind particularly is not nearly so exhausted at the end of the day, and I lie thinking or wishing I might read when I go to bed – I have been sleeping on a divan in Mummy's room so that I can get anything she needs and so do not like to keep the lights on too long.

It would seem to me worthwhile to be your wife, dear – that we should live a full and happy life together. Thank you for being so sure of everything, because you make me feel sure, too.

Chrysanthemum-time, Tony, and I treated myself to some dainty pink ones yesterday. I arranged them in a cutglass bowl, and they look so alive and beautiful, the dark-green leaves a lovely 'gown' for each proud lady.

Your letters were really interesting and helped me to know you better and better, Tony. Go on telling me all your plans, Tony; their contemplation does make the time pass more quickly.

My loving thoughts,

Joan xxxxxx

## 5 November 1944

My darling Joan,

You wrote how Kath, Margaret and you would lie on the grass on the common and pour out your thoughts to each other, and your words reminded me of the lovely poem by Rupert Brooke.

*Breathless, we flung us on the windy hill, . . .*

Darling, the day is not far distant when we shall be together again to help each other, to soothe away each other's worries, to resolve each other's wonders, to reassure each other and to live a life made wonderful by our love.

This present time is an interval between the acts of our life. Our normal existence has been relentlessly covered over by the curtain of war, and we are left bewildered, trying to adjust ourselves.

For you it is very difficult. Your life has been broken up, you have to work hard and your work is dull; it does not even seem to be directly connected with the war. It needs real courage and perseverance to carry on cheerfully, although the smiling face hides a lonely heart. If only I could see you again, even for a little while, and hold you in my arms and tell you how much I love you and how much you mean to me.

Your love is the only real thing in the changing, uncertain world in which I live. Nothing else seems definite. I am losing my ability to rest and think quietly; there always seems to be something that could be done, and yet when I try to settle down to hard work I find myself thinking of something else and unable to concentrate.

I love music but find that very often I cannot even sit and listen to it. My whole life is restless and unsettled.

In this uncertainty you are my only help, and your letters and thoughts remind me that this is but a passing phase and that, once we are together and able to share our puzzles and cares, our love will melt them all away.

It is, then, in the glorious hopes of the future and tender memories of the past that my consolation lies.

Today I was listening to the wireless, and the lovely strains of Handel's 'Largo' carried me back to a wonderful evening a year ago. Do you remember, dearest? It was at the Winter Garden Theatre.

The grey cloisters gave a touch of tranquillity and calmness and a contrast to the colourful scene which confronted us.

The stately, scarlet-clad figure of the Lord Cardinal Archbishop of Rheims dominated all others as he sat in his great chair, with his court around him: 'Many a knight, and many a squire, with a great many more of lesser degree.' His monks were respectfully gathered to the right and even the jackdaw was subdued. The interest of all was centred on the surplice-clad choir.

How clearly the lovely young voices rang out in the glorious anthem – it was like an echo from the Courts of Paradise. Joan darling, those happy days will come again, and war and destruction will be nightmares lost in the wonderful promise of the sunrise of peace. Then there will be one joy of my life: to surround you with love and happiness and wander with you, hand in hand, towards the lovely reality of our hopes and dreams.

If things seem dull and weary now they will merely serve to enhance still further the true and lasting happiness that awaits us.

Goodbye, sweetheart, with all my love,

Tony xxxxxx

## 5 NOVEMBER 1944

Joan darling,

As you are feeling puzzled and lonely I have written to try to comfort you and to tell you how very proud and grateful I am that you should confide in me. I hope and pray that I shall always be able to help you and know that you will always be able to calm and soothe away my doubts and worries.

With all my love and constant thoughts,

Tony xxxxxx

## 8 November 1944

Dearest Tony,

I am settling quite successfully into the second week of housekeeping, with no worse tragedies on my record than two cut thumbs and a scalded wrist! It is hard work running a home these days without help even of a cleaning woman and with all the shopping to carry and rationing problems. Overwork and tired nerves account for Mummy's illness. I wish I might stay home and help her, but that is impossible. In London I would not have cared to do this, but now that I do not like my office – the work is so trying, and there is so little fresh air in my life – I am enjoying my present home work. Mostly, I believe, because, although I work longer and busier hours in the house, I have not felt that extraordinary tiredness that I do from my office duties. In fact I wish so much you were home; I feel just in the mood for tripping out and having fun in the evenings!

Your desk-muddle seems an interesting one, Tony. Mine is a different kind of untidiness, Tony. I do not like to see muddles, even neat piles, around me, and so bundle everything into drawers and cupboards. Unfortunately I rarely remember which contains the article I happen to want, and I scramble things wildly in my search!!

I often regret not having joined the forces early in the war before I was reserved. Now that it is slightly easier to get one's release, the women's services are requiring recruits to sign on for three years. I fear that would mean my being just about trained and shipped overseas when you were returning to England!

This little 'nurse' has just had an order for cocoa and buttered toast from the patient (and incidentally the patient's younger daughter!) so must leave you.

My love and thoughts, dearest,

Joan xxxxxx

## 9 November 1944

Joan darling,

I arrived in Cairo at about one o'clock in the afternoon and found it very, very cold.

There was a rather good film on at the 'Metro' – Cairo's best cinema – *The Cross of Lorraine*. The 'Metro' has wonderfully comfortable leather armchairs. There is no cinema organ, and instead we had gramophone records. Then back to 'Music For All' – I had dinner there and met a Palestinian with whom I had a very interesting conversation. I will tell you of it in my long letter.

And so my short leave was over. I caught a train at seven o'clock next morning and soon was back at Shallufa.

It made a pleasant change, though, and I felt much better for it.

Goodbye and God bless,
Tony xxxxxx

## 10 November 1944

Joan darling,
I have just heard about the V-2 on the wireless. How I wish I could get back onto operations against Germany so that I might feel I was doing something to stop this ruthless and indiscriminate attack on a civilian population. The German government must be made to pay dearly for this destruction.

Goodbye and God bless, my darling.
With all my love and thoughts,
Tony xxxxxx

## 11 November 1944

Joan darling,
Today is an anniversary: the anniversary of our first kiss. It was a year ago, and we were driving back from a show at the Opera House. The night was dark and cold, and we were grateful for the warmth of the car. We left the busy streets behind and turned along the front and then, suddenly, we were in each other's arms. How beautiful that first kiss was, and how lovely the drive seemed with you close beside me with your cheek against mine. It seemed like a wonderful eternity and yet passed far, far too quickly.

And then those two happy days together when, even then, I was too shy to tell you how much I loved you. I was so very, very happy just to be near you. I treasure the memory of those two days more dearly than anything else in my life. Soon, dearest, we shall be together again and there will be nothing to cast even the faintest shadow on our joy. Let us never lose this sweet wonder of being in love for the first time and make our life a long and ever happy romance.

Whenever I hear lovely music I think of you and long to be with you so that we can enjoy it together. We shall have so much time to make up for when this weary parting is over. It will make everything seem even more precious and lovely, though, so we should really be grateful.

With all my love and impatient thoughts,

Tony xxxxxx

## 12 NOVEMBER 1944

Joan darling,

I think that one of the most wonderful and exciting things about being in love is being able to share each other's thoughts and dreams. To confide in you is so natural and easy. Your thoughts are so much the same as mine. We must truly be very much and very deeply in love to be so closely linked together.

I mentioned in one of my air letters that I had met a Palestinian in Cairo. He was in the army. His mother and father had been in Switzerland when war broke out but had to go to Holland on business. Unfortunately while they were there the German invasion started and as Jews they were deported to Germany. He has never heard of them since. It made me realise how lucky we really are. How terrible it must be to be in suspense about one's loved ones and never hear a word about them.

I was sitting in the lounge the other morning, and everything was very still. Someone had left a cigarette in an ashtray, and the smoke was curling lazily upwards in a transparent veil of lovely blue. The grace and beauty of the slowly curving whirls was so striking that I began to wonder how I could describe it. It was then that I realised suddenly the utter inadequacy of words. It was impossible to describe the loveliness of even so small a thing.

I think that one of the most precious things one can have is one's freedom. I was watching a bird soaring gracefully around and envying it its freedom in the air, and I thought how terrible it would be to be enclosed in a small space and never able to wander out into the open, to watch the beautiful things of nature: the birds, the sunshine, clouds, the stars and everything that we take so much for granted. I could never be a judge. No matter what a man had done, to sentence him to spend months or years in a confined space, seeing the same surroundings every day and feeling every moment that intense and bitter yearning to be free, would be impossible. It sounds absurd, but I think death would be infinitely preferable.

My thoughts today have been with the one I hold dearest in all the world. I have wondered what you are doing, what you are wearing, hoping that you were happy and that perhaps you were thinking of me. You are the only thing that matters in my life. You are part of everything I think or do, and all my hopes and plans are directed to bringing closer that happy day when we shall be together for always, when my whole life can be devoted to making you happy. I shall never be able to write a third of what my heart wants to say. I love you so very, very much. Perhaps it will be easier when I can hold you close in my arms and whisper how much you mean to me and how you are my life.

God keep you safe always.

With all my love,

Tony xxxxxx

## 15 NOVEMBER 1944

Joan darling,

I have spent a lovely afternoon reading through all your letters. As there are so many now (thank you, dearest, for writing so often), I have sorted out those that I like best of all. A difficult task, for they are all very precious. These I shall keep in my writing case so that I can read them often. The others I shall put in a box to keep them safe and sound.

Your letters are so lovely, Joan. I always look forward eagerly to their arrival.

With all my love and thoughts,

Tony xxxxx

## 16 NOVEMBER 1944

Tony darling,

Thank you for your dear letters and the very lovely poem. I have read them over and over grasping the reassurance of life that they contain.

Please forgive these troubled moods of mine, Tony. Many things have worried me lately and made me sad; but usually I am a very happy and 'purry' puss and hope that soon my joyful heart will return.

I am glad you bought some more of your beloved books. I am afraid I will not allow you to stay at home and read all next leave; I long so much to 'fling us on a windy hill, laugh in the sun and kiss the lovely grass'. That is a wonderfully lovely poem, dear – I read it once long ago and thought how beautiful it was.

And when will you return to make the lovely peace?

My love, dear,

Joan xxxxxx

## 16 NOVEMBER 1944

My darling Joan,

How I wish I could be with you this Christmas that we might share the love and happiness of this lovely season. May it be the last we shall ever spend apart, dearest.

Since I shall not be able to whisper to you how much I love you, I have written a poem which I offer as a Christmas present. It tries to tell you a little of what my heart longs to say.

Goodbye and God bless you, my darling.

My ever-loving thoughts,

Tony xxxxxx


*Oh radiance of your presence*
*Dims the sun at noon on high,*
*And your star-eyes hold the glory*
*Of a wondrous evening sky;*

*Your dear lips the dew-pearled petals*
*Of a lovely English rose;*
*Sweeter than the calm of moonlight*
*Your bright loveliness e'er glows.*

*Yours the promise of the sunrise,*
*And the fragrance of May morn;*
*Your voice the glad sweet music*
*Of birds heralding the dawn.*

*Your gay smile is sunshine breaking*
*From the clouds across the sea.*
*And your laugh, Oh Dearest Joan,*
*It means all the world to me.*

## 18 NOVEMBER 1944

Joan darling,

We entertained the sergeants in our mess yesterday evening, and I think that everyone really enjoyed it. I stayed for a while and then slipped discreetly away as things became a little hectic!

I stood outside the mess looking at the lovely sky and, as I watched, a bright star flashed across the heavens, leaving a glowing trail behind it. The Norsemen had a legend that our life was like a shooting star. We appeared, stayed a little while in the world and then vanished into the unknown. Still, if we can leave a bright trail behind us as an example we shall have helped the world a lot.

People are inclined to be very materialistic and cynical nowadays, but I think that being able to do good for others and helping them to lead fuller, happier lives would be its own reward.

I miss you more and more, dearest, each day, and long for the time when we shall be able to sit close together and share our thoughts and ideas, knowing that we shall be able to understand each other perfectly. How wonderful our lives will be.

Goodbye and God bless, my darling,

Tony xxxxxxx

## 20 NOVEMBER 1944

Dearest Tony,

A very tired me, sitting on the end of a divan in Mother's room, stealing a little while in the afternoon to write to you.

Mother is a little better and sleeping again, but it seems she will not be able to do all the work for perhaps a long while. The very great problem is who is to do it! I should have returned to the office today when my sick leave expired, but Mummy was not well enough to get up. I may have to work only part-time, but it seems a pity to give up my establishment. Oh dear, how full of problems life is!

My love and thoughts and blessings,

Joan xxxxxx

## 21 NOVEMBER 1944

Tony darling,

Dearest, what a lovely anniversary to remember. Yes, please let us always remember dear things like that, for so is life made softer and more beautiful. Some people seem so afraid of expressing emotion that I think others can never really understand them. Anniversaries, birthdays, Christmas, or little personal ones are such precious reasons for expressing happiness, for remembering past joys and dreaming of future ones; it is a pity to drift away from them as so many people do.

Thank you for your sympathy, too, Tony. I am sorry to have written of my worries instead of the happy inspiring words I should write to you. But it is so good to be able to shift a little of one's load on to another's shoulder – someone one feels very capable to help. Perhaps I have always turned to Mother for comfort when I have real need of it, and so miss her help now, when she is not fit to manage these problems that I must decide for the whole family. I will only say thank you, then, for all your love and wonderful thoughts for me. I do cherish them, my darling, with all my heart.

Though reality often falls so far short of dreams, I do hope and hope our story may prove as lovely as you paint it. Yes, I believe that you will gently, confidently, understandingly, lovingly make it so. My love, dear one.

Good night,

Joan xxxxxx

## 21 NOVEMBER 1944

Joan darling,

Yesterday evening we had a programme of recorded music on a gramophone and amplifier built on the station. It was quite good. We had Tchaikovsky's *Piano Concerto No. 1*, a selection from *Carmen* and *Manon* and, best of all, Beethoven's *Symphony No. 1*.

Beethoven is, I think, my favourite composer, and when I hear a great orchestra playing one of his symphonies I just drift off and am lost in the grandeur and beauty of the music. The second movement is a lovely minuet and minuets are my favourite dance music!! How typically impractical of me!

I really must learn to dance, Joan, then perhaps I shall find modern dances as enchanting as my minuets. And, anyway, with such a lovely partner I should never hear the music or think of the dance but have room in my heart and mind only for you. We shall be so happy, darling, that merely being together will be wonderful fun, and nothing will ever be able to spoil our happiness. How I long and long for those bright days.

Goodbye and God bless, dearest.

With all my loving thoughts,

Tony xxxxx

## 22 NOVEMBER 1944

Dearest Tony,

Is it strange that I, too, feel intensely about being shut in? My greatest horror of the air raids was being confined in a small shelter, and I used to creep into the house some nights when the family was sleeping, longing to move outside those close walls.

It would be so good if we knew just when you would be in England, when we might see each other. It would seem like a lovely dream made real. Do you feel like that, Tony?

Good night, dearest; may you be very happy,

Joan xxxxx

## 23 NOVEMBER 1944

Joan darling,

Thank you for your Christmas card. It looks very bright on my table and makes the room seem much more friendly.

I do wish I could come home to take you away from all your work and care and look after you and help you recapture your happy, carefree laugh.

Yesterday I was reminiscing with the dentist. We talked of the quiet lovely lanes we knew in Cheshire and drew little diagrams and maps to explain how to find them. The hours skipped by very quickly. Then we drifted on to theatres and Shaftesbury Avenue, Charing Cross Road and Leicester Square. We discussed shows and plays and then London in general, and it seemed like a breath of home. How wonderful thought is, that it can carry you across time and distance back home and to the ones you love.

All my friends are being posted away now, and soon I shall be all alone among comparative strangers. I have formed some very close friendships since I have been in the Air Force. Living and flying together, one soon smoothes out any little differences and accepts people at their true value, although one's tastes and inclinations may differ. If only the spirit of comradeship can be carried on into the peace. It is so much stronger than class or race barriers. Then we would really be a united nation.

With all my loving thoughts,

Tony xxxxxxx

## 27 November 1944

Joan darling,

I am so sorry that your mother is not well yet. And you, Joan dearest, at risk of making you cross, must *not* work so hard! If you get ill there will be no one to look after you.

Oh, how I wish and wish that I could come back to take you out and brush the worries and care from your mind and watch you grow gay and carefree again and look after you and love you. I am so glad that my letters make you happy; I try to write as often as I can because I know you must often feel lonely.

When I come back to you I shall be able to spend all my time making you happy and bringing all our wonderful dreams and plans to life.

They must come true, darling; we have been parted and lonely too long, and so the future will be a beautiful story of love and happiness. It could not possibly be otherwise. We love and understand each other so well, and there will be so much for us to do. I know we shall be happy, caring for each other and helping to make our beloved England the land of freedom and beauty that we both want.

With all my loving, happy, confident thoughts,

Tony xxxxxx

## 30 November 1944

My dearest Tony,

Picture me tonight, Tony, sitting very close to the fire, wearing a housecoat and with my hair long and fluffy and not quite dry from its recent washing. Your navigation folder is balanced on my knees, the box containing your letters open on a chair beside me; the two latest letters, note paper and an open pencil-case are scattered within reach.

Thank you for your dear words – that you are working for me. I shall think of that always when I feel impatient with things I have to do, impatient to see you and live our plans, and these war years will seem less fruitless to me.

But keep well, Tony, and don't overwork. Life is so much more enjoyable when one does not feel tired.

How ugly these grey letters are, and how badly I write in my eagerness to pour out my thoughts to you. I wonder which can be your favourite letters? I wish they might be written beautifully on fine paper. Please come home, and I will be neat and beautiful for you, not like my scribbly letters!

A sweet good night to you,

Joan xxxxxx

## 1 DECEMBER 1944

My dearest Joan,

I am very sorry to say, dearest, that there does not seem much hope that I shall be able to come home by February. I have tried very hard, so far without success. It *will* be like a lovely dream, Joan, for no matter what happens we shall be able to love and help and comfort each other always.

Thank you, darling, for all your loving thoughts and confidence. I am so longing to see you so that I can really tell you how much your love has meant to me while I have been away.

Goodbye and God bless, sweetheart,

Tony xxxxxx

## 2 DECEMBER 1944

Joan darling,

So you are having a white Christmas! Some airmen have just arrived from England and remarked how warm it was. One of them said that the temperature must be over 90 degrees. The sergeant laughed and went to look at a thermometer, and it was! And everyone else had been saying how cold the weather was.

Tomorrow I am going climbing among hills I described to you. They are not really high. Mount Attica, the peak, is about 2,000 ft. It will help to keep me fit, though.

With all my love,

Tony xxxxx

## 3 DECEMBER 1944

My dearest Joan,

I have just returned from my mountain-climbing expedition. It was great fun. The rock is all volcanic and apt to break and be rather treacherous, but everything is all right if you go carefully.

Joan darling, please always tell me all your troubles, and even if I am away and cannot help you, it makes me so proud and happy that you confide in me. True love must share sorrow as well as joy, for life is not always all happiness.

Goodbye and God bless, dear heart.

With all my loving thoughts,

Tony xxxxxx

## 6 DECEMBER 1944

My darling Joan,

Joan dearest, please don't worry if your letters are not neat and tidy – it is the love and wonderful thoughts that they bring that matter.

I wonder if I can tell you how much they mean to me? They give me sweet, confident messages of hope, of faith in a lovely future, of something to really work and fight for. I cannot bear to think what life would be like without them. I'm afraid that may all sound rather exaggerated, but it is all true. I think that the real danger out here is that the feeling of loneliness, and being far from those you love, may make it seem that nothing is worthwhile and that the only escape is in apathy. It is your love and understanding that helps me to carry on.

Goodbye and God bless, my darling,

Tony xxxxxx

## 8 DECEMBER 1944

Dearest Tony,

Our plans are all for Christmas just now. This year the food situation will be greatly eased by the extra rations of fat and meat and the promise of oranges and nuts. As usual, our fare has to stretch a long way to accommodate the servicemen Mother always invites on Christmas Day and friends and, of course, the children who come for tea. The tree is the greatest, though I think the nicest, problem. We always 'undress' the tree after Christmas tea, Santa Claus distributing the gifts in the firelight. Then 'lights-up' and the exciting scramble of unpacking.

It is difficult to buy presents now, and especially for strangers, but we usually have an inspiration which saves the situation! Last year I made glamorous dolls after Veronica Lake with dusters and shoe polishers, adding finishing touches of gay silk and yarn 'hair'. So far I have thought only of making stockings for everyone filled with useful oddments, plus as funny a toy as I can find.

I am sure we shall be together long before next Christmas, Tony. Good night, dear; my love to you,

Joan xxxxxx

## 10 DECEMBER 1944

Joan darling,

Shall we spend our holidays this year in Cyprus? I am sure that you will like it; it is so quaint and beautiful.

I think it will be nicer if we fly. We can leave Alexandria after breakfast and be in Cyprus in two hours.

Isn't the sea a lovely blue, with the creamy-white caps dancing across it in the bright sunshine? How quickly the flat Egyptian coast has vanished – we are now in a world of our own. Wait a moment, though, there is a tiny sailing ship below, racing merrily in front of the breeze. How brave it seems, all alone in this wide expanse of sea.

The sky looks a little darker over there; surely it is not a storm coming up? The dark streak grows and then suddenly takes shape: the hills of Cyprus rising from the sea.

Gradually we approach the long coastline, and the silvery beaches and cliffs and inlets pass underneath. There is the harbour of Limassol, with the neat houses clustered round the pier. All is quiet, and the little fishing vessels ride serenely at anchor.

At first the land seems a little sandy and flat, but now the hills are looming ahead. The slope rises and rapidly becomes tree-covered, with little streams winding their way across it.

That lofty peak on the left is Mount Olympus: home of the gods. We are back in the golden age of Greece. Will the gods smile benevolently on two mortals who have braved their stronghold to seek still more beauty and happiness? I think so – they were always kind to true lovers, for they knew the greatness and glory of love.

We brush lightly past the summit and race onwards into the valley beyond. More trees, but now little fields wind along beside the streams, and peaceful cattle graze. Absurd little red and white houses are perched on the hilltops, pretending to guard them.

The plane circles the airfield inquisitively and then swoops gratefully down to rest. There is a car waiting, and we jump in and drive off down the narrow road to Nicosia. Here we notice the first change from Egypt: we are driving on the left of the road, instead of the 'continental' right.

The road is very winding and is tree-lined all the way. We pass between orchards, and the sight of all the ground between the trees ploughed up reminds us that we are on an island where cultivatable land is scarce. Something about the scene seems strange – why, of course, all the workers in the fields are women, with shawls wrapped over their heads! The men do only the easy work! Another unusual sight: a field with a giant cactus around it instead of an ordinary hedge. The road is very rough, and our difficulties are added to by the donkey carts that go jogging slowly along, swaying dangerously from side to side.

The houses are mostly whitewashed and very neat with clean curtains fluttering in the windows. The walls are almost hidden by fresh green creepers, and the gardens are gay with flowers.

We cross a wide bridge across the old moat and we are in Nicosia, chief town and capital of the island. The streets are very, very narrow and the pavements practically non-existent. The road turns and twists, and there are innumerable little side streets cutting across it. And the chief fascination: the cyclists. Everyone on the island seems to have a bicycle, and they ride in and out of the traffic with completely reckless abandon.

We are fortunate in having a Cypriot driver. His plan is quite simple: he drives steadily on, ignoring everything! Perhaps it would be better for our peace of mind if we got out and walked!

The people are very different from those of North Africa. They are more a European type but very, very sunburnt. Most of them are Greeks and Turks, although there are considerable numbers of Armenians and some Arabs. Nearly all of the notices are in English, Greek, Turkish and Arabic, and it is quite amusing to try to pick out similarities in each language excepting, of course, in Arabic, which is very graceful but wholly unintelligible! The shops are dark and sell most contrasting things, but best of all is one dark Ali Baba's cavern with the simple legend in English outside: 'postage stamps'!

The real beauty of Cyprus, though, lies away from the towns and villages, so let us recall our driver and continue on our quest of the Golden Fleece of loveliness.

Out into the quiet lanes again where we can relax after the energetic bustle of the little town. But a strange apparition fills the way in front of us. What can it be? We draw near, and it resolves itself into a bus – but the sort of bus that could be found nowhere except in Cyprus. It is a small lorry, rather on the lines of a shooting brake, but with rows of wooden seats behind the driver. On the top and sides are perched precariously large boxes of fruit and vegetables, tied on, it is true, but rebelling at every bump. But what is that looking out at us from the back? Surely it cannot be . . . but yes, it is, a sheep!! Pigs, sheep and even a cow are part of the normal load of this strange bus service! We creep past and on into the hills.

The names themselves are full of the traditions of the island. There are hills named after prophets – John and Elias – after apostles – Andrew and Luke – after saints – Nicholas and Ambrose – and after sultans and Greek heroes.

We turn off here along a narrow track and pause at the foot of a hill. On its slopes are ring after ring of breastworks and fortifications: the castle Hilarion of the crusaders.

On and along the coast road, through little villages, past the ancient Roman ruins of Salamis, past Famagusta with its memories of Ulysses and Argive chiefs, and Larnaca with its ancient remains of Turkish palaces.

We pass through the little town of Limassol that we saw from the air and then turn back, up into the hills once more, higher, higher. The road takes us almost to the summit of Olympus, and we climb to the peak.

The whole of the island lies at our feet – the fertile valley and hills beyond to the north, the mountains rising from the sea to the west, the beaches on the southern shore, and to the east our only rival: lofty Mount Adelphi.

All is green; the snowcap has not settled as it will later on, and the grassy slopes are wonderfully fresh as if they knew that soon they will be covered over by the soft white carpet of winter and wished to make the most of every precious minute.

My darling, the time has come for us to part once more, but on this ancient hill I promise you that I will come back to you soon and pledge you my love, now and forever.

A sweet good night to you, then, until we meet once more in this precious land of make-believe.

With all my loving thoughts,

Tony xxxxxxx

## 11 December 1944

Tony dear,

Thank you for cabling greetings, but Mother wishes me to reprimand you for sending telegrams unnecessarily just now, because her thoughts fly to possible bad news from her family! It is because my granny is ill and there are the V-2s. I had a crazy, Christmassy mood on Saturday and spent all my coupons on woolly jumpers! It is so cold, and I could not choose between two blue and an emerald-green one, so I bought them all.

It snowed all day yesterday; it was not crisp snow but melted into slush as it reached the ground. I fear before February I shall regret not having bought warm nightdresses with those coupons! The damp makes the house so cold. But I shall remember the lovely feeling of buying what I felt inclined without considering the wisdom . . .

I chatter too much!!
Only room to send my love, dear,
Joan xxxx

## 15 DECEMBER 1944

Tony darling,
So at 90 degrees Shallufa grows cold! If only it were as cold as that
here. My chilblains would vanish, and I might cease to resemble an
Eskimo!

I am glad you are not travelling further away, Tony, although I wish
so much you might be posted home. But I always hope you will not
go to the Far East, wherever else you may travel.

We made stockings with red, white and blue frills last night and
plan to fill them with sweets, nuts, etc. for grown-ups and children
alike! That is, if our nut ration increases – the greengrocer sent six
almonds, six other nuts and about half a pound of peanuts for the
family rations today! Mother suggests sending them to the Minister
of Food as a Christmas present.

There will be ten at our table on Christmas Day, and I expect lots
of fun. But I wish we might have been together, Tony, to spend the
holiday we dreamed.

May this letter arrive to bring my thoughts to you on Christmas Day,
thoughts of spending the next one as we wish, carefree and at peace.

And may we meet again before 1945 is very old.
Happy Christmas, Tony, and a wonderful New Year.
My love, dear,
Joan xxxxxxx

## 15 DECEMBER 1944

Dearest Joan,
My determination to make a success of my political handbook was
strengthened today when one of the more senior officers confessed
that he had no idea at all as to how we are governed and laws made.
I worked all the afternoon on it and hope to have it ready in a few
days.

Goodbye and God bless you, darling.
With all my loving thoughts,
Tony xxxxxx

## 17 December 1944

Dearest Joan,

I have just returned from Cyprus once more! I flew over to attend the wedding of a friend of mine. I will tell you all about it in an air letter. Coming back, another friend and his bride were trying to get to the mainland again so we flew them down. So many weddings made me feel very wistful and long even more for the day when I shall be able to see you again.

Goodbye and God bless you, darling.

With all my love,

Tony xxxxxx

## 18 December 1944

Joan darling,

I enjoyed my last visit to Cyprus even more than the first, strangely enough because it was rather stormy. This time the hills were veiled in clouds, and there were little rainbows dancing on the rocks. The sky just overhead was a wonderful clear blue and suddenly four lovely snow-white pigeons flew by. They looked like birds of peace breaking out from the clouds of war. It seemed a happy omen.

I wish we had more lovely memories, Joan dear. I pray that it will not be long before we are together for always. It seems so very selfish of me to ask you to wait so long for me. Then, too, it is so much harder for you because your work is more difficult and not so exciting as mine and you must often feel very lonely. Oh, Joan darling, I promise you that as soon as I return I will make up to you with companionship and joy and love for all the long and weary days you have waited.

I feel the same way when I try to tell you my thoughts. Words seem so meaningless, and the only thing I can say is I love you and without you life would be empty and valueless.

My life and my love are all yours,

Tony xxxxxx

## 19 December 1944

Tony dearest,

Thank you for your letter about Cyprus and your dear words to me.

Your description brought a sunny world into this damp cold one and your promises, dreams of a happy future, were as happy as dreams can be.

It is late already; I have been painting a few Christmas cards for people I had forgotten in the scramble of shopping. It has been a rather breathless time altogether this year to find and dispatch gifts and cards, with so much else to do. The purchase tax makes things so very expensive that shoppers look despairing or converse in indignant tones in the shops! I have found it more successful in the end to make many of my presents.

Oh, for the wonderful days when Christmas shopping is a really joyous and exciting experience again! Why, one could buy far better things at Woolworths before the war than one can for pound notes now. I often remember long ago when, with sixpence clutched in my hand, I was Queen of that enchanted store, to buy anything I chose. Woolworths and Punch and Judy were the ordeals of my daddy's Saturday afternoons. Good night; I think of you,

Joan xxxxxx

## 21 DECEMBER 1944

My darling Joan,

Thank you for everything you mean to me. I had been feeling rather tired, and we had been talking about the war and affairs in Greece and about how very long and weary everything seemed, and I was feeling very bewildered and unhappy. Then I remembered another occasion when I had been feeling miserable, and I opened my writing case and began to read through your letters. I read two and then found I was smiling and humming the 'Sleeping Princess' waltz. Suddenly everything seemed to sort itself out and all was well again and I felt so very, very grateful to you, far more grateful than I can ever tell you. It means so very much out here to have someone whose thoughts and hopes you can share, someone you can confide in, someone you know will understand and sympathise. Thank you again, dearest.

The preparations for Christmas are well under way now. The airmen have all decorated their quarters and the CO will judge them and award prizes. A donkey derby has been arranged as well as a donkey polo match – officers versus sergeants! There will be carol singing and a special gramophone programme of Christmas music.

In order to let the newspaper publish my book sooner, I have decided to divide it into two complete parts. The first will deal with the political side of government, its defects and possible reforms, and the second will deal with the administration, local government, education, justice, etc. This has the additional advantage that the two parts will be simpler than if I had to link them together.

Goodbye and God bless you, my darling. May every happiness and joy be yours throughout the coming year.

My loving thoughts,

Tony xxxxxx

## 23 December 1944

Dearest Tony,

The Christmas we hoped to spend together will have passed, but, having reconciled ourselves to the disappointment, we can look forward just as happily to meeting again in the year lying so promisingly before us.

Let us then cheerfully look forward to a happier time for us and all the world.

Perhaps it will be spring or summertime for our holiday, Tony. Except for the wonderful festival of Christmas, summer is so much more pleasant than wintertime.

Perhaps buds will be breaking and primroses flowering in the hedgerows on those Downs we long to roam. And the spring sunshine cheering the dusty streets of London, baskets of lovely spring flowers on sale at every corner.

Or will it be bluebell time, the countryside all green in its full pride? And we can laugh and get brown in the sunshine. I shall think of you during these Christmas celebrations to come, think of you opening your presents on Christmas morning, wish that you were by my side in the firelight in the evening, helping unfasten the gifts from the tree or walking under the stars to blow away the sleepiness of the exciting day indoors.

And I will meet you, dear, when the bells ring in the New Year.

My love and all my wishes to see you again,

Joan xxxxxxx

## 26 DECEMBER 1944

My darling Joan,

It was very cold on Christmas morning when I awoke, and I jumped out of bed to get my fur-lined flying jacket – and retreated hastily once more out of the cold. I had left your parcel and a pair of scissors on the table and now proceeded to open it, feeling very impatient with the scissors because they would not cut fast enough! At last the wrapping was off and I was searching eagerly among the gay Christmassy paper. Thank you for everything, dearest, you are so very thoughtful. The diary is lovely, and I was delighted to find the tiny snap of you on the stocking.

After breakfast we all went down to the sports ground for the donkey derby. It was very amusing. Many of the airmen had dressed themselves up, and the races were quite colourful. The donkeys were very strong-willed and often went off in quite the wrong direction. Some were restive, and one or two riders fell off. Among the unfortunates was the Station Adjutant, who had been a very reluctant competitor! Next event was the airmen's Christmas dinner, which was at midday. The officers and NCOs waited on them, and the airmen thoroughly enjoyed it. There were quite a number of them, and it lasted for over three hours, by which time we were all feeling exhausted! We went back to our own mess and had a cold buffet lunch.

Dinner was a formal one with the CO as President and it very soon became a truly festive affair. The great moment was when all the lights were put out and the pudding carried in blazing triumphantly! Unlike the Scottish Christmas of last year it was not piped in! We all sat talking for a long time after dinner, and by the time we rose it was time to go to bed.

Darling, I pray this may be the last Christmas we shall ever spend apart. It is such a lovely time, and it is so very much happier if you can share it with those you love. The year is drawing rapidly to a close now, and I shall be thinking of you as the New Year, with all its hope and promise, dawns. It cannot be long now before we are together again and all our dear hopes and dreams a lovely reality.

Goodbye and God bless you sweetheart,

Tony xxxxxx

## 28 DECEMBER 1944

Tony dearest,

I, too, long to see you, Tony, to share all the happy things of life. And I confess, since you guess it already, that waiting does try me sometimes. The time I have spent here has seemed apart from my own life, because my plans have never centred here. Except for the one great and dear fact of our meeting here, I would completely forget St Annes.

These are very vague explanations, but I believe you will understand how I feel. I know that there are so many millions of people all over the world whose share it is to wait patiently. Only I tell you partly because your courage and sympathy help, and partly so that you may know that I am very human and not an especially wonderful person! It is said that if people have too brilliant a conception of one another, they are often bitterly disappointed at discovering faults after they marry. So I take care not to conceal my failings, that I may be loved for my true self! We had an air-raid warning last week. My first thought on its waking me was to dive under the bedclothes in case of flying glass – until I realised the years and distance I was from those Blitz days! How very much habit governs our actions.

There were over a hundred children at this year's Boxing Day party. Daddy was Santa, and I helped entertain the children. The evening party was fun, too, some ATS girls adding greatly to the merriment. They, with one of their Scottish officers, danced a reel and joined wholeheartedly in the singsong at the end of the party.

I am glad, so very glad, of your patient, courageous confidence, Tony. Particularly now, when we are feeling the length and weariness of the war so much.

Soon I will take a firm hold of my cheerfulness again. From your replies I am ashamed to think I must have been grumbling.

God bless you dearest,

Joan xxxxxx

## 31 DECEMBER 1944

My darling Joan,

Your letters always arrive wonderfully, dear. I received your dear thoughts and message for the New Year this afternoon, only a few hours before the end of 1944.

I am starting this letter in the evening; it is six o'clock now, and I will complete it at one o'clock, just as the New Year dawns for you in England.

This year has been an eventful one with its excitements and disappointments and joys, but I think that it has been a happy one. This is because during 1944 I have found out from your sweet letters how much we care for the same things: music, poetry, books, beauty and high ideals. I loved you very dearly before, but you seem even closer now, and with the pattern of our lives so closely woven together we cannot be anything but wonderfully happy.

We have made many plans and dreamed many dreams during the year, and I long for the time of their lovely fulfilment. Even if we cannot make all of them come true – as you wrote – our hopes are so much the same that if we are disappointed we shall find just as much happiness sympathising with and consoling each other.

1945 will see peace once more in troubled Europe and perhaps throughout the world, and our task of rebuilding will begin. Side by side we shall be able to help and encourage one another towards a goal of a life built on trust and beauty, in which anger and envy will have no part. If only the nations could be taught to trust and assist each other, what a wonderful world we could make.

I will leave you now for a little while, darling Joan, until the New Year is dawning.

It has been raining heavily for nearly 48 hours now – an event unparalleled in Shallufa's history. It seems as though the elements are mourning the departing year.

The seconds are flying by now, and I know that Big Ben will be chiming. So begins 1945. A great and wonderful New Year to you, my darling. May all your wishes come true, and may the year see us together again very soon. Especially at times like this I feel a little lonely and wish and wish that I could see you once more. How beautiful it will be when we can enjoy holidays and anniversaries together for always. Our present parting will make it an even dearer time.

Goodbye and God keep you safe, sweetheart.

With all my love and every thought throughout the year,

Tony xxxxxx

## 4 JANUARY 1945

Dearest Tony,
Our New Year dance was a little different this year, beginning with three words on the notice: 'Evening Dress Optional'. Some of us took this opportunity to add a little gaiety to the dance. I wore my black velvet dress, a white camellia and my 'diamond' pendant and bracelet. My friends wore one black and one blue taffeta dresses; we enjoyed dancing a lot better than the actual dance, I believe.

The news seemed a bit more heartening tonight. You worry too, don't you, Tony? But happiness will return. There seems about half measure of joy and sorrow for each of us.

God keep you and speed you homeward.

My love,

Joan xxxxxx

## 5 JANUARY 1945

Dearest Joan,
I am so sorry that I have not been able to write for a few days, but have been flying round with the Group Captain visiting other units.

At one unit the Commanding Officer lived in a house built by natives. It was oblong, with two domes, one above each room. It was a creamy colour and looked delightful. Inside, the walls were also creamy plaster, and it was rather like being inside a bell, with the dome rising above you. It was very cosy with a blazing fire in a brick fireplace. Everyone else slept in tents, and, as there was no room in the CO's house, we shared one. It was very, very cold and I slept with a pullover over my pyjamas and in a silk dressing gown – I must have looked a very comical sight!

Goodbye and God bless you, sweetheart,

Tony xxxxxxx

## 7 JANUARY 1945

Dearest Joan
I am going on leave tomorrow. I shall start at Cyprus and then go to Alexandria. I may possibly get to Lebanon as well. I will write you wherever I go and tell you of my experiences.

How I wish and wish that you could be coming with me.
All my love,
Tony xxxxxx

## 9 JANUARY 1945

Dearest Tony,

My morning has been spent almost entirely in interview about my special leave! It is considered detrimental to my future career, adding to rather a lot of sick leave since 1940 etc., etc. I have not been a very successful CS, and I am sorry because I like to make a success of everything. But I shall not be sorry to relinquish this career, although I said nothing so reckless to my concerned seniors!

My love, dear, and may you soon be home,

Joan xxxxxxx

## 10 JANUARY 1945

Dearest Joan,

Still my leave is delayed!

By the way, there is a ruling now that we cannot send letters with parcels. I tell you lest you should search for a letter with the 'carrots'!

Goodbye and God bless, sweetheart.

With all my love,

Tony xxxxxx

## 16 JANUARY 1945

Joan darling,

I am now in Alexandria, having returned from Cyprus via Palestine. We flew to Cyprus and followed the coast of Palestine for quite a long way. There is a wide stretch of sand about three miles across along the whole length of the coast, broken only by occasional little streams and the white buildings of towns and cities. Inland, the fields are green and everything is fresh and beautiful. In the distance are great ranges of hills hazy with cloud and mist.

At first the sea was fairly calm and the waves broke lazily, leaving a delicate lace fringe along the shore. We passed the twin cities of Jaffa and Tel Aviv, with their modern seafront and streamlined buildings, and continued on our journey northwards. The hills began to creep out towards the sea until we came to Haifa, dominated by Mount Carmel. All this time the wind had been rising, and now we could see a storm raging over the Sea of Galilee. We hurried on out of its path, past Acre and Tyre and Sidon, all rich with memories of the past.

Now the mountains of Lebanon began to come into sight, each with its snowy mantle and veil of clouds. Another modern city drifted by underneath: Beirut, with its orderly streets and creamy houses. Soon it was time to leave and turn from the coast, with its green hills and white road, out over the blue sea towards Cyprus.

This time, alas, Cyprus was very, very wet, and I was thankful for my greatcoat!

I stayed for two days and then set off for the mainland once more. I have some bad news to report. The 'carrots' I ordered had been sold as I had not been able to collect them, so I ordered them all over again with dire threats if anything happened to them. I will collect them next week and dispatch them. I do so wish that you could be with me. What a wonderful holiday we could have.

With all my love,

Tony xxxxx

## 21 JANUARY 1945

Joan darling,

While I was in 'Alex' I met a friend who is out here in the Wrens. I had not seen her for over six years so we had a long talk. She was very busy, but we had dinner and went to the cinema. I was very pleased to see her, but I must confess that I spent most of the time wishing that it had been you.

It rained a lot, but one fine afternoon I went riding. It seemed strange at first, but I soon settled down again. The horse was a nice chestnut but very lazy. I managed to get him to canter, but he refused to gallop!

I returned by train. There was a little goat tethered by the side of the railway, and he was very interested in a flamingo which was strutting up and down near him. He kept putting his head down and eyeing it, but the flamingo just hissed at him indignantly and walked round and round.

The fields are all very fresh after the rain, and the Arabs were busy cleaning out the ditches. They form a chain right down into the water and pass up the mud and rushes from hand to hand. The women were filling containers with the water and going home balancing them on their heads. Nearby a patient, blindfolded ox was plodding round in an everlasting circle, turning the wheel of a primitive pump. Further on an Arab was turning a cylinder with a spiral shelf in it, forcing water from the ditch to the land. All life centres round the water that is the lifeblood of this dry land.

I long for the day when we shall be able to tell each other all the interesting things we have seen and share our interests and thoughts and our whole lives. Oh, Joan, how wonderful and beautiful it will be, and how impatient I am for it all to come true.

Goodbye and God bless, my darling,

Tony xxxxxx,

## 22 JANUARY 1945

Tony darling,

I don't know how long it is since I last wrote you. I am so sorry, dear, but please forgive me, because I have been ill.

In spite of all your advice I fear I could not have looked after myself well, because after trying to shake off feeling rotten for a long while, I caught flu.

Don't worry, Tony, because I am on the mend now and will write properly when I feel stronger. And please forgive me for not attempting to write sooner – everything did seem to hurt at once.

My love and 'thank yous' for your letters,

Joan xxxxxxxxx

## 23 JANUARY 1945

Joan darling,

I realised that you must be lonely, dear, and am so glad that confiding in me helps you a little. I hope and hope that the day is not far distant when I shall be able to help you and keep all worries away from you for always.

I do love you, Joan, for your sympathy, your love of beauty, your understanding, your courage, your power of making me so very, very happy and, above all, you yourself for everything you

Joan Charles in 1942.

Crest of 603 City of Edinburgh Squadron.

Officers' Mess, Gambut, in 1943.

My tent, Gambut,
in 1943.

My Beaufighter: 'H'.

INCERTI QUO FATA FERANT.

Motto I designed for 'H'.

Three Ju 52 transport planes, shot down 27 January 1944.

One of four Arado 196 fighters, shot down 27 January 1944.

German destroyer Francesco Crispi, sunk at night by rockets 8 March 1944.

Standing on the beach in Libya, April 1944.

Our wedding, 21 June 1946.

The Old Manor Hotel at Witley, Surrey, where we spent our honeymoon.

'Charters', Epsom Downs: the house Joan designed for us in 1950.

Joan and our son,
Christopher, in 1950.

With Christopher, 1951.

Joan's favourite home, Dorset, 1988.

Our son Christopher at
his computer in 1995.

Our Golden Wedding, 1996.

France, 2009.

are – and for me you will always be a very wonderful person.

I was very amused to hear of all your interviews and feel sure you did not take them too seriously. How lovely it will be when you are free of the restrictions and regulations of the Civil Service!

The watch night service and the bells sounded beautiful, dear; we must go to the next one together.

You must have been very lovely for the New Year's dance, Joan, and I do so wish I could have been home to take you. I must try to improve my dancing in anticipation.

We will build a beautiful home together, darling, and you shall have all things you like. I, too, love cheery fires, but we will have electric heaters and draughtproof rooms as well! We must draw plans for our home so that we shall not waste any time when it can really come true.

Goodbye and God bless you, sweetheart,

Tony xxxxxx

## 26 JANUARY 1945

Tony darling,

I am determined to write a long letter in an attempt to make up for the gap in my mail to you. If you have been puzzled or worried, please forgive me, Tony – I felt so ill.

But all bad things come to an end, and I am downstairs today – *and* I ate my dinner. I am longing now to go out, as soon, anyway, as the 'newborn calf' feeling goes from my legs.

Although those who have to go out do not seem to think so, the outside world is very beautiful just now. Through the Jack Frost-painted windows I can see a fairyland, carpeted in snow and trees pure white to the tiniest twig – if only the snowy branches could be preserved and used for house decoration!

The cheekiest of our girls recently got special leave to spend with a quite new boyfriend, by saying she was to marry. On returning unmarried she unblushingly explained that her father's consent was not granted in time!!!

Your round house has fired my imagination. I think round rooms would be lovely. In fact, I've been wondering a little if one day I might have a round room of my own – I can see the creamy walls, thick red carpets and curtains, and blazing log fire. I *am* silly.

Only room now to send my fondest love, dear heart,
Joan xxxxxxx

## 28 JANUARY 1945

Joan darling,

You must be having terrible weather in England at the moment. We hear of blizzards and hurricanes and of such severe icing that Big Ben refused to chime! I can hardly bear to think of it! I expect that the weather is causing the hold-up in mail from England. The last letter I had from you was dated the ninth, but as everyone else is the same I am not worried. I expect it will all arrive together.

I shall be flying over to Cyprus in a day or two to collect the 'carrots' for you. I shall only be away for one day and will post them on my return.

Don't worry, darling, I feel sure that we shall soon be together again and able to forget all the unhappiness of parting in a new and wonderful life.

My love,
Tony xxxxxxxx

## 31 JANUARY 1945

Joan darling,

I was very, very sorry, dear, to hear that you were ill and do hope that you will be well again by the time you receive this letter. You really should not have written, dearest; I know how much effort it needs when one is not well, and it was very sweet of you. I hope you will not be ill again while I am away, but if ever you are, please don't try to write; I really hear from you very often, and I want you to save all your strength for getting well and happy again. How I long for the day when I shall be home again and able to take you away for a long holiday to enjoy the sunshine and bring roses back to your cheeks.

Surely peace is in sight at last. Oh, there are so many lovely things we must do, Joan. May it be very soon.

My love, dear, and all my hopes for a speedy recovery,
Tony xxxxxxx

## 31 JANUARY 1945

Tony dearest,

Two dear letters from you today cheered me very much. Your words succeed in taking me far away from these worrisome days into a gloriously calm and happy existence. And our lives will be truly our own in those days.

I shall feel little regret at relinquishing my Civil Service position. The fighting services could not equal its regimentation! I believe a gleam appeared in the eyes of Those-Who-Like-To-Exert-Their-Authority when we were reserved, for now by petty rules, regulations and nagging they might hold despotic sway (their staffs could no longer get transfers or leave for the great outside world).

Your amusement at my many interviews for a small concession came as a warning that I have been taking it all too seriously. So may one's spirit be slowly and imperceptibly crushed! By the way, our 'little Hitler's' reckoning may be approaching. The Chief Establishment Officer's wife complains of her. A complaint which, though of course this should not be so, will no doubt attract more notice than the many voices which do not belong to Anybody-in-Particular's wife!!

You send me the loveliest of 'carrots': a home to plan. We shall no doubt have to be very patient (unless you have a friend in the building trade!) because of the terrifying shortage of living accommodation, restrictions on building and just about everything else. But, of course, we can plan just what we should really like, and I shall try to be as confident as you always seem of getting it!!

It was my childhood ambition to be an architect, but recently, when I tried to plan a bungalow for Mother, though the outside looked fine, there just wasn't enough window space or plumbing for the rooms.

You have so many experiences to talk about. Although you have written so much to me, I look forward to hearing it all again from your own lips, through long contented hours. I often picture us, dear, lying on a sunny hillside or curled up by a glowing fire, talking, or just quiet with our thoughts.

God bless you, Tony, and send you soon and safely home.

My love to you,

Joan xxxxxx

## 1 FEBRUARY 1945

Joan darling,

I flew over to Cyprus this morning and at last managed to get the 'carrots' for you. I do hope that you will like them and that they arrive safely. I could only spend an hour on the island, as I had to return the same day.

There were scattered storms the whole way with sunshine breaking through occasionally. Once, we found ourselves in the centre of a complete rainbow; it lasted quite a long time before slowly fading away. The sea was very rough with white caps racing across it and the foam being dashed from their crests.

Dear heart, I long for the day when I shall be able to tell you how much I love you instead of trying vainly to find words to write.

With all my love,

Tony xxxxxx

## 6 FEBRUARY 1945

Tony darling,

In a state of mingled exasperation and depression over the unreasonableness of my 'Powers That Be', please may I be pardoned pouring out my rather dull troubles – for your amusement, if you like, but sympathy too, please, since I am truly worried.

My special leave has been refused on the grounds that Mother could go into the sick bay and we three remaining members of the family could muddle through housekeeping in the evenings.

That may sound possible to 'Powers' unacquainted with the size of the house, shopping difficulties and mothers who would not go to hospital for the world, sisters who are busy studying for School Cert and daddies with fantastic ideas of housework. I wasted my time pointing this out, for I received a reply that if I were in the ATS, married with four children, a man, or Mother was childless, she would have to manage without my help! Can you believe that people who are such sticklers for facts in their reading of the rules would make such vague and stupid remarks!

The specialist may again press me to resign, and I agree with him that it is stupid for me to be buried in the CS anyway! But – *several* 'buts' – should, as we hope, Mother get very much better in a few months of rest, I should probably be recalled to National Service. Dad suggests I would be drafted into the ATS and sent overseas; the Treasury might take ages considering my resignation anyway, and might refuse it, and, a little consideration, I should miss my marriage dowry! The first is the only possibility that really worries me – it would be bad if we were parted again when you did come home. For all the welcome change in the world, I do not want to chance that.

Oh, Tony darling, how would you solve this problem for me? I believe it has something to do with a woman's fight for equality! She has had to do the same work as man to gain equal respect, instead of being given equal respect for her special capabilities. Now she is expected to combine *both* jobs. It is the home-life, the children of our country that are suffering. But that is another problem, and not my very own! Do you follow the wondering and queerly connected thoughts I write, Tony? I promise my next letter shall be more interesting.

Join me then in being *very* indignant with 'Powers That Be' in general and resolving to elect more sensible 'Powers' in our lovely world.

I send you my love and constant thoughts,
Joan xxxxxx

## 8 FEBRUARY 1945

Dearest Tony,
Thank you for No. 200! I know that before you left England, you would have considered it impossible to write so many letters, and so I appreciate them even more.

Conversation here has turned to the war service gratuities and post-war rehabilitation. It seems to me that you will have to be very much on your toes to see that promises are kept and that you are given a good chance. The gratuities are scarcely generous to compensate for years in which men might have gone so far in their work. My friend Mary's brother has been discharged, far from well. His nerves are so bad he is scarcely fit to apply for pension and look for work. Surely there should be a state organisation to see men through this period? Daddy laughs at my indignant concern. 'It is,' he says, 'the same old army; as in 1918, men will have to fight and fight for their rights.' It is so *wrong*, Tony.

Looking forward to seeing you, my dear.

My fondest love,

Joan xxxxxx

## 10 FEBRUARY 1945

Joan darling,

I am most indignant over the stupidity and muddle-headed thinking of our bureaucracies. They seem to be run on red tape by officials without enough courage to act on their own judgement but who must be governed by rules of procedure and regulations in everything they do. The remarks they made seemed to be entirely irrelevant and made only to give some semblance of an excuse for their refusal. I think that the trouble is due to the entire system. Officials who spend their entire lives in the Civil Service are afraid to show any initiative in case it should meet with disapproval from someone higher up. If they do everything blindly from the book they think they will be safe.

As regards a solution, though, I think that it would be best for you not to resign yet as you would probably be called up for National Service and be even worse off. At the moment you can spend a certain amount of time at home, whereas it would be impossible if you were posted away in the services. Would it be possible for you to be granted a certain amount of time off each day to help with housekeeping? Or can you find anyone to help at least part of the time? Please forgive my asking, dearest, but is there any question of financial difficulty? If so, I may be able to help a little. I do so want everything to be right for you so that you have no worries or hard work to do. I know you will understand and not be offended.

Thank you, Joan darling, for your lovely valentine – you are very sweet and dear to me. Oh surely, surely I shall be able to come back to you very soon so that we can start making our wonderful dream-world come true. God bless you, sweetheart, and thank you for your trust in me.

My love,

Tony xxxxxx

## St Valentine's Day 1945

Dearest Tony,

Thank you very much for your valentine greetings.

A most blessed springlike day after so much snow, greyness and rain. It, together with a good night's sleep, has made me feel very, very much better. If Horlicks and the weather continue their good work I should soon feel really sparkly again!

Sorry, dear, that I have not written sooner this week, but my first two days back at work tired me extraordinarily. After helping a wee bit at home on Monday I tumbled into bed and last night sat by the fire, reading a little but mostly yawning and wishing my washed hair would dry quickly so I might go to bed! That sounds terribly lazy, but I had not been sleeping well, and lots of sleep is a thing I cannot do without.

My crusading in the interest of health at the office is at last having effect. Our 'Führer' has been asked by greater powers to air the office daily. This she is doing by blowing us out completely, but it is indeed preferable to suffocation! She has, we understand, had a severe 'dressing-down' on her behaviour towards her staff, and I feel a little bit sorry for her. One must be joyless to be so disagreeable.

I bought cherry-red, wooden-soled sandals on Saturday. These are only two coupons instead of the seven for leather-soled shoes! They look quite cute too, and one ignores Daddy's remarks about the strength of the ceiling when one walks about upstairs!! I went looking for a black coat (with a thought to our visit to London, Tony) but failed to find one I like – at least among those that wouldn't completely break the bank!

Keep happy and smile your way home.

I send my love and a good night blessing,

Joan xxxxxx

## 19 February 1945

Joan darling,

Yes, I agree that the war service gratuities are far from generous. The average amount will be about £50, and I don't think that that will go very far in the post-war world. We shall indeed have to see that our interests are safeguarded and all promises kept.

I must confess that I do *not* want to go overseas again after the war – at least not for long periods. Of course our world cruise is a very different thing!

I have seen so many interesting things that I am longing to tell you about, but, as I said in my previous letter, I fear they must wait, at least for a little while.

The weather is getting quite warm now, although it is very cold at night. The countryside is beautifully green though, and it makes a delightful change from the sands of Egypt. It is surprising how quickly one gets used to grass and trees once more. No matter how pleasant the climate and countryside though, I always long to be wandering with you along some quiet English lane, happy in the certainty that we are together for always.

All my loving thoughts, sweetheart,

Tony xxxxx

## 20 FEBRUARY 1945

Tony darling,

You are the kindest, funniest, dearest person in the world. Thank you for thinking so much about my problems, dear – I feel very guilty about worrying you with them.

You are perfectly right about the Service; most everyone is afraid to depart from the strictest letter of the law. An amusing typical example occurred during one of my interviews. It was suggested that an office cleaner might help us in her spare time, and I enquired if she was trustworthy, since Mother might sometimes be in bed. 'Oh yes,' Miss Hosking replied, then added hastily, 'But, of course, I would not be responsible for her!' Actually, the woman never came (cleaners and maids are almost as scarce as bananas, and less use) but things are much better now, since I am working only a 42-hour week for a short while.

Thank you, too, for offering to help me, Tony. I am not offended, because I do understand, and appreciate more than I can say, your thoughts for me. But no thank you, dear. Daddy would have been glad to keep me home for a few months had it been possible, and, independent daughter though I am, I should have been glad to stay! But there it is; it is not possible. The 42-hour week, however, does help tremendously. (I wonder how long such a great concession will be allowed!) And, best of all, my health and spirits are much better.

It is great to feel myself again. I felt so hopelessly depressed, I must have been a trial to everyone while I was ill.

But no, darling, I sleep now, and sometimes the sun shines. This morning I breathed deeply and tossed my head and smiled at the lazy sun getting up and I said, 'Oh, Tony, it's so good to be alive, to be you and to be me.'

I am looking wonderingly forward to reading about your ideal home. I have always loved beautiful homes. But please do not be too ambitious, Tony. We don't want to save and store until we are 50!! Teasing apart, it will be wonderful to spend our hours together, in rooms we have planned together, in contentment found together. I wasn't sure, but you have made me sure; I feel I should love you if we had never met. As though I was *meant* to – is that possible, Tony?

God bless you and our love dear, that it may make the world, as well as us, more beautiful.

Joan xxxxxxx

## 22 February 1945

Joan darling,
The weather is cold and rainy, and I have been sitting quietly dreaming of our home.

I would like our home to be in spacious grounds, set on a hill overlooking the lovely surrounding countryside. Over to the right a silver river winds its way leisurely through the valley, past the quiet fields with their sleek contented herds of cattle. There are woods too, with lovely silver birches, sturdy oak and beeches and, near at hand, a grove of noble pine trees.

We can catch a glimpse of the grey Norman tower of the little village church among the trees, and from time to time silvery chimes come stealing across the quiet air. A broad winding drive leads up to our house. It is tree-lined and neat and guides us through the park and past the rose garden. The day is warm, and the roses seem very inviting. Shall we leave the drive and wander among them?

The garden is enclosed in a trim dark hedge, and flagged steps lead down to it. The paths through it are all grey stone, and in the centre is a tiny formal pond. The roses themselves twine over rustic archways and are continuously falling rebelliously across our path. There are all shades from the full, regal-looking red to the faint, delicate colours of the tea rose. Wooden seats in a flowery arbour are tempting, but we must continue to explore our domain.

Passing through the hedge at the far end we find ourselves facing the terrace in front of the house itself. It is a fairly long building of rough-faced grey stone. On this side French windows open out onto a path running round the velvet lawn, which extends down to the broad terrace itself. Wide steps lead down from the terrace to the path on which we stand. The other windows are spacious and mullioned and are set in a smooth, creamy stone which breaks up the somewhat quiet colour of the rest of the house.

Hand in hand we walk eagerly towards our so-long-hoped-for dream home, now a wonderful reality.

Until we meet again in a little while to continue our exploration, goodbye and God keep you, dear heart.

Tony xxxxxx

## 27 FEBRUARY 1945

Dearest Tony,

Your gifts from Cyprus arrived today. Thank you very much, dear, from everyone.

And the mats are lovely, too, Tony. They are so dainty – I can imagine them fitting into a room with frilled muslin curtains! Yes, I can see everything in that room if I close my eyes a moment. Faint-pinky ceiling and walls, thick creamy carpet, low beds with very simple walnut heads and blue brocade spreads; the mats on a long, low dressing table and cream spotted muslin crossed over the windows. Oh yes, and one picture: a watercolour of flowers perhaps. Does it sound rather a girlish room? It might be best for a spare bedroom. The Vale of Aylesbury would, I think, be lovely, Tony. People should begin their lives together in a new place, I believe.

So long as we are together anywhere we shall find a lot of happiness, dear one.

I wish and wish and wish you were not going back on 'ops', but that wish is in so many hearts, and we must all be 'plucktons' a little longer.

I do feel much happier and braver since I am well again and am determined to revert to cheering you instead of your having to cheer me!

My love and thoughts and prayers for you,

Joan xxxxx

## 27 FEBRUARY 1945

Dearest Joan,

I shall be going back to Shallufa in a few weeks' time, although my stay there will be only for a short time. I shall be quite pleased to see everyone again. I shall be pleased to get away from the rain. The roofs here are metal, and as soon as the rain begins the sound echoes round and round inside and makes it impossible to hear anything else.

A thing that rather amuses me is the audacity of the birds. They venture right into the rooms and sit on the window ledges chattering to each other. Often I wake in the morning to find them flying about overhead and, I am sure, trying to wake me up!

Shall we continue with our visit to our dream home? Let us take it in proper sequence and walk round to the front, along the gravel drive.

The entrance is a stone porch with a dark, iron-studded, oak doorway. We pass through it and find that it opens, through another door, into a large hall running across at right angles. The floor is of polished oak, and the walls are dark oak panels. The hall is not dark though, for there are large windows at either end. Heavy brocade curtains hang on either side of them, and the upholstery of the chairs matches them. Over to the left is a large open stone fireplace, and it is easy to picture a log fire blazing in it on a wintry evening.

At the far end of the hall a wide stairway leads upwards, dividing either way from a landing near its head. It is covered by a deep-piled, sombrely rich carpet which invites us to go over to admire it.

The ceiling of our hall is a delicate cream, and there are no lights to break up its smooth sweep. The lighting is concealed in the cornices.

Once again we must pause before continuing our tour of exploration.

Goodbye and God bless you, sweetheart.

With all my love,

Tony xxxxxx

## 2 MARCH 1945

Dearest,

I am writing at the table, but in a less businesslike position I confess. My feet are occupying a second chair, and somehow I have contrived to rest my head on my hand, my arm on my upbent knees, and it seems quite comfortable. Although I am often told of it (!), I have never realised, until I thought to describe myself to you, in what unconventional positions I sit!

I cannot help wondering and wondering if you will soon be home, Tony? The war goes so well.

I stayed in on Saturday evening and only went out for a short walk and to church yesterday. The service was very uninspiring, and I almost regretted venturing out in the teeming rain. A young soldier, sitting close by me, fell asleep, and I anxiously awaited his deep breathing attracting the attention of the whole congregation! He was aroused, however, by the organ and rose, singing joyfully as though he was heart and soul with the service all the time!!

My love to you wherever you may be.

Joan xxxxxx

## 2 MARCH 1945

Tony darling,

The sea was a beautiful colour this evening, the still greeny-blue of a zircon and pink sunset fading into misty lavender, and way up in the sky the perfect evening star.

I wanted to tell you that before I forgot in my excitement over the main subject of this letter: my carrot of carrots!

All the 'thank yous' in the world, dearest, for the beautiful bag and gloves. You seem to choose exactly the things that I would choose, Tony. These will look lovely with my blue summer dresses, and I wish and wish you might be home to share my pleasure in using them.

I was so excited to open the parcel that my fingers got in each other's way and it took quite twice the necessary time! And it was the loveliest of surprises. I have the tiniest worry that I believe I told you I should need a new bag to worthily carry my silver compact. Oh, Tony, I would hate you to think I dream of your sending me the things I chatter about having. Please tell me you did not think this, darling, to make my present perfect, and so I will not have to worry if 'wishes' find their way into my letters in future.

Perhaps you will laugh at my anxiety. I am often chided about being too sensitive. But I know you will understand.

I am glad you have left the desert but am puzzled where you can be. I am happy not to know, so long as it is pleasant.

It is snowdrop time, Tony, and sunny days, though still cold, make spring pictures crowd one's mind. I think so much of the spring beauty of Lakeland and am looking forward to spending a day at Windermere in bluebell time.

I walked home today with a friend and her two-year-old daughter, Jennifer. Oh, Jennifer's tiny smile holds all the sweetness in the world. It seems so sad that her father has missed her babyhood; she is so lovely.

Could I write so, I would have written this to you:

*I wish I could remember the first day,*
*First hour, first moment of your meeting me,*
*If bright or dim the season, it might be*
*Summer or Winter for aught I can say;*
*So unrecorded did it slip away,*
*So blind was I to see and to foresee,*
*So dull to mark the budding of my tree*
*That would not blossom yet for many a May.*
*If only I could recollect it, such*
*A day of days! I let it come and go*
*As traceless as a thaw of bygone snow;*

*It seemed to mean so little, meant so much;*
*If only now I could recall that touch,*
*First touch of hand in hand – Did one but know!*

The clock ticks round to bedtime, and although I should like to continue talking to you, dearest, I am being very firm with myself about getting plenty of sleep, so as not to get too tired in the long days. I want so much to feel wonderful for our holidays.

Bless you, bless you, bless you, Tony.

Joan xxxxxx

## 4 MARCH 1945

Darling Joan,

I agree that people should begin their lives together in a new place. Then they can build up all their happy associations from a fresh start, and it is all really their own.

I may not be going back on 'ops', Joan; there is a possibility that I shall be required for something else. I shall know definitely in about a month's time.

It was lovely to hear that you are feeling so much better now and that you are happy. One feels so dispirited when one is ill.

It will not be long, Joan, before we can spend our evenings and all our days together and our long parting will be a memory of far-off days.

Until then, dear heart, my thoughts are always with you.

Goodbye and God bless,

Tony xxxxxx

## 6 MARCH 1945

Joan darling,

I am so glad that you have been able to solve your problems at least partly. The Civil Service must consider a 42-hour week a tremendous concession!

No, dearest, I certainly agree; we must not save and store to make an ambitious home, but I feel certain anyway that we shall have a beautiful one.

There was a most lovely sunset this evening. The lower part of the sky was a dark purple, and it was fringed with a wide border of blazing orange and gold. I stood watching it for quite a long time.

Shall we continue to discuss our dream home?

A door leads from the far side of our hall into a short corridor. Let us start exploring from the far end of it. The room we enter is the drawing room: a corner room with windows on two sides. Its walls are a creamy pastel colour, and there are two or three Peter Scotts hanging on them. The curtains are a deep-red velvet, and the carpet is cream with a red border to match. On the right is the fireplace, and on either side of it are low built-in bookshelves packed with books in gay-coloured paper dust jackets.

The bookcases are the same creamy colour as the walls. The alcoves over them are rounded at the top, and in the centre of each is a light with a frosted-glass screen casting a soft, diffused glow over the wall. Over to the left is a large radiogram in a polished walnut cabinet.

There is a deep sofa and two easy chairs near the fire, their rich red covers blending in with the rest of the room. The picture is completed by a small low walnut table on which stands an off-white vase full of red and white carnations.

Darling, I have felt, as you, that we were always meant to love each other, and I know that our life together will be one of lasting joy and happiness.

All my love to you,
Tony xxxxxxx

## 7 MARCH 1945

Tony dearest,
I wonder if I am more modest in my plans because women are more practical-minded or because I am closer to the difficulties attendant on building and running homes promised after the war? Probably the latter, because I remember dreaming quite happily before the war of being a fairy princess!

Perhaps if everyone else, as seems the trend, decides to live in service flats, the village gardener will be free to attend to our roses! I should so love the roses. They would make me feel almost a 'Mrs Miniver'!

How often I, too, wonder how long our parting must yet be.
Bedtime again. Good night, dear.
My love and thoughts,
Joan xxxxxx

## 8 MARCH 1945

Joan darling,
I am so glad that the 'carrots' arrived safely and that you liked them. I had tried to get a rather brighter shade of blue, without success. I really can assure you, dearest, that I had quite forgotten your mentioning a new handbag. I saw one being made for someone else and felt sure you would like one of a similar design. I do understand about your sensitiveness, Joan, and think it is very lovable, but then I am always finding things to make me, if it were possible, love you more and more.

The poem is beautiful, dear, and so very, very apt. Our first meeting has slipped away into the land of forgotten things, but it is in the bright future that our true and lasting happiness lies. I remember many things of that meeting though: how we four walked back together from the pier and the coffee-making!

I am glad that you are being strict with yourself and resting well. I shall take you away for a really good holiday as soon as I can get home again.

Until then, take good care of yourself, sweetheart.
Goodbye and God bless.
All my love,
Tony xxxxx

## 9 MARCH 1945

Dearest,
I was very cast down last night because you frowned at me from your photograph, when I went up to bed! I intended writing to you during the evening but found, to my dismay, that my stock of airgraphs and letters was exhausted.

I heard the good news that the airmail service is reinstated. The clerk told me, however, that it is not very reliable and advised me to use air letters a bit longer: all ordinary letters will soon travel by air to the Middle East as they do to the Far East. With this happy thought in mind we went in search of nice paper to write 'blue letters' to you. There is none in the shops here just now, so it must be added to my Blackpool shopping list.

Bless you, darling, my fondest love,

Joan xxxxxxx

## 11 MARCH 1945

Dearest Joan,

The days are racing past, and soon I shall be on my travels again. I wonder where I shall go. I have seen a policy letter stating that, except in most unusual circumstances, anyone who has been overseas more than a year will not be sent to the Far East, so that should limit the area at least somewhat. All my wonderings will be of no avail, however; I must just wait patiently!

At the moment there is an unearthly howling going on outside. Packs of wild dogs and, very often, jackals wander around the countryside and make a terrible noise every evening. They are very cowardly though, and are soon chased away.

I spent the rest of the afternoon very pleasantly – reading through my favourite letters from you. It has been so very difficult choosing those that I like best; they are all very dear to me. It is so very wonderful to be able to share each other's thoughts and hopes and wonderings; it makes us seem so very, very close together.

I hope that it will not be long now before the war and all the parting is over and we can really begin reshaping the world together. I miss you so very much, darling.

Goodbye and God keep you, Joan.

My loving thoughts,

Tony xxxxxx

## 12 MARCH 1945

My dearest Tony,

So nice to spend a whole evening talking with you alone, Tony.

I was glad indeed that it was tiredness only and not worry I detected in your letters. I wish with every wish of yours that we might be together, Tony. Long, and weary sometimes, as it seems, I begin to agree that parting has made us sure. The number of broken loves, engagements and sometimes even marriages consequent upon parting bewilder me. Are minds made up so lightly about their whole lives, or are our hearts so accommodating, that they change with change of company? Many of my friends seem to be so!

Is it strange, then, or proof of love more wonderful, that we do not doubt our waiting?

I fear I shall puzzle you with my wonderings forever and ever. Sometimes, it is surprising I have not turned into a question mark long ago.

Good night then, dearest.

God speed you soon and safely home.

My love,

Joan xxxxxx

# 4

## AN INTERLUDE IN PALESTINE

I was sent to a top-secret radar station in Palestine for intensive training.

### 13 MARCH 1945

Joan darling,

There is very little I can tell you of what I am doing; in fact since I have been here I have only left the station once. I can, however, dream of more plans for our home.

The last room that we peeped into was the drawing room and we can go straight from it into the dining room.

The walls of the dining room are panelled with dark oak, and the electric lights are in the form of branched candlesticks. There are rich-blue velvet curtains on the window, and the carpet is light blue with a dark-blue border to match them.

Over to the left is the fireplace: a large open one of grey stone. The framework is a basket of wrought iron.

There is a large mahogany table in the centre of the room. It is already laid with gleaming silver cutlery, and there are two triple-branch silver candlesticks, one near either end. There are creamy lace mats and crystal glasses, and in the centre is a crystal ball of roses, its image reflected in the table's glossy surface.

Around the table are graceful Chippendale chairs with padded leather seats. To the right is a massive mahogany sideboard with a row of decanters.

This, then, completes our dining room. There are many more rooms we have to explore yet, but we must wait for a little while before continuing.

Please forgive me this time if I finish hastily, Joan, but I have to return to work, and I want this to catch the post.

Goodbye and God bless you, sweetheart.

Tony xxxxxx

## 15 MARCH 1945

Dearest Joan,

I am so glad that you liked the home I plan and the roses. I think that a garden is a very important part of any house.

No, I do not want to leave England again after the war, except to carry you away on our visits to other lands and peoples. England seems so beautiful and gracious after all these foreign lands. I could not bear to live anywhere else for very long.

I, too, am longing for the day of our own wedding. How excited Janie will be. Would you like her as one of your bridesmaids? How wonderful it will be to know the rest of our lives will be spent together with no more partings. As you once said, even if all our plans do not come true, we shall always have each other and we shall sympathise so much with each other's joys and disappointments that we shall have no regrets of our own.

Earlier this evening I saw the new moon for the first time. It was a lovely golden sickle, low down on the horizon, and I wished and wished you might have been here to watch it with me. There are so many beautiful sights and scenes, but they will always seem empty until I can share them with you. One of the nicest things about being in love is being able to share all your thoughts and hopes and joys and to know that you will be understood.

Bless you, dearest, for all you are and for everything you mean to me. I love you so very much but never seem to be able to find words to tell you properly.

My loving thoughts, sweetheart,

Tony xxxxxxx

## 17 MARCH 1945

Joan darling,

This afternoon I went for quite a long walk and thoroughly enjoyed it. I went across some little hills and past an Arab village. The huts were mud and straw and were roofed with turf. One noticeable thing was the fact that none of them had windows or even openings which could serve as windows – they must have been very dark inside. Some

Arabs nearby were ploughing a field. The plough itself was merely a sharpened branch with a handle fastened to it. It was drawn by two oxen and a camel! The people can have changed but very little throughout the centuries.

I have been trying to find out what is going to happen to me – so far without success. If the RAF adheres to its policy regarding Far East postings I shall be all right!

I feel very sure that it will not be long before I can see you again, dearest, so keep happy and don't worry.

My loving thoughts,

Tony xxxxxxx

## 19 March 1945

Dearest Tony,

My very own evening again. I have drawn the sofa close to the fire in the little room, and I am comfortably leaning back against the cushions with my knees drawn up to provide a writing desk! The glowing fire seems an extra special treat since we were nearly without coal this week. The coalman rescued us from this fate at the eleventh hour. We have been very much more fortunate than many people to have coal all through winter.

Last night I lay in bed thinking, smiling a little, of the things I like about you and one fault I've discovered!

I love your graciousness to everyone, the way you talk to people. I remember how it pleased me to discover you talking to the usher and usherette at the theatre. Your hands, Tony, they are so firm and gentle you might have been a surgeon, a children's doctor. Your restfulness. Your love of life. Your love for me.

Never mind the fault; someday, maybe, I will tell you.

I seem to remember your not seeming to think our children will be handsome. I think with your dark thoughtful eyes and brown curls they might be beautiful. Do you want children, Tony? When I think about things I always wonder what you think about them too. And I like to think about life, about all its possibilities, its hope, fears, joys and disappointments. Just to think and think. It gives me a calm feeling.

I feel happy now, Tony. I am well; I feel I have learned how to live. I am glad I met you when I did. I used to get so terribly excited, bitterly disappointed, so easily hurt. My nature hasn't changed, of course, but from trying to understand the experiences of the world, one's friends and oneself I believe one gains some understanding, ability to see things in right perspective, patience – and so is able to live more happily with other people.

I appear about 84 from my grave discussions on life and living! And I expect I shall make hundreds of mistakes, laugh and cry a lot my life through. I just try, not succeeding very well, to write my thoughts to you, muddled and puzzled as they often are. I do so long to talk with you. I want to know how you came to be you, the things that shape your character, your thoughts, a million other little things I wonder about you.

Sleep almost overcomes me. I have slipped down flat on my back and feel all blinky and yawny!

So good night, dearest – don't think I am too funny.

My love, my love, my love,

Joan xxxxxx

## 20 MARCH 1945

Joan darling,

I love your letters very much, dearest, and do understand them very well. They are so very much you – your thoughts and wondering. I sympathise with all your wonders. I, too, like to find out why things happen and why people act as they do.

The number of broken engagements and marriages after partings does indeed seem to be very great. I think that people are very often lonely and bored and meet someone who interests them at the time and they imagine that they are in love. With parting they find that their interests and hopes are not strong enough to survive the test of waiting, and they lose interest very quickly.

It may prove to be, then, that the time we have had to spend apart has not been wasted since it has shown us that our love is so very real and lasting. We have found our dreams and hopes to be so closely woven together that we cannot be anything but wonderfully happy in our love.

Until that lovely day when I can come back you again, my thoughts are always with you.

All my love, sweetheart,

Tony xxxxxx

## 23 March 1945

Dearest Tony,

I wonder if you are feeling as contented and 'purry' as I am this moment? I am sitting in bed; my table is piled high with poetry books, a novel and your letters. Bathed, hair brushed and smelling faintly, satisfyingly, of lavender. The evening before me, how could I feel otherwise than contented? It is nice to be a woman when one can slip into silky things or dig into sweetly perfumed jars of cream. But other times, in big things, I think it is best to be a man. I have not thought about this *very* deeply, though, because it is certainly best to be content about unchangeable things!

I am glad that you do want to live in England, not so much because I would not care to live abroad, but because it reassures me that England is a lovely place. I believe people do have to work too much to earn a reasonable amount of leisure and pleasure here. But if that could be altered, so that everyone could have *time*, they could live happily indeed. (The other extreme – the life of passing time in card-playing and amusement, of British people in India, for example – terrifies me!) I do hope, Tony, that we may *do* some, at least, of the things that other generations, in other wars, have talked about. Of course there has been progress, marvellous progress, in science, the standard of living and so on, but I wonder have men progressed in learning to live together happily, at peace? If only that could be the aim above all others, instead of it becoming crowded out by business, militarism, greed, ambition.

Tony, have I any grasp of politics at all? I am eager to know a great deal; I want to use my vote rightly, for the future of mankind and not just the business of my town or even my country. But I have only the vaguest idea of the political parties, local government, etc. even. If only we were taught a little of this at school instead of birth dates of romantic kings and battles, how much more useful citizens we might be. For the unstudious it is indeed hard, driven as one may be by one's conscience, to apply oneself to political literature (heavy and bewildering stuff that it is!).

When I heard of the injustice of a divorce law to a woman recently, my immediate reaction was to tell you about it. Then, thinking, I realised that woman's weakness lies in that very fact: she turns to man always to solve problems, to make laws, and then wonders why he solves the problems, makes the laws in his own favour!

I expect you are smiling at my trying to understand the age-old puzzles of the universe! But I know you will admit that if I am not very knowledgeable, my interest is very healthy indeed! I am glad, so glad, that you are patient, Tony, to listen to all my wonderings and help puzzle them out.

I wish and wish you could come home, to talk of lovely things. So many, many plans we have to make.

My fondest love, dear,

Joan xxxxxx

## 23 MARCH 1945

Dearest,

Mother gave me a very dainty swing mirror, the base and uprights made of twisty oak. It is hard to describe, but I know you would just like it, so I shall keep it for our home. 'Our Home' sounds so cosy, beautiful, Tony. I suppose all lovers feel the same, but I like to think there will be a more lovely spirit in ours. I want so much to keep love lovely always . . .

My love and thoughts and prayers for you,

Joan xxxxxx

I forgot to tell you I have a sweet bowl of primroses in my room.

This is the loveliest, sunniest spring, dear. I think so often, as I walk to the office, how fine it would be if you were with me and we might go on walking, dreaming, talking, enjoying just being alive and warmed by the sun.

Joan xx

## 24 MARCH 1945

Joan darling,

There was a pleasant surprise this morning: I went into breakfast early and found a large bowl of freshly cut lemon blossoms on the table. It looked really lovely.

For a change, yesterday afternoon we played hockey. Only about three people in both teams had ever played before, but it was a good exercise, and we all enjoyed it.

Our bird-life here has increased by a little grey owl which is now living in the mess. Its favourite resting place is an electric light flex, and it swings to and fro on it.

Goodbye and God bless you, sweetheart,

Tony xxxxxx

## 26 March 1945

Joan darling,

I agree that it is very nice to be welcomed to someone's home. I remember a certain person who invited two airmen home for coffee and made them feel very welcome indeed. They did appreciate it, Joan, and that evening will always be one of my fondest memories.

Thank you for your kind words about me, dearest. I am glad that you have found one of my faults – I am very far from perfect – and I know that you will still love me in spite of them. Please, I would like to know what it is so that I can correct it.

Yes, darling, I am very fond of children. What a responsibility and what a privilege to think that the shaping of their lives and characters would be in our hands.

I am so glad that you are really well again and that you are feeling calm and happy. I can sympathise with your feelings and moods very much because I so often experience the same feelings myself. How I long to be able to talk to you and to discuss all our thoughts and wonderings.

I shall know my fate very soon now and will write and tell you as soon as I can.

Goodbye and God bless you, dear heart,

Tony xxxxxx

## 28 March 1945

Joan darling,

Safely back at Shallufa once more! I returned by train, and the journey took me nearly twenty-four hours, although when I flew there going it was a mere two-hour trip.

Now that I am back I have decided to take some leave and shall be departing on Saturday afternoon. This time I am going down to Luxor and Aswan to see the Valley of the Kings and all the tombs and temples. I shall be away just over a week and expect that my fate will be decided by the time I return.

I am very sure that this will be the last Easter we shall be apart. Next spring, we shall be able to walk together across the fields and watch the buds breaking into lovely flowers. I think that spring is one of the nicest of the seasons: everything is so wonderfully fresh and new. The whole world seems to be reawakening. Until that happy day when I see you again, goodbye and God bless you, darling.

With all my loving, impatient thoughts,

Tony xxxxxx

## 29 MARCH 1945

Joan darling,

A letter to tell you of my explorations in Palestine.

We started off very early one morning and drove across the Plain of Sharon. The land was fairly flat with a few little hillocks and for miles was carpeted with purple flowers. These soon gave way to intensive cultivation, and we passed through wide orange and banana groves. Around each grove was a line of stately cypress trees as a measure of protection against the wind.

From time to time we passed great creamy-yellow buildings, each with a grim square tower. These were the outposts of the Palestine police. The police wear khaki uniforms and black astrakhan caps, rather like the one presented to Mr Churchill when he was in Russia.

Hills now began to rise on the right, and we skirted along the seashore, past Caesarea and into Haifa. Haifa is a pleasant stone town with streets climbing up and running down at crazy angles. The buildings are all very modern, and the architecture is quite pleasing.

While in Haifa we visited the Jewish Technical College: a large sandstone building excellently equipped. The pupils' ages varied between 16 and 20, and they were studying engineering, electricity, physics, architecture, etc.

The winding road now led us into the plain once more and under the towering heights of Mount Carmel. Here again all the land was cultivated, and once more there were groves of trees, this time including eucalyptus.

Our next stop was at a Jewish smallholders' cooperative settlement called Ginegar. Later on in this letter I will tell you how these settlements are run. The houses were sandstone and all grouped together at the foot of a ridge of hills. There were pleasant rock gardens and flowering shrubs, and a cypress-lined avenue led through the tiny village. Behind the houses was a tall whitewashed tower, and we climbed to the top of it to see the surrounding countryside. Behind us was a thickly forested ridge named after Balfour, for the good work he had done for Palestine. To the right were the distant hills beyond Haifa. On the left was the village of Endor of biblical fame and, further over, Mount Tabor.

Time was short, and we hurried on into the hills. The road twisted and turned, always climbing and often running along the edges of steep escarpments. At last the summit was reached, and we drove through a rocky pass and into Nazareth.

The buildings here were nearly all stone, and the old houses and churches were all thickly clustered together. Largest of the churches was the Church of the Nativity, and next to it was the large stone building called Jacob's Workshop. Further on down the main street was a well known as Mary's Well. From this the Holy Family were reputed to have drawn their water supply.

Suddenly the road twisted and began to climb once more, this time to the top of the hills overlooking Nazareth. There was a wonderful view from here of the village below and of the plains beyond stretching into the distance. Down the other side and through the village of Cana and then began the steep descent to Tiberias. A sign beside the road stated in a matter-of-fact way 'sea level', and still we continued downward. The road crossed a small ridge, and below us lay the Sea of Galilee and the town of Tiberias. This time the surface of the lake was calm and serene, and the green slopes of the hills on the far shore looked very inviting. At last our headlong descent was checked, and we entered the town, 650 feet below sea level.

In odd corners of the town were traces of the Roman buildings, some of which had been used as a foundation for more modern houses by the Arabs. On the outskirts of the town were the famed hot springs, concealed in a somewhat dilapidated stone building.

The route continued along the shore towards the south. It was getting late, and the fishing boats had all put in to shore. At the end of the lake was another Jewish settlement – this time one depending on fishing for its living. We crossed over the River Jordan and followed its valley past the great hydroelectric plant which supplies all Palestine with electricity.

Now there was a barrier across the road, and we stopped while our passes were checked. Everything was in order, and we crossed the frontier into the Arab state of Transjordan.

Our progress here was very slow; first the road was blocked by a wildly milling flock of sheep, and no sooner had we negotiated them than another flock took their place ahead. Another delay, and we were free again.

A turn in the road soon disclosed another obstacle; this time a herd of goats. These were rather more intelligent than the sheep and soon dispersed. Our triumph was very short-lived, however, for we encountered successively yet another herd of goats, a herd of cattle and finally another flock of sheep!

After all this we were quite pleased to see another frontier post ahead, and we crossed back into Palestine.

The road climbed slowly back across the hills and down into the coastal plain. It was dark now, and we were all quite pleased when the lights of Tel Aviv began to gleam ahead. A sudden contrast as we broke out from the lands of the Bible into a modern streamlined city with flashing, many-coloured neon signs.

So ended quite a memorable tour of the Holy Land. Apart from the large cities, it has changed but little throughout the ages, although the farmers are gradually adopting more and more modern methods of cultivating their lands.

I promised that I would tell you more of the Jewish settlements, Joan, and will describe two that I visited during my stay.

The first was a cooperative smallholders' settlement. It had been in existence for quite a long time and seemed to be very well run.

First we were invited to one of the houses and sat under a lattice of grapevines, drinking milk and munching home-made biscuits. The farmer told something of the methods of the settlement. Each farmer held three or four acres of land which had been given to him by the Jewish National Fund. It was his, but he could neither sell it nor use it as security. It was not one plot of land but was divided up into several small portions in different parts of the village.

Because of the small area, very intensive methods of farming were used and advice was given by an experimental station, which we visited later.

The farmer had poultry and ducks, some potato crops, vegetables and fruit. He also had two cows of his own and about six pigs. The fruit was especially interesting; he had some lemon trees which had been grafted, and so on each tree were tiny buds, small fruit and fully ripe lemons so that there was always a ripe fruit crop available.

All the food produced was sent direct to a cooperative store and sold. Seven per cent was deducted for expenses, and the rest went to the farmer. The women had to work in the fields with the men, for the farmer was not allowed to employ any labourers – everything had to be done by his own family.

Next we visited the experimental station. The approach was along a wide tree-lined avenue, and the buildings were all creamy and modern.

We were taken to a laboratory which specialised in citrus fruit and shown the dehydrated oranges and lemons in the form of thin rolled sheets. We tasted some, and it was very good! This section also dealt with bottling and preserving and jam manufacturing.

Another department handled all other fruit – apples, pears, bananas, guava, etc. – and here they had dehydrated bananas!

There were sections for the study of soil, for developing crops and for insect extermination, but we had no time to visit them all, so we went on to the central laboratory. Here the chemical side of agriculture was dealt with, and there was a great deal of research into the manufacture of synthetic drugs.

Our next visit was to an agricultural college not very far away. The pupils here were all girls with ages ranging from 8 to 17.

The younger children were given a general education until they were 12 and then began with farm work. For one year they worked in all branches and then were allowed to specialise. If they showed promise on completing the course they were sent on to a university abroad.

There were no charges at this college – all the expenses were borne by the Jewish Fund. Most of the younger children were refugees from European countries, and there was the great problem of languages. First, each child was taught Hebrew, and then English. In many cases the refugees were frightened and suspicious, and then it was left to the other children themselves to win their trust and confidence.

First, we looked over the building. There were large airy classrooms with concealed lighting and long glass windows, each with its rows of potted plants and flowers. Next were the kitchens: these were spotless, and in the pantry everything was in neatly labelled glass jars. All meals were planned by an expert dietician. In the dining hall a large notice was hung. It was in Hebrew, and its interpretation read 'You live by your work'. There was another notice in the entrance hall: 'It's no use trying to reach heaven unless there is soil under your feet.'

Outside were orange groves, fish ponds, a chicken farm and herds of cattle. There were incubators, and the chicks passed from one hut to another as they grew, until they were large enough to venture outside on their own.

All the children seem so very happy and laughingly threw oranges to us as we left.

Then came the second type of settlement: the communal settlement. This was mainly a transition period. Everyone lived in wooden huts in a close encampment. The huts were squalid and crowded together. We had a meal, and the food was poor, consisting merely of sauerkraut, with milk poured over it, and bread. For the children, however, the accommodation was excellent. They did not live with their parents but were in a communal playroom together. They had toys, and classes were held on the settlement for them. They were sent to secondary school at age of 14 and worked in the settlement in their spare time. At 17, if they showed promise, they were sent to a university. Each child had to learn to play at least one musical instrument and each settlement had its own orchestra.

The girls were sent away and trained as nurses and then came back to teach and look after the children.

The settlement we saw had been granted some very poor land in the south and certain members lived on it, trying to make it fertile by irrigation. They were also building houses. There was an almost fanatical ardour about everything – the land would need at least 20 years before it could support the settlement, and yet they were all as enthusiastic as if it would be ready within a week.

No one had any money; everything was pooled. If someone wanted clothes or cigarettes etc. he asked for them, and they were given to him. All the financial dealings were handled by committees which changed each year. The source of revenue in this instance was furniture and box making.

This then, dearest, is the story of Palestine today. The life is a hard one, and the reward seems far distant. In spite of this, wonderful progress has been made.

How wrong it seems that some people should have to strive so hard to obtain so little, and what a long way it will be to our ideal world.

Goodbye and God bless you, sweetheart.

My loving thoughts,

Tony xxxxxx

## 31 MARCH 1945

Joan darling,

In an hour or so I shall be starting my leave. I am very pleased that I shall be able to visit Luxor and Aswan, because the season ends in April and after that it is far too hot. This, then, will be my last opportunity, as I hope that before the winter comes I shall be back again with you.

I love to be able to visit these places, because then, when I can bring you out to see them with me, I shall know all the beautiful things that you would like to see. I always dream of the time when you will be standing beside me and we can enjoy them together.

With all my love and thoughts,

Tony xxxxxx

# 5

# THE HISTORIC DELTA

I took advantage of two weeks' leave to visit some of Egypt's antiquities.

## 4 APRIL 1945

Joan darling,

I am now at Aswan, about 600 miles south of Cairo.

In Cairo I visited the Mohammed Ali mosque for the first time. I think that it is one of the most wonderful buildings I have ever seen and the only thing in Cairo which is worth visiting again.

The train left Cairo on Sunday evening and arrived in Luxor at eight o'clock the next morning. I had a sleeper, and the journey was very comfortable.

In Luxor I visited the Valley of the Kings, including the tomb of Tut Ankh Amen; the Valley of the Queens; and many temples, including the great temple of Karnak. We also sailed along the Nile in a dhow to watch the sunset across the river.

The hotel was excellent and was set in a garden full of lovely flowers.

The hotel here, the Cataract Hotel, is even better, and my room looks out over the river towards the west and across a small island with some picturesque ruins.

I am enjoying every minute and am looking forward so very much to the time when I shall be able to bring you with me to see all wonders and beauties of this lost civilisation.

With all my love,

Tony xxxxxx

## 5 APRIL 1945

My dearest Joan,

Here begins the first chapter of my 'Arabian Nights' entertainment. The journey starts in Cairo, where I left you.

We drive away from Opera Square through the narrow and twisting streets of the Mousky and begin to climb the hill overlooking the city. The road passes between two tall sandstone mosques; shall we stop and look at one?

The one on the left is the Coronation Mosque built by the Khedive Ismail for the crowning of the kings of Egypt. We climb up a long flight of steps to the door. Here we must pause while canvas sandals are placed over our shoes lest we should defile the sacred place. This accomplished, we pass on. The interior of the mosque is lofty and the walls of grey stone. We turn to the right, and above us rises the great central dome. This is beautifully carved stone, painted in rich blue and gold and skilfully dovetailed together. A wrought-iron circle hangs below the dome, and from it are suspended silver oil lamps. The chains supporting them terminate in silver globes; these were to keep the rats from climbing down and stealing the oil. Nowadays electric lighting is used, but the lamps still remain. Under this dome the coronation of the king takes place.

On the far side of the dome is a strange-looking wooden structure: a platform with a raised section along one edge. This is for the head of the university. He sits cross-legged on the platform and rests the open Koran on the raised portion.

To the left is a large grill gateway. Mohammedans do not allow their women to mix with them in prayer – they must remain in a separate portion of the mosque.

We retrace our steps, and on the right near the entrance we find another doorway. Inside is an intricately carved wooden screen surrounding the tomb of one of the Mohammedan saints. The shrine itself is covered with a green veil indicating that he was a descendant of the Prophet.

There is a more wonderful sight awaiting us so let us hurry out to our car and continue.

We drive on up the hill and pass through first one and then another deep stone archway. These are part of the citadel built by the great Saladin. Beyond the second archway is a wide-open space, and in front of us is the great mosque built by Mohammed Ali. It is an oblong building, the upper part being sandstone and the lower sections being gleaming white alabaster. In the centre is the great dome, and on either side of it is a graceful minaret. The mosque is modelled on that of St Sophia at Istanbul but has only two minarets instead of four.

We pause once more to have sandals fitted and then pass through into a large open courtyard. The walls are all snowy alabaster, and the floor is white marble. Around the side runs a colonnade of graceful pillars. At the centre is a great carved shrine with verses from the Koran inscribed on it in letters of gold. Around the shrine are taps so that the faithful can purify themselves before prayer. Towering above us are the twin minarets from whose lofty heights the muezzin calls Islam to prayers. On the right is a slightly smaller tower with a great clock presented to Mohammed Ali by Louis Philippe of France.

We pass now through an archway on the left and find ourselves in a true wonderland of the East.

The mosque is bathed in a soft golden light which reveals a myriad of rich stone carvings. Four massive yet beautiful alabaster pillars rise from the centre to support the great dome. The inside of the dome is blue and gilded stonework, exquisitely wrought. Around it are pierced intricate arabesque windows, each with multicoloured panels of stained glass. There are four smaller domes around the main one, and these again are beautiful almost beyond description.

As we move about, the great dome appears to be continually changing in its hues. Suspended beneath it is a massive crystal chandelier, another gift of Louis of France. Around this hang two great circles of lights. The floor is covered by a rich-red Turkish carpet. Above and behind us is a gallery for the women – for, as we have seen, they cannot pray with the men.

Around the dome itself are four carved plaques bearing the names of the four great Mohammedan caliphs, and beyond these are more plaques bearing the names of Allah and of Mohammed, his prophet.

The inside of the mosque is completely panelled with translucent alabaster. Over to the right is a small flight of steps leading up to a canopied pulpit. From this the muezzin reads the Koran. The whole of this structure is carved from wood and gilded and painted a rich green. The entrance to the steps is barred by two elaborately carved gates. In spite of the richness of this pulpit, the King decided that it was not worthy of the mosque and decreed that another of alabaster with wrought, gilded brass gates should be made. This now stands beside the wooden one, waiting to take its place.

To the left is a rather smaller dais on which the repeater stands. His duty is to repeat to the faithful the prayers read by the muezzin, lest they should pass unheard.

Beside the alabaster pulpit is a great alcove with a large pillar on either side. This is the Mecca arch and shows the Mohammedans the direction towards which they must pray. The pillars are to guide the blind if they should chance to be alone in the mosque, trying to find the arch.

Now that we are beside the pulpit we can admire its wonderful tracery. An arch is pierced through it below the platform of the muezzin; this is the Arch of Wishes. Let us pass under it and wish that we may be together happily and for always. To make certainty more sure we can also walk under the wooden arch of the old pulpit.

Beside the door through which we entered is a great brass-work screen. This surrounds the tomb of Mohammed Ali. Around it are silver candlesticks, and the tomb is covered with rich velvet drapes.

We cast one last long, lingering look around and pass into the bright courtyard once more.

Walking round the outside of the mosque we come to a wide courtyard with a stone parapet. This looks across the city of Cairo.

We can see the remains of the great aqueduct leading across from the Nile. Among the houses and towering buildings are many mosques and minarets. Behind us is the city of the dead. In the distance to the right is the ancient city of Memphis, former capital of Egypt and now a ruin. Beyond the Nile are the pyramids of Giza.

Fronting the courtyard is the palace of Mohammed Ali – closed, alas, for the moment. Beyond it is the Roman wall and, on the heights still further away, the fort of Napoleon.

So the ages seem to have gathered their treasures together to spread them before us. It has been a wonderful sight and one which we shall never forget.

In the next letter I will take you to scenes far more ancient, traces of a civilisation which existed 4,000 years ago.

Goodbye and God bless you, dearest,

Tony xxxxxx

## 5 APRIL 1945

Joan darling,

While I am writing a long letter to tell you of the places I have
visited, I thought you might like to hear one or two amusing incidents
which happened on the journey.

We left Shallufa at about midday to drive to Cairo. We were
driving in a car belonging to the person who was arranging the
trip. About a mile from the camp we were blinded suddenly as the
top of the bonnet flew up in front of the windscreen. We stopped
and, after searching along the roadside for a minute or two, found
a piece of wire and tied the car together again. Soon after this we
drove into a sandstorm and, as one of the windows was missing,
we were soon covered with sand. About this time there was a
very strong smell of hot oil in the car and, when we stopped to
investigate, we found that the belt had come off the fan and that
the engine was overheating. This was worse as the fan belt also
drove the pump for water-cooling. It was impossible to replace it so
we crawled on through the sand at about five mph until we came
to the NAAFI halfway house – although the 'house' is merely a
collection of tents! Here we had some tea, and the fan belt was
replaced. We drove gaily off only to find after about five minutes
that the fan belt had completely broken. For about an hour we
crawled along at a snail's pace until we came to a tank unit where
some Good Samaritans repaired our untrustworthy vehicle. The
fan belt also drove the generator, and the battery was now flat, so
we had to push the car to start it. The last straw was about a mile
from Cairo, when we ran out of petrol! We managed to get two
gallons eventually, but by now the fuel pump was choked with sand
and the car refused to start. So, in despair, we abandoned it and
continued our journey in a taxi.

I was very, very grateful for a hot bath and went to bed quite
early.

In spite of the start, everything has been wonderful, and I wish
and wish you could be with me.

All my love, dearest,

Tony xxxxxx

## 10 APRIL 1945

Joan darling,

Back at Shallufa once more.

Before I answer your letters I will give you a few pieces of news.

As you may have guessed, I was away on a course, and the results have just come through. Although I cannot tell you what the course was, I can give you the result. I was fortunate enough to obtain a 'Distinguished Pass', with the highest mark in the Mediterranean and South East Asia Commands.

The second piece of news: I have seen my chief and will very probably know my fate on Saturday!

And the last item: I managed to get one or two 'carrots' for you while I was away on leave. I am posting one today and also a rather more prosaic present concerning which, however, I refuse to satisfy your curiosity!

The other two 'carrots' require some alterations and additions, and I will send them as soon as possible.

Having now aroused your wonderings once more, I will leave you, sweetheart, and hope that everything arrives swiftly and in good order.

With all my loving thoughts,

Tony xxxxxx

The course was on new secret radar for Pathfinder squadrons.

## 11 APRIL 1945

Joan, my darling,

I love all your wonderings and long for the day when I shall be able to talk with you about them. I sympathise with your indignation over the injustice to women. I believe that men and women should be equal companions both to each other and in the eyes of the law. They should realise that they are complementary, and that while there are many things a man can do better than a woman, there are very many things that a woman can do far better than a man.

Your mirror sounds lovely, Joan, and how wonderful it is to think that we are furnishing our home already! That reminds me: I saw an exhibition prefabricated house in Cairo the other day. Darling, we must never live in one of those; the terrible sameness of row after row of identical structures would be unbearable. I suppose the government have done the best they can, but we must make very certain that these houses are not allowed to become permanent. I was heartened by your thought that a flat would be preferable. One of my friends had a good idea: to live in a flat and start building or furnishing a house in the country. Time could then be taken to build up the home we really wanted, and we could take time to choose or look for really lovely things. What do you think of this, Joan? I am so interested to hear of your wishes. I think that the idea of the rose bushes is wonderful.

With all my love,
Tony xxxxx

## 15 APRIL 1945

Good morning, dearest,
I am thinking soon, very soon, we shall be rejoicing; there will still be the peace to struggle for in Europe, many people to comfort, countries to rebuild. Japan must still be conquered. But we shall rejoice because a great strain will be lifted.

And I am thinking Tony will not be going on 'ops'. He will be coming home. Our hopes, our dreams, will no longer bear the reservation 'after the war'.

Our plans were changed by rainy weather yesterday. We had tea at the Savoy and were charmingly entertained by a young man, his sweet smiles and brilliant conversation winning our hearts away. He was fair and had truly navy-blue eyes, and his name was Peter. Now, Peter ate his buttered toast with a pastry fork and told us his daddy had no toes!

Peter was not yet two years old. I am rather pleased I met him, because Jane's brother had really scared me off baby boys!

My love, dearest,
Joan xxxxxx

## 17 APRIL 1945

My dearest Tony,
Congratulations on your very distinguished pass. I am proud for you,

Tony. It is a wonderfully satisfying to do well, whatever the subject of one's work. I am not exceptionally clever at anything but sometimes have a pleased feeling that I have done some little thing as well as it could be done.

The only time I remember experiencing the thrill of being 'top o' the class' was once at art school. Each week, the headmaster had all the nature drawings pinned on the wall and publicly criticised them. I was very much younger than the other pupils and felt my childish drawings quite hopeless. Imagine, then, my joy when the HM said of my painting, 'This plant looks as though it is really *growing*', pointing it as an example to the much more clever painters whose plants did not grow from good brown earth!

My love to you,

Joan xxxx

## 19 APRIL 1945

Joan darling,

I have been posted to Cyprus and am leaving on Monday. However, I may be moving again in a little while.

I know that it is very hard for you and that you are feeling lonely, dearest, but it will not be for long, and our eventual happiness will be so much greater, if possible, after our parting. I love you so very much, Joan, and am longing for the time when I shall be with you for always and able to keep all unhappiness and worry from you.

All my eager, loving thoughts,

Tony xxxxxx

## 20 APRIL 1945

Tony darling,

I have arranged myself in a very businesslike manner this evening, seated at the table with paper, ink and a pile of unanswered letters spread before me. But I do not feel at all like answering them: I would rather chatter to you.

Answering your letters: Yes, dear, a flat would be the best idea, I believe, until we can build a house which would please us always. It might have advantages, too. We should not be tied so when we wished to scamper off on holidays! I like to know what you think about 'us', too, Tony. Have you thought when you would like to be married, Tony? There are many considerations, perhaps, but I confess my most important one will be a trousseau! I do not think I should like to forgo this delight, even the shopping and sewing. In her joy at gaining a son, Mother will no doubt do magic for me, but there will have to be a very drive of coupon saving and borrowing! And Jane must have a white dress, even if I do not!!

Am I not vain tonight?

My eyes are going to sleep without me, so good night, dearest.

My love and love to you,

Joan xxxxxx

## 22 APRIL 1945

Joan darling,

I started to read through the *Heritage of Poetry*, and all the tiredness fell away as I read Walter de la Mare's lovely poem on England.

What wonderful things words can be, dearest, and what a great effect they can have on us. I often think that a mastery of English would be one of the finest things to possess. How often I feel lost for words to express something I want to say. Something that I have, oh so clearly, in my own mind, but when I try to write it the words seem so inadequate and unsuitable.

That will be one of the nicest things about being together again. We shall be able to share our thoughts and dreams so much more fully.

Something that might amuse you. The other day I was speaking to one of the warrant officers about aircrew and happened to mention that I thought they were rather young now. He said, 'Excuse me, sir, but how old are you?' I told him and he was most surprised. He said, 'I thought you were about 19!', so I must be growing very youthful out here. Perhaps I shall be a Peter Pan!!

All my loving thoughts,

Tony xxxxxx

## 27 APRIL 1945

Dearest Tony

Yesterday's mail brought another disappointment: we cannot go to Kathleen until Monday. Hers is a tiny flat but it has the greatest luxury in the realm nowadays: oceans of hot water, day and night! Kathleen, unacquainted with empty coal cellars, runs the water unconcerned. I confess I run it too, right to the top of the big bath, but feel terribly guilty about the King and the rest of his subjects in their five inches! I am very bad.

You *are* growing young out there, Tony. I thought you looked very grown up for your age, except sometimes when you were shy and a wee bit nervous! I am told I still look a 'teen'y', too, but sometimes I feel I have been old a long, long time. The war years seem much, much, much longer than all the rest of my life. It is difficult to explain, but I believe many people feel the same.

Good night, dear one.

My love to you. God bless you,

Joan xxxxx

## 27 April 1945

Joan darling,

About our wedding, dearest (how wonderful and important that sounds!), there are indeed many considerations, but I think that your trousseau is the loveliest. I should like it to be as soon as possible, but the choice shall be all yours.

Descending to facts like this is even lovelier than making plans – it makes everything seem so very certain. I wonder how our housekeeping will manage, Joan. Please may I act in an advisory capacity as economist?!!

Goodbye and God bless you, sweetheart.

With all my, happy, loving thoughts,

Tony xxxxxx

## 29 April 1945

Joan darling,

I arrived yesterday evening and soon met very many of my friends. My room here is smaller, and I have nowhere to put any of my things. I am writing this letter resting the pad on a suitcase on my bed. I must see what I can do about furnishing.

By the way, dearest, you still have not told me of the fault you discovered! I wonder what it can be? I think that perhaps my greatest fault is vanity – I care too much for what people think of me. It is quite a serious fault, because I am sure that sometimes it sways my judgement, although I try not to let it.

Goodbye and God bless you, my darling,

Tony xxxxxxx

## 30 April 1945

Joan, my darling,

Let us continue from the Mosque of Mohammed Ali and back into the town again. We have some time to wait before our train leaves; let us stroll down to Gezira.

How full of traffic the Midan Ismailia is; it is worse than Piccadilly! Safely over, though, we cross the stately 'English Bridge', with its flanking lions, and so to Gezira island. Shall we turn to the left along the road running beside the river? A light breeze is ruffling the water, and big and small yachts are sailing gaily down the broad Nile. How peaceful everything seems, the river and the boats, the green trees and grass and the graceful buildings along the banks.

The road turns slowly and takes us back around the other side of the island to the continuation of the bridge. On the other side of the road are the great white buildings of the Agricultural Hall. There is an art exhibition being held here; let us wander in.

The paintings and statuary downstairs are by the leading Egyptian artists and are very stereotyped and conventional. There is one exception, though: a charming portrait of the Crown Princess of Greece. Shall we go upstairs? The work shown here is by the students of the College of Fine Arts, and the freshness of the young artists is in striking contrast to the somewhat jaded work of the 'masters'.

The time has passed quickly, and it is growing dusk outside. We had better go along to the station.

The hotel has seen the luggage safely on board, and the tickets are all in order. A few endless moments of waiting, and the train draws slowly out. It is almost dinner-time, and a page passes down the corridor sounding a gong. The dining-car is next door, and we are soon settled at a table for two. The train is quite steady, and dinner is not so much of an ordeal as on some transcontinental lines.

We pause at a station, and once more the contrast of Egypt strikes us. From the comparative luxury of the dining-car we gaze on the peasants, young and old, men, women and children huddled together, sleeping on the platform. How many aspects of our world there are which must be changed.

We linger over coffee, chattering happily, and at last make our way drowsily to our sleepers.

The dullest, most uninteresting part of the journey passes rapidly while we rest, and when we get up it is quite light.

Gazing out of the windows we see a bluish haze, and the acrid smell of wood fires drifts in as we pass through little villages. The fields are drenched with dew, and in the distance are misty hills. A pelican, startled by the sound of the train, stretches his great wings and flaps protestingly away.

The attendant brings us coffee – we shall have breakfast at the hotel – and tells us that we are due to arrive in 15 minutes.

At last the station, and the dragoman from the hotel takes efficient charge of our luggage and shepherds us out to the waiting car.

We drive through narrow streets, as yet still deserted, and then through a gateway into the hotel grounds. The gardens are a blaze of wonderful colour, and purple bougainvillaea climbs the side of the building. All around pigeons are sleepily cooing. As we enter, the manager comes forward to bid us welcome to Luxor.

A brisk wash, and we are eager for our long-deferred breakfast. A morning spent lazily unpacking, and a stroll along the riverbank, and after lunch we are ready to start exploring.

Our first expedition is to the great temple of Karnak – the largest of ancient Egypt. An open horse-drawn carriage takes us through the town and out into the countryside beyond. About five minutes at a leisurely pace, and we alight.

Before us is the temple. An avenue of sphinxes leads up to the massive doorway, awe-inspiring merely in its proportions. There were many smaller temples in the main one, dedicated to different deities, but greatest of all was that of the Trinity of Thebes: the sun god and his wife and their son, god of the moon.

The great walls are coloured with carvings of the mighty kings who built the temple and with the figures of the gods.

We can climb to the top of the gate and are rewarded by a magnificent view. Immediately below us lies the temple itself; in front is the avenue of sphinxes which once led all the way to the river, the river itself and, in the distance, the Hill of the Dead, with the Valley of the Kings just visible. How wonderful it must have been when all around was the might and grandeur of ancient Egypt. Descending once more, we pass into the great Hypostyle Hall – a truly wonderful spectacle with its forests of mighty pillars towering high above us. Further on are two great marble obelisks, which have miraculously survived ancient earthquakes and the ravages of time.

Two more halls, and we reach the sanctuary itself, where the statue of the god was kept. The Pharaoh alone could worship here; his family, the nobles and the people were separated, each in their own hall. The statue has been removed and is now in the Cairo Museum.

All around are rooms where the offerings to the god were stored, and on every wall are the rich carvings.

We turn to the right and pass through a doorway into the bright sunlight once more. On the left is yet another marble obelisk, this time lying on the ground, toppled by a great earthquake nearly 2,000 years ago. Beyond it is the sacred lake, its origin shrouded in mystery and its purpose unknown.

We walk slowly down another avenue and between the walls of another gateway, this time greatly ruined, its stones still balanced precariously as the earthquake left them. Beyond it is the gate of the Ptolemys, built much later and in almost perfect preservation.

And so we return to our waiting carriage and back to the world of today.

But first is the transition period. We pass through the native village. We are soon surrounded by little children clamouring for 'baksheesh'. A few coins thrown into the distance, and they go scampering away. How primitive the mud houses are; look at the quaint round pigeon cotes on their roofs – like rows of flowerpots.

The carriage reaches the riverbank and then turns to the left along it. The sun is setting beyond the hills on the far side, and a flaming crimson carpet stretches across the water towards us.

To the ancient Egyptians the sun left the world as it passed beyond the mountains, and so they buried their dead there, so that they could continue in its train.

Once more we are back in the hotel and can bathe luxuriously, grateful for modern comforts. After dinner, if you like, we can play table tennis on the floodlit veranda, before we sleepily retire.

There is no need to rise early this morning; we are not venturing far away, only to the Temple of Luxor, which is beside the hotel, so we can lie lazily daydreaming.

Breakfast over, we set out. Part of the temple is still buried, but the uncovered portion is magnificent.

Flanking the entrance are gigantic statues of King Rameses, wearing the double crown of Upper and Lower Egypt. Once more we have the series of courtyards and then the sanctuary.

This time, though, many things have been altered. In the first courtyard is a mosque: a very recent addition not more than 700 years old. To the right of this courtyard are some slender pillars erected by the Romans a few years before Christ, when they worshipped here. The sanctuary itself has been partly plastered over, and on the plaster there are paintings of the Apostles, drawn by the early Christians about AD 100. They still retain their brilliant colour, and the work is excellent.

So, once more, we have a panorama of the ages: the ancient temple built 3,000 years ago, the Roman remains 2,000 years old, the early Christian sanctuary and the fourteenth-century Moslem mosque. Will someone gaze on the ruins of our civilisation so in the far years to come?

Rest a little, dearest Joan. Long ages of happiness lie before us, and we continue on the morrow.

All my love,

Tony xxxxxx

# 6

# Cyprus, an Enchanted Island

Appointment to a senior administrative post with a staff car gave me the opportunity to explore Cyprus.

## London, 2 May 1945

Dearest Tony,
London and Londoners are sadly scarred by V-bomb attacks, Tony. It will be a long, long while before it recovers from its shattered buildings, homeless, helpless people with their frayed nerves, oh, and shabbiness.

I expected the bomb damage, the nerves, for of these I had experience, but the shabbiness of 'the greatest city in the world' shocked me. Almost all the pretty clothes seem to be on the inside of shop windows, Tony. Of course, it is not very important and explained by most of the 'glamour girls' being in the forces, rationing and so on, but how much it adds to the dreariness. The people are extremely weary, Tony, or the girls would have put a gay face on it with crazy shoes and hats as the Parisiennes did.

A woman's way of looking at things!? Perhaps, but I have many other impressions to give to you. I will leave them for another letter.

Good night, dear. My love,
Joan xxxxx

## 3 May 1945

Tony dearest,
I am pleased to be able to write much more happily of Surrey than I did of north London and Kent – it has not suffered nearly so severely from the bombs.

The countryside is full and green, flowers bloom everywhere, and the people look bonny and happy too.

Goodbye for a little while, dear. May we be together very soon.
My love and thoughts,
Joan xxxxxx

## 4 May 1945

Joan darling,
I have noticed in one or two letters I have censored lately that some
people have written to men out here reproaching them because they
did not take part in the Second Front. Surely people cannot have
such short memories that they have forgotten the great campaigns
fought out here, and surely they realise that the men cannot influence
their own postings. Very many out here wanted nothing more than
to take part in the invasion.

All my thoughts and longings will be with you during the victory
celebrations and all my prayers that we may soon be together once
more.

Tony xxxxxx

## VE Eve, 7 May 1945

My dearest Tony,
We arrived home a short while ago to hear the VE announcement. I
feel deeply grateful, but not excited. It seems strange that the war is
over for the continent of Europe, and yet we still have a bitter foe to
conquer before we turn to peace.

I should like to marry soon too, sweetheart, but want to be very,
very sure we shall be happy. If only we might know when you will
come home. When we meet we shall probably know the answers
to many of our wonders. I will think and think about this most
important wonder and write tomorrow, dear.

My love and special thoughts,
Joan xxxxxx

## VE Day, 8 May 1945

Dearest Tony,
Do you disagree with divorce altogether? It seems very wrong to
break vows, but then it seems dreadfully wrong, too, for people to
live together if they are ruining one another's lives. I have known

marriages that really do seem a waste of lives.

Your discussion about happiness, Tony: my impression is that about half of life is happy, contented – so on this I disagree with you a little! I believe you must have been exceptionally happy, dearest.

Here lies the fault I've told you of, Tony: you seem to take happiness for granted. It makes one terribly afraid of disappointing you. There, now I have told you so much, I am going to tell you how it worries me particularly, and more the longer you are away. Forgive me, but I cannot help thinking of the possibility that one of us, or both of us, may have changed. I know many people who have worried so, only to find their fears vanish, but then there are over-confident ones who are bitterly disappointed. Please do not let this upset you, dear. I wonder if you have thought about it yourself?

How much I hope my fears will vanish when we meet again. Is it selfish of me to ask you to share them? Only so could I explain why I would rather wait to decide about our marriage until we are sure beyond all doubt.

It was dear of you to explain all possibilities, and here are my thoughts about them. If, as please may it be, you come home very soon, we could be married and I live near wherever you are stationed or have a home in some pleasant place where you could spend your leave. This would be quite possible, I believe. The Essential Works Order relaxes now, I think, to the extent of allowing a wife to go with her husband so long as she registers for work. (This opens all kinds of interesting possibilities to my fertile imagination, from helping in a children's nursery to selling porridge and liquorice strips in the village general shop!) The accommodation problem, too, would probably be eased, except in London, by the numbers of troops leaving Britain. We should not have to worry about money while you were in the RAF and could save for our home.

I have thought carefully and believe we should need £7 a week to live reasonably in London, Tony. It is quite probable that this budget would need a lot of adjusting! I am practical, Tony, but not one of these terribly efficient women! Neither irresponsible nor terribly careful with money. I should, at least, until I got the hang of housekeeping without supervision, need a better system than my personal one of spending as I go along without account! (Though it causes much merriment amongst my friends, because I scarcely ever know how much money I have. It has the beautiful advantage that I often discover some money tucked away in an odd purse, just when I imagine myself completely broke!)

That is about enough of my comical and contradictory ideas for one letter.

I am not quite sure about your 'vanity', Tony. I like everyone to like and be pleased with me, too. I thought it might be a trace of my childhood inferiority complex, but maybe it is vanity!

Thank you, dear, for all your letters.

May you soon be home now.

My love,

Joan xxxxxx

## 12 MAY 1945

Joan darling,

I don't believe I have described the drive over the hills in detail.

The road leaves Nicosia town, and it runs along fairly sedately with trees on either side. On the way, it passes through tiny villages with the houses right against the road. From time to time, sideroads branch off, signposts pointing along them with most intriguing names.

The mountains over to the right are drawing steadily nearer, and the road, growing suddenly playful, begins to twist and turn – the journey upwards has begun in earnest. Wooded slopes rise around us, and we zigzag slowly between them. Higher and higher. If we glance back we can see the plains stretching away to the mist – coloured giants to the south which dwarf our own tiny range. The road has now begun to bewilder us in earnest and rushes forward, only to double back on its tracks around an overhanging shoulder of rock.

A magpie, startled by our sudden appearance, beats angrily up in front of the car and settles itself by the side of the road further along, and, as we pass, it is setting its ruffled feathers once more. A gleam of bright blue plumage is shown, contrasting against its glossy black wings.

We are now at the summit of the pass, and a headlong descent begins. To the right is a deep narrow valley with a tiny burn rushing along towards the sea. Its slopes are a mass of lovely green foliage. A sudden bend, and the blue Mediterranean lies before us, flanked by the hilly range through which we have just broken, triumphantly.

In front and below is Kyrenia, its tiny houses gathered round the great, grim-seeming castle. The road twists and turns desperately and then, with a tremendous effort, straightens itself and leads us demurely into the little town. A steep cobbled street with whitewashed buildings, another turn, and we are on the seafront beside the hotel. The Dome Hotel is a long, rambling, creamy building with red-tiled domes scattered liberally across its roof. It is a gay, airy place, and, joy of joys, from its windows one can look straight down to the sea below.

What a lovely place for one of our so-longed-for holidays, sweetheart. Join with me in hoping that it may be soon.

Goodbye and God keep you, darling.

With all my loving thoughts,

Tony xxxxxx

## 14 MAY 1945

Joan darling,

You fear that one or both of us may have changed. We shall have changed, look different physically perhaps and perhaps grown a little more mature mentally – but that is all. Now is the time for my second confession; a difficult one, this, and something which I tell only because I think it will help you – I know you will sympathise and understand.

I spent two gloriously happy days with you before I left England, days happier than I had ever known before. I did not stop to think; I only knew I loved you, and so I wrote from Plymouth. Then, if it had ever been possible, there might have been some slight doubt. We had known each other such a short time, knew little of each other's tastes and likes and dislikes. I acted on the impulse of my heart.

In the long days of parting that followed, however, I began to learn very many things about you from your letters. Before, I had only known that I felt wonderfully happy whenever I was near you; now I began to understand why, and the knowledge strengthened my love for you still more.

Our interests and outlooks are almost identical. (Although we do not always agree completely – hence this 'apologia pro vita sua'! That is as it should be, though; a life in which we had no questions to discuss with each other would be very dull.)

They make an imposing list, you will agree. Some are small things, but then life is made up of small things: great and momentous events are generally few and far between.

We are both young and enthusiastic, and we both like children. We both love England, not merely the outward England but the life that is England. We love beauty in all things, flowers, music, poetry, the countryside, art, ballet and opera. We are both fond of animals, especially dogs (do you remember the golden retriever of my dream home?). We are interested in life in foreign lands. We share common ideals as regards child education and welfare and the necessity for helping people to appreciate the loveliness of life. In the realm of sport we both like riding and sailing and – less exotic taste – table tennis! We like plays and generally the same sort of films, and we are both fond of dancing. I protest this last very strongly, although you may disbelieve it! My main reason for not dancing is that I know how bad I am, and I feel that until I can dance properly I should only spoil my partner's pleasure.

These, then, are some of the reasons for my confidence in a great and happy future for us. The plans we plan and the dreams we dream blend perfectly with each other. Last and most important: I love you so very much for yourself, for everything you are, for all the things I can never put into words. These are the things that can never change. Do you remember the poem of Elizabeth Browning that you sent me? Love me for love's sake, 'that evermore, Thou mayst love on, through love's eternity'.

That love will always be true, my darling, and passing years and changing circumstances will never alter it. Here is another poem for you by an even greater, wiser poet: Shakespeare.

*Let me not to the marriage of true minds*
*Admit impediments. Love is not love*
*Which alters when it alteration finds,*
*Or bends with the remover to remove:*
*O, no! It is an ever-fixed mark,*
*That looks on tempests and is never shaken;*
*It is the star to every wandering bark,*

*Whose worth's unknown, although his height be taken.*
*Love's not Time's fool, though rosy lips and cheeks*
*Within his bending sickle's compass come;*
*Love alters not with his brief hours and weeks,*
*But bears it out even to the edge of doom.*
*If this be error and upon me proved,*
*I never writ, nor no man ever loved.*

Do you wonder now, sweetheart, at my confidence? If it is possible to be happy even in adverse circumstances, how much greater and more enduring that happiness can be with all our heart's desire to encourage it.

Your budget seems wonderfully comprehensive, Joan dear, and as I know nothing of present-day values I am well content to leave it in your hands. What grand economic conferences we can have.

Bless you, darling, for all your thoughts and cares for me.

With all my love,

Tony xxxxxx

## 15 MAY 1945

Tony darling,

But before I chatter any more I must tell you wee bits of news. There are private cars being driven proudly around already. I should not be surprised if they were on the road ten minutes after the petrol ration was announced! The garage on St Leonard's Bridge is, apparently, from the display appearing this weekend, knocking together anything which will travel on four wheels!

Daddy is advertising for a house in any southern county, and we are enquiring of friends. Alternatively, should this effort produce nothing, Mama and Papa are considering storing the home, selling this house and travelling around until they find a suitable house. I should like to go along, but may be unable to obtain my release. Let us hope the Essential Works Order will soon be cancelled or at least modified to affect only urgent work. Oh, Tony, I could not bear to live in a 'state-run' country. Perhaps I am too individualistic; even school discipline irked me! But I do hate doing anything unless I am impressed that it is the reasonable and best possible thing to do!

I am desperately tired of the work I am doing. I could train someone else to do it perfectly in two or three months. There are several capable people who are doing work which only exists through lack of organisation and forethought. But unless I do something desperate I shall continue doing that same work for as many years again perhaps. Any mention of change or promotion elicits hurt surprise: 'Why, Miss Charles, you have only been in the Ministry six years, and the work you are doing is most important . . . !!'

Our service has certainly the value of incorruptibility which some nations' 'servants' lack, but of resourcefulness and imagination it knows so little. (Here I have the farmers' full support!) Fortunately, the war departments are more businesslike. For instance, the Admiralty hold promotion boards frequently, before which one may choose to appear, thus being judged on one's obvious merits as well as record. But in our Ministry one modestly awaits one's name being put forward by one's superior officer, and the promotion board judges on this recommendation and the record, also largely compiled by the superior officer, without knowing the personality involved by more than a name! It seems to me that an officer might be of great use to his country and yet not be popular with his immediate superior?!

Oh, Tony, am I not always 'carrying the banner' about something! Now I cannot imagine why I poured all that out to you, for it must be very uninteresting. I fear I am a wild thing, Tony, and not very well tamed. It is perhaps because Mother used so often to take me out in the country on a lovely summer day, instead of sending me to school!

Too tired to start on another long page.

Good night, dearest.

My love,

Joan xxxxxx

## 16 MAY 1945

Dearest Tony,

Our house is in the agent's hands for sale, but the next move is not decided. You have no bright ideas as to finding accommodation anywhere in the Home Counties, Tony? It would be fine if we could stay at an inn or flat or cottage in the country and wander round from there to look for a more permanent home. Daddy invites me to go along for a three-month 'treat', if I can get my release. That 'if', however, is a big one at the moment.

Another friend has her man home from Germany. About every one of our office sweethearts has had leave or been repatriated. It is definitely our turn, Tony!

My love to you,

Joan xxxxxx

## 17 MAY 1945

Dearest Joan,

Today has been beautifully warm, and I went swimming and sunbathing at Kyrenia. Some of the natives caught a baby octopus near the swimming pool. They are quite harmless and are very, very frightened. This one was gaily coloured – red, blue and orange – and as soon as it managed to get into the water it scuttled away and hid under a rock.

Somehow they never seem to grow very big out here. It is just as well for our peace of mind when we are swimming! The natives go out at night with powerful lights and shine them in the water. They can then see the octopi (is that correct?) on the seabed, and, as it is quite shallow, they spear them. They are considered a great delicacy, but I resolutely refuse to be tempted!

With all my love,

Tony xxxxx

## 26 MAY 1945

Dearest Tony,

I have been thinking about us and all you say about us, dearest, not for the first time, of course, but all over again. You are wonderfully right; we have a great deal to look forward to happily and confidently: love, companionship, sharing things. But I cannot help growing impatient for these things, to feel they are sure and secure again; it is so long since our world tumbled down.

If all goes well, we shall be leaving St Annes within a month.

All my love,

Joan xxxxxx

## 28 MAY 1945

Joan darling,

Today has been very warm again, but fortunately the warmth was slightly tempered by a fairly strong breeze. The chief trouble is the heat in our rooms. The buildings are like Nissen huts with stone walls. The roof of each is corrugated iron, and there is no lining. You can imagine how hot it gets inside when the sun has been beating on the metal roof all day. Then again, the rooms are quite small, smaller than those at Shallufa, and the smallness accentuates the discomfort.

We have some wonderful 'Heath Robinson-ish' ideas for cooling them, though, and I will tell you how we succeed. One is to rig up a curtain to collect any breeze there is and direct it into the room!

With all my love and thoughts,

Tony xxxxxx

## 28 MAY 1945

My dearest Tony,

It is very sweet of you to send presents, Tony, and I love them. My chiding arose only out of concern at the high cost of living. We shall both, I guess, have to give up some of our extravagances if we are to be married soon! We shall have lots of necessary, but not necessarily dull, shopping to do, and it will be fun doing it together.

Now I am going to melt my weariness in a hot bath and lazily decide whether to make some coffee or tumble into bed and leave Daddy to make the coffee!

My love and thoughts and longing to see you,

Joan xxxxxx

## 30 MAY 1945

Dearest Joan,

I, too, think it important to be able to discuss the things one cares for and wonders about. Very often my own view is one adopted hastily and without proper thought, and you show me so many aspects I had not considered.

No, darling, you did not hurt me in suggesting that I might be over-confident of happiness. Looking back I can well see that it was a most natural thing for you to think. A sheltered childhood is a wonderful thing. If all life could be as happy and serene. If one experiences many disappointments and cares in early life, it is so very, very easy to become bitter and cynical.

I can especially sympathise with your unhappiness at being teased by your classmates, for when I was at school I was often told that I looked like an Indian. At first I was desperately unhappy, but later realised that the more I showed my resentment the more the others teased, so I soon began to display an indifference that I did not really feel, and the teasing died away.

I never think your ideas or scraps of memories silly or funny, dearest. I love them because they let me share a part of your life that I do not know and help me to understand you better and better. That is why all your letters are so precious to me.

So you have applied to resign from the Civil Service. I was pleased to hear it, because I know how restricted and regulated its life is. The dowry is certainly a most unimportant consideration; your happiness is the only thing that matters.

You say you have inherited your mother's practical nature to counter your 'artiness'. Please, Joan dear, do not think that I am flattering you – I think that your nature is ideal. You love and appreciate beautiful things and ideals and yet take very good care always to keep the ideals within the realms of possibility. (Something, I fear, which I often disdain to do when I make sweeping plans. All I want then is boundless power to improve the world in spite of itself!)

With my eager, loving thoughts,
Tony xxxxxx

## 1 JUNE 1945

Darling Joan,
There is a test case before Air Ministry at the moment. Some people have been put up for home leave, and everyone is waiting for their decision.

I think that you have made a wise decision in resigning from the Service. The great part of the war is over as far as the people in England are concerned, and considerations of health and happiness once more take their place as things of importance. The whole Civil Service atmosphere seems so narrow and uninspiring. I am sure you will find something that you will like far better.

With all my love and happy, hopeful thoughts,

Tony xxxxxx

## ST ANNES, 4 JUNE 1945

My dearest Tony,

Daddy had a terrible time in Surrey. He found a small house for sale at New Malden and is negotiating for it. None of the 'chosen' towns – Dorking, Reigate, Wimbledon, etc. – offered any house under £4,000!

I confess, at this news and disappointment over the holiday, I burst into tears. That was not very considerate of me after all Daddy's trouble, but for the moment the bottom seemed to fall out of my world! Dad comforts me that, by the time you and I are seeking a home, conditions will be better, and you have a priority claim to a house anyway. Things probably won't look nearly so black either, when I am less tired!

All my love,

Joan xxxxx

## 4 JUNE 1945

Dearest Joan,

I suppose that it is no use telling you not to work so hard. I know that you must help your mother. One of our first purchases must be a washing machine, although a laundry is far simpler, if more devastating!

I have just been over to dinner and was startled to see white sugar with the coffee. I had almost forgotten that sugar was ever white. How quickly one can get used to things!

Good night and happy dreams, my darling.

Tony xxxxxx

## 6 JUNE 1945

Darling Joan,

I am feeling a little cross today. I have a slight touch of fever, and the doctor insisted that I go into hospital. It is nothing very much, and I hope to be out again in a few days. I do not feel like writing a long letter tonight, dearest, but know that you will forgive me. I will write again tomorrow when my head is a little clearer.

With all my loving thoughts,

Tony xxxxxxx

## 7 JUNE 1945

My dearest Joan,

I am feeling rather better today but fear I have to resign myself to a few more days in bed. I am not allowed to eat anything. For 48 hours all I have had, officially, is 8 pills and two glasses of Horlicks!! I say 'officially' because the padre came in this morning, and he and the MO had tea and cheese and biscuits. The MO went out for a few minutes, and the padre smuggled two biscuits and a piece of cheese to me. These I ate hastily before the doc returned!

How lovely it would be if I were in England and you could call in to visit me. I should recover rapidly!

Goodbye and God keep you, my darling.

Tony xxxxxx

## 8 JUNE 1945

Dearest Tony,

Thank you very much for the sugared almonds; they arrived in perfect condition.

It might be a wonderful idea for MPs to join the food queues; they would learn much about the temper of our people. For a little instance, the potato shortage is taken uncomplainingly, because, I suppose, the harvest weather was so bad and it was not possible to supply sufficient labour. But there is much dissatisfaction about the fish muddle, because, with abundant fish in the sea and the boats and men to bring it in, the fault lies apparently with the government departments concerned with its transportation etc. You see, plentiful fish was promised to make up for the cuts in meat, bacon and fat rations, but so far the little available is always at the end of a long and early-morning queue!

Goodbye for a while,

My love,

Joan xxxxxx

## 9 JUNE 1945

Joan darling,

I have been promoted to a 'light diet' but fear that I don't feel hungry. Yesterday I ate one cherry and a tiny jelly!! I must go up to the invigorating mountain climate.

Apart from a rather drowsy feeling, I am really quite well, but the doctor will not relent.

Don't worry about me, dearest; I shall be up long before this reaches you.

With all my loving thoughts,

Tony xxxxxx

## 14 JUNE 1945

My dearest Tony,

I am sorry you are sick and hope you do not feel too bad. By now I hope, too, a pleasant convalescence will be making up for being ill. Is it a serious fever, Tony? The biscuit-and-cheese episode encourages me to think that it is not.

I wish I might come to see you and smuggle you some cherries I have bought, although if you were very ill I should be quite as strict as the MO!

My news: my release has not been approved yet, and I can get no more information than that my papers are in London, and the service departments have no desire to hurry or encourage such releases. They guardedly agree that it would probably be possible to transfer me, if my resignation is not accepted, to a London office. Perhaps that won't be so bad, although it will mean long, busy days – I used to be happy in town.

God bless you, dear.

My love,

Joan xxxxxx

## 14 JUNE 1945

Joan darling,

I am on the road to complete recovery now, although I expect I shall have to remain here a week or so while they keep an eye on me.

My appetite has at last returned, although I have to be very careful what I eat – this, needless to say, is completely out of my hands!

Goodbye and God bless you, sweetheart. Don't worry – I am almost well again.

With all my love,

Tony xxxxxx

## 17 JUNE 1945

Dearest Joan,

I am pleased to be able to report that, today, I feel almost completely recovered. I even got up and had a shower (without permission, I must confess!). The fever has gone entirely, although I now have jaundice. The main trouble is that, although I feel quite well, I shall not be allowed to leave the hospital for some weeks.

It is rather trying having to stay in bed when I would so much like to be up and out in the fresh air and sunshine. Still, I shall appreciate it all more when I am eventually free.

With all my love and thoughts,

Tony xxxxxx

## 18 JUNE 1945

Dearest Tony,

So you are being really contrary about your food! Is your nurse not firm, or not pretty, enough to persuade you to 'eat it all up'?! Teasing over, I sympathise greatly. It is beastly to eat when one does not fancy to. But I must admit that when I was ill I made no recovery until I was forced, by threat, entreaty and every other method of persuasion, to eat. And I have not yet recovered from a loathing of Brussels sprouts formed at that time!

My resignation has not been accepted, and so I must return to the office on Thursday and take a transfer to London on the 28th. Unfortunately, this news has come when Mother is feeling bad again and counting on me to straighten out the new home, and I was rather looking forward to this. We can only hope there will be a miracle in the form of a domestic help in Malden!

Good night then, dear. I hope you feel well again.

My love to you,

Joan xxxxxx

## 20 JUNE 1945

Joan darling,

The MO today said that I should be in bed about another two weeks and then spend about two weeks up, but in the hospital. After that I expect about two or three weeks' sick leave! So you will see that my programme for the next two months is well mapped out for me and I must just drift where the stream takes me. Then, and only then, can I begin to wonder what will happen to me next.

God keep you, my darling.

Tony xxxxxx

## 23 JUNE 1945

Joan darling,

Our wireless has been returned after an absence of over a week. It makes a great difference; I get so very tired of trying to read all day, and if I sleep I cannot sleep at night. The really annoying part is that I feel perfectly well and have an enormous appetite. My diet, fortunately, is not limited in quantity, as long as I do not have anything with fat in it. This is a sad blow because my fellow patients get fresh milk every morning and I am compelled to watch them drink it and envy them in silence!

What a wonderful time I shall have when I am released from all these restrictions. I expect that will be in about three weeks from now.

Goodbye, sweetheart.

Tony xxxxxx

## 27 JUNE 1945

My dearest Joan,

Today I had a special treat. There was an ENSA concert in the evening, and the MO allowed me to get up and dress and go to it. He insisted on my going and returning in an ambulance, although the concert was held in a building only 100 yards away.

After such an exciting evening I feel quite tired and expect I shall sleep very well tonight.

Goodbye and God bless you, dearest,

Tony

## 28 JUNE 1945

Dearest Joan,

I am feeling very fit today after my evening out. It was really great to be able to dress again after living in pyjamas for weeks! The doc refuses to let me get up yet and said it was only in a moment of weakness that he let me go to the concert! It made a wonderful change though, and I feel much better for it.

The wireless worked beautifully for two days after its return and then lapsed into a sulky silence from which nothing can shake it.

By the time this reaches you I shall no longer be a 'bed' patient but will be allowed up all day and able to go out for short walks.

Don't worry, dearest, everything is progressing splendidly, although I am so impatient!

With all my love and eager thoughts of you,

Tony xxxxxxx

## 1 JULY 1945

Joan darling,

Yesterday I sunbathed for an hour. I retired to bed again shortly afterwards, but it made a pleasant change. The doctor says I may get up for a little while longer tomorrow and promises that I should be fit to leave at the end of the week.

I shall be very glad to get into the outside world once more. I plan a week in the crisper air of the mountains and then a week in Kyrenia, where it will be quite hot but where I can do plenty of swimming to get really fit.

With all my love and constant thoughts,

Tony xxxxxx

## 2 JULY 1945

Dearest Joan,

Today there was a big break in routine. At ten o'clock, after the doctor had seen me, I got up and dressed and have spent my time since sunbathing and sitting reading. It is now five o'clock, and I do not intend to go to bed before eight.

Already after these few hours up I feel much stronger and in a day or so shall be completely well again.

How little we value health and fitness until it is taken away from us. Then the country and the world outside are things we long for more than anything else. Perhaps it is a good thing to be ill occasionally; it teaches us to appreciate our ordinary life more.

God keep you, dearest,

Tony xxxxxx

## HOOK, SURREY, 3 JULY 1945

Dearest Tony,

Just to let you know that I am home and tremendously happy about it. How I wish you might be home too.

I am very happily installed at Auntie Nina's – the most light-hearted of households.

The 'powers' at the office have been most unexpectedly charming to me and promised me an interesting career if I will stay. My friends are happy to see me back and I am very happy to be among my ain folk again.

I came down on Sunday and began working here on Monday morning; we have had visitors until midnight each night, so I am completely breathless but very happy.

I do hope I shall hear from you soon – no doubt the letters are wandering around between my 'possible' homes. And I hope you're feeling much, much better, dear.

My love to you.

A very excited,

Joan xxxxxx

## 5 JULY 1945

Joan darling,

Great news today! The doctor has decided that I am fit enough to leave hospital tomorrow.

On Tuesday we had a visit from Lady Wooley, the Governor's wife, and General Manifold, who is in charge of Red Cross work on the island. The General is very old, and I felt quite sorry for him walking about in the heat.

Goodbye and God keep you, my darling,

Tony xxxxxxx

8 July 1945

Darling Joan,

I am writing from the officers' mess at the leave camp at Troodos. It is really delightful; we are in the midst of a pinewood near the summit. It is just over 5,000 feet above sea level, and the air is cool and wonderfully refreshing.

We left the aerodrome yesterday at about ten o'clock and drove across the plain towards the west, almost as far as the sea. Then we turned south and were soon climbing the first range of hills, passing through a succession of delightfully picturesque villages. From time to time we crossed quaint stone bridges over dried-up river beds. One bridge was curved downwards, like a humpbacked bridge reversed.

Soon the smaller hills were left behind, and we approached the giants themselves. The road twisted and turned as it climbed, and slowly a wonderful panorama of the island began to spread itself before us. Behind were the hills of the Kyrenia range and the broad valley which we had just left. To the right was the sea, glinting and sparkling in the sun. In front and to the left were the wooded hills. Often the road ran along the edge of slopes, falling away 1,000 feet to the valley. The woods now began to gather around, and the ferns and flowers made it seem like an English scene. Hollyhocks, growing wild, made a lovely patch of colour, and there were irises, although the flowers were faded away.

At length the road levelled out, and we reached the camp. The mess is a stone building with a central porch and is quite small and cosy. From my room I can look right down into the valley and watch the birds soaring and tumbling about below. Two swifts have built a nest against the wall, and there are four hungry young mouths to feed. They spend their time bringing back morsels to the nest and each time, as they approach, four tiny heads with wide-open beaks appear!

There are tennis courts and a cricket pitch, but alas I am not allowed to play. I may not even go for long walks, so I think I shall be content to sit in the sunshine and read.

It gets quite cool at night, and yesterday we gathered round a blazing log fire in the lounge. It seemed very strange in July!

I plan to stay here until Friday and then return to Kyrenia on

Saturday. The keen air up here should soon revive me. I must climb to the top of Mount Olympus before I leave – it is only two miles from here and about 500 feet up.

I will write a day-by-day account of my adventures so that you may know how I am progressing.

With all my loving thoughts,

Tony xxxxxx

## 10 July 1945

Dearest Joan,

Yesterday we went out on an all-day expedition to an old monastery. We left at nine o'clock and drove along the road for a little while, then turned off on to a dusty track. This led us between the pine trees and skirted around the peak of Olympus. At first, the view was obscured by the woods, but soon we came into the open once more and the whole of western Cyprus lay before us.

Below were hills, lofty themselves but dwarfed by the majesty of our own great range. Beyond these hills lay the plains, with tiny toy villages scattered across them, and then the graceful sweep of Morphou Bay.

The track continued on, always descending gently, and at length we came to another road. We turned right and passed through the village of Prodhromos. We kept to the road and continued our downward flight. We were now driving along the brink of a deep valley, and soon, 1,000 feet below us, we saw the neat red and grey roofs of Pedhoulas. Our own road led into it, twisting tortuously down the side of the valley. We were just preparing for the headlong descent when we left the road and swung down yet another track. This remained fairly level and followed faithfully every twist and turn of the hills. For a while we kept the valley, with its neat villages dotted along its length, in sight – then we turned and lost all trace of human habitation in the wilderness that lay ahead. We could see the track stretching endlessly before us, disappearing behind one peak only to reappear as it swept round the next. Our way was always narrow, with the hillside rising steeply above us and on the other side a sheer fall to the stream, which we could see dashing its impetuous wayward course among the trees below. All around were towering crests, and we felt intensely our own insignificance.

We continued thus for nearly an hour, and then the path began to climb again. The ascent was short but steep, and we rounded a shoulder of the hill to find the monastery of Kykko before us.

The monastery was a long white building with a red tiled roof. A great arched doorway in the centre led into the first courtyard. Here two black-clad Greek monks bade us welcome in quite good English and said that they would show us round the monastery.

The first courtyard had cloisters running along one side with a balcony above them. From this balcony were stretched wires supporting grapevines. Onto it opened the rooms of the monks. We crossed and passed through a smaller archway and down some wooden stairs into the inner courtyard. Again there were cloisters along one side, and opposite was the chapel. Above and to the left was a small belfry.

We entered the chapel, and to the right was a great brass and wood screen, most ornately carved. In each panel was a painting of a saint. From the roof were suspended silver oil lamps and several silver ships. These ships commemorated the bringing of a precious ikon to the island by St Luke.

The ikon itself was in the centre of the screen, entirely concealed by a brass cover, except for one great emerald. The monk told us that much of the elaborate metalwork had come from Russia before the revolution.

The present church was just over 130 years old and was built on the site of an older church, which had been destroyed by fire. The rest of the church was quite plain – the walls and ceiling were of white plaster, and all around were the stalls of the monks, with a larger and more ornate throne for the abbot.

Behind the church was a grim, but very interesting sight: a tomb with a stone slab on the top, old and not very well cared for. On the slab were the names of previous abbots and the dates of their tenure of office. The monks moved the slab aside, and we saw an untidy heap of bones. As each abbot died, he was buried and his body left undisturbed for several years. His bones were then removed and placed in the shrine.

We re-entered the church and came to the inner courtyard once more. Our guides now led us upstairs to the balcony and into a small lounge. Rather incongruously, this was furnished quite comfortably and had maps of Cyprus and of the world all round its walls. One of the monks had left us, and he now returned with a tray on which were glasses of water, spoons and a jar of jam. This he offered to each in turn. We took a spoonful of jam and a glass of water and found that the jam was really delicious. It was made from cherries from the garden of the monastery.

The monks now took us along the balcony and stopped before a small door. This they unlocked, revealing a flight of narrow, winding stone stairs. We climbed up and emerged on the platform around the belfry. The pride of the monastery was the great bell which hung in the centre: a gift from Moscow many years ago. Beside this there were four smaller bells, each with ornate inscriptions and designs. The method of ringing these was ingenious. A rope was attached to the clapper of the big bell and passed, via a pulley, to a pedal. Two more ropes were attached to the smaller bells, each rope ringing a pair of bells. The ends of these ropes were led to a point near the pedal so that one monk could ring all five bells.

On our return to the balcony we were cordially invited to stay for lunch, and we gladly accepted the offer. As there was just over an hour to wait, we all went outside, and two of my friends decided to climb up to a small shrine on a hill above the monastery. The other was intent on discovering a church in the valley below, and so I was left alone, talking with one of the monks. He told me he was studying English and produced a copy of *The Prisoner of Zenda*, from which he read one or two passages aloud, asking for correction.

Time passed quickly, and my friends returned, tired but triumphant, and we went into lunch. This was very interesting: we were given a whole loaf each! The main dish was a mixture of white and runner beans, and there were also olives and some sour, whipped cream. Afterwards there was watermelon.

Lunch over, we chatted for a while and then set out on our return journey. We reached Prodhromos once more and then drove to see a government experimental fruit farm nearby. It was small and not nearly so well run as the one I had seen in Palestine, but the director told us that it was being expanded.

We returned to Prodhromos for tea and then to the camp again. The whole day was most enjoyable and very interesting.

My appetite is even greater than before in this keen air, and I am beginning to feel really well again.

I am obeying orders and not doing anything strenuous but must confess that I am looking forward to some swimming at Kyrenia next week.

God bless you, dear heart,

Tony xxxxxx

## 11 JULY 1945

My dearest Joan,

Today I fulfilled my ambition and climbed Mount Olympus. It was well worth it – the view was magnificent. I am enclosing a flower I picked at the very peak – the highest point on Cyprus. I fear it does not look so nice now; I did not press it properly. I must be quite well again, because I walked over five miles and have not felt the slightest effect. It is wonderful to feel really well again.

There is to be a bonfire on Olympus tomorrow night, and there will be Cypriot music and dancing. I think I will stay in the mess, though. It will be very late by the time it finishes. They plan to roast meat and have a real feast.

With all my loving thoughts,

Tony xxxxxx

## 21 JULY 1945

Joan dearest,

Yesterday morning I set off from Kyrenia very early – at five o'clock – to scale the peak that I could see challenging me from my bedroom window.

The sun had not yet risen, but it was quite bright and beautifully cool. The first part of the journey lay along a country road and through a tiny, silent village. On leaving the village I struck across the fields, determined to go direct. My plan was to follow a stream which had carved a valley down the hillside and so avoid having to climb up and down several smaller hills on the way.

Crossing several orchards painfully carpeted with thistles, I reached the foot of the range and began the ascent.

As I climbed, the sun began to rise, glowing warmly through the light mist. The little stream wound in and out among the rocks, and all along its bed were lovely wild flowers.

At first the ascent was gradual, but, as I went on, it grew steeper and steeper. At last I reached the broader pathway which led from the main road to the east, and now my journey grew easier.

I stopped at the house of a friend of mine, built at the summit of the range. The stones and general outside design are the same as the castle, and from below it looks like a well-preserved part of a tower guarding the approaches. Fortunately, the house was open – it is used but rarely – and I drank a long, cool squash very gratefully.

Fortified by the rest, I set out again and in about half an hour had reached the entrance of the castle, St Hilarion.

The castle is built in three rings around the peak of the hill. The outer ring was the military castle; the next the quarters of the monks, for the castle was built around a still older monastery; and the topmost part was the royal apartments.

Although the castle is now in ruins, it is a truly wonderful sight. Towers peep from behind rocky crags, windows open onto glorious views, and there is always a fresh treasure to be discovered around the next corner. Two of the loveliest windows are the 'Queen's Window' in the Queen's apartments and the window called 'Bella Vista', which opens onto a circular plot, formerly the scene of gay tournaments. From this window the royal ladies watched and applauded the efforts of their champions.

I paused again at my friend's house on the way back and chatted for a while, and he very kindly offered to take me back in his car. I gratefully accepted, for it was now 11 o'clock and I wanted to swim to cool me down before lunch.

So I achieved one of my ambitions and 'stormed' a fairy-like castle. May other ambitions be as successful.

With all my eager, loving thoughts, sweetheart,

Tony xxxxxx

## 23 JULY 1945

Joan darling,

My leave draws rapidly to an end. Yesterday morning I walked into Kyrenia and looked over the castle. Although I have been past it many, many times, I have never bothered to go inside. How little we value things that are easily attained.

It is not so interesting as the other castles as it was completely rebuilt by the Venetians in the sixteenth century. The walls are extremely thick as a countermeasure against the still novel use of cannon. As it is in an excellent state of preservation, it is now used as a prison. Hence many of the rooms cannot be seen.

There was little time before lunch, so I did not go down to the sea but swam in the pool. Numerous bees fall in the pool trying to get water, and I always rescue them with a piece of wood. A young doctor who was staying at the hotel picked one up, and it sat quite quietly on his finger while it preened itself. Opening its mouth, it extended a tongue almost as big as the entire rest of its body. Balancing on its back legs, it proceeded to wipe away all traces of water with its front legs, and then, changing its balance to its front legs, it completed the process. When it was eventually satisfied, it tried its wings once or twice and then flew off quite unconcerned by its narrow escape.

I hope that someday you will come to this lovely island to enjoy its beauty and peace with me, too.

God bless you, my darling,

Tony xxxxxx

## 25 JULY 1945

Tony dearest,

Tony, I could not resist the temptation to use my blue bag and gloves today! I have a big hat and shoes to match and wore just a flowered blue silk dress. Mm, I felt nice.

Take care of yourself, Tony.

God bless you dear.

My love,

Joan xxxxxx

## 25 JULY 1945

Joan dear,

Early this morning I left Kyrenia and returned to Nicosia. Leave was over, but I had many memories. Perhaps the loveliest was that of sitting on the terrace in the evening, with a cool breeze blowing from the sea. The sun was setting in the west, and in the distance the Taurus mountains of Turkey were shrouded in a purple mist.

The light-grey stone pillars of the colonnade were tinged with a faint pink, and the young pine trees beyond them grew darker and darker. From the road came the sound of singing as young Greek boys and girls slowly wended their way home. Then the sun had set, and the rose changed to green and then blue, and the bright stars began to gleam.

With all my love and dreams of you,

Tony xxxxx

## 26 JULY 1945

Darling Joan,

The election results have been announced, and we now have a Labour government. I am disappointed, but since they are in power I am glad that they have a clear majority. Any faults will be entirely theirs, and if they succeed they can justly claim all credit.

Now, to answer your letters: I asked the doctor what could have caused my illness, and he said that it was impossible to say, so little was known about it. They knew the symptoms and the remedy but not how to prevent it.

Please don't worry about a birthday present, dearest; the only present I want is to be able to hold you in my arms and tell you how much I love you and how much I have missed you.

As I walked over to my room this evening I saw a great tawny full moon rising with a beautiful golden halo around it. Here the halo brings no threat of rain; the summer is perfectly dry.

Goodbye, my darling.

Tony xxxxxxx

## 28 JULY 1945

Dearest Joan,

I am going to Cairo tomorrow and returning on Monday. I thought that, after so long in hospital, I ought to do some flying again. It will seem quite strange!

I have very little work to do at present; I am President of a court of inquiry, but that should not take very long, and then I shall be 'unemployed' again. I hope that you are still on your 42-hour week – it makes things so much nicer for you. Perhaps the 'Powers That Be' will find something interesting for you after all.

Goodbye and God bless, dearest,
Tony xxxxxx

## 31 JULY 1945

Tony darling,

This is my first experience of living in another home than my own,
and, although I have been enjoying the company and fun, it will be
nice to be in my own home again. To be able to say when I want to
write or read or sleep instead of talking or going out. To be able to
do things when it *isn't* convenient! And to be untidy sometimes!!

This wobbly old train is nearly home to another busy evening for
me. Never before have I so rushed through life. I have to run all *up*
the escalator at Waterloo to catch a train in time for dinner!

Continuing Wednesday morning

My Auntie Nina is terribly particular about mealtimes and quite
the most house-proud woman in the world. You can imagine
how careful I have to be, specially not to curl my feet up on the
cushions!

I feel ashamed of saying so often that I am tired. Time perhaps
that I explained.

Tony, when I was ill in the winter, it was awful bad nerves. Mother
said you would worry unnecessarily, so I did not tell you. I am feeling
well now, except I still get bad headaches when there is not enough
sleep in my life, and rushing about exhausts me. Are we getting *old*?!

My love,

Joan xxxxxx

Worried a little that there is still no mail from you. I do not deserve
any but know you are too generous to be so very cross with me.

## 1 AUGUST 1945

My dearest Joan,

There are so many flying people these days I have high hopes that
release will be very rapid.

Regarding home leave: at the moment all space is being used to
give personnel posted to the Far East home leave before they go, and
this is only fair. In my new job I may possibly have opportunities

for travelling, but it is only a very vague chance. Perhaps policy on leave will be crystallised soon.

Goodbye and God bless you, darling,

Tony xxxxxx

## 2 AUGUST 1945

Dearest Tony,

Lunched with an old friend on Wednesday and found her very glamorous. Very much a career girl, 'Taffy' (not at all Welsh indeed!) surprised me with the news that her younger sister has recently blossomed into a film star, with the lead in *Pink String and Sealing Wax*.

You seem so happy and enjoying life, bless you. I am glad your holiday was so good. I wonder about the posting.

Love to you,

Joan xxxxxx

## 3 AUGUST 1945

Dearest Joan,

I am going to Cairo again this afternoon and then on to Alexandria. I shall be returning tomorrow.

I remembered something that I had intended to tell you about in my last letter, about my earlier visit to the Delta.

I stood at a window of the hotel in the evening and saw searchlights playing over the harbour, illuminating silver, fairy-like ships. More searchlights lit the Royal Palace, and a statue of Ismail Pasha. Above the palace an Egyptian flag floated in a sea of light, the crescent and stars seeming to glow against their green background. It was so lovely that it tempted me out, and I walked along the seafront ablaze with light. It seems such a short time ago that Alexandria was blacked out that I could hardly realise that the blackout was a thing of the past. How much I look forward to the time when I shall be able to see the lights of London with you and buy you violets in a Piccadilly gay with flashing, coloured signs.

Goodbye and God keep you, dearest.

Tony xxxxx

## 7 AUGUST 1945

Dearest Joan,

Today I went to Famagusta. I set off at about eight o'clock and arrived at half past nine.

The old town of Famagusta is completely enclosed by a massive wall, built mainly by the Venetians in the fifteenth century, although the town is very much older. At intervals are mighty gates flanked by towers, one called Othello's Tower. Legend has it that here Othello murdered Desdemona.

Near the gate, inside the city, is the old cathedral of St Nicholas, now used as a mosque and called St Sophia. The nave of the building is still intact, and the lovely Gothic windows remain, although the glass has been replaced by oriental plaster tracery. Two ornate flying buttresses remain, and these have been copied, to a certain extent, by the Turks who repaired the others. Thus on either side are plain and massive buttresses, contrasting strikingly with the airiness of the original Gothic. The front of the cathedral is pierced by three graceful Gothic doors, with pointed arches and wonderful carving. On either side rises a tower, and on the left-hand one a minaret has now been erected. The other remains almost intact.

The interior has been whitewashed throughout, and Islamic characters have been painted on the columns. All other traces of decoration have been swept away.

Facing the cathedral is the remains of the facade of the Venetian palace. This is of creamy stone and consists of a wall with three rounded arches. Beyond are the courtyard and the ruins of the walls. An old cannon remains trained on the entrance, and around are numerous stone cannonballs. In one corner is a still more ancient siege piece and a pile of battered, rusty morions.

To the left of the palace is yet another ruined church – in and around Famagusta are more than 360 ruins. Among all these traces of ancient splendour are the houses of the present-day peasants. Many are built of mud bricks and others with stones taken from the palace and churches.

The winding road leads on to the west wall, and by climbing to the top a wonderful view can be obtained. Dominating all else is the stately cathedral. It is possible to follow the wall along the ramparts until the main gate is reached. This is a most elaborate structure with gates, portcullis and covering towers and strong points. Little wonder that Famagusta has withstood more than one siege.

There is one more ruin of interest within the walls: another church. In this are the remains of many frescoes, with the original colours still fresh. What excellent craftsmanship it must have been to have weathered so many centuries.

Chief of the more mundane attractions of Famagusta is a lovely silvery beach, the nicest place for swimming on the island. As you will guess, I spent quite a long time sunbathing and lazily swimming.

At each village we passed on the way back, the peasants were threshing the winter harvest. First, the whole ears are laid on the ground, and a peasant drives a pair of oxen over them, harnessed to a flat board on which he usually sits on a wooden chair. When he is satisfied that the grain has been separated, the whole is swept up into a heap. As soon as there is a wind, the peasants get fine forks and throw the chaff and grain into the air. The chaff, being light, is blown away, and the grain remains.

Other peasants were busy making the flat mud bricks from which their houses are built.

The contrast was almost as great as in Egypt between the primitive present and the splendour of the past. Present-day civilisation has affected the peasant but little. I think that the chief boon it has given him is the two-gallon petrol tin, which is used for everything from carrying water to roofing houses!!

Goodbye and God bless you, my darling,

Tony xxxxxx

## 8 AUGUST 1945

Dearest Joan,

I am going down to the Delta again on Friday, this time to Cairo. I shall be coming back again on Saturday. How strange it will be to return to England, where 200 miles is a long journey. Cairo is over 300 miles away, and I am merely going there to do some shopping.

I heard the news today of the new atomic bomb. How terrible are the uses to which science can be put. Let us hope that it will help to shorten the war considerably. I thank God that you are safe and out of range of possible reprisals.

I long always for the day when we shall be able to set out together for the places that you would like to see, in our quest of loveliness and peace.

Goodbye, darling,

Tony xxxxx

## 9 AUGUST 1945

Dearest Tony,

Our picnic is the nicest thing to tell about. It was just a simple family picnic on Sunday. We did not have to walk very far to find a quiet, sunny field close to a tiny wood. The corn stood straight and golden in the sunshine; there were blackberries ripened already in the hedgerows and shelter from a sudden shower 'neath the trees. I felt a great contentment, long foreign to me. I must have looked happy because Daddy remarked to me, 'You do love Surrey, don't you?'

We lay in the sunshine, reading and chatting drowsily all afternoon. Merryl buried me in straw; we enjoyed lots of fruits, then roamed slowly home, longing to pick berries and to talk to a wee pony.

There is a great drive of fruit-bottling and jam-making with the abundant harvest of apples and plums (and a great deal of fruit-eating on my part!). It is lovely to see the trees laden with fruit, the lovely flowers, the rich harvest. Is it not terrible that with all the abundance of the earth, mankind should have brought itself so near starvation as it is today?

I wonder how you think about the A-bomb, Tony. Dare we hope that its awesomeness will prevent war? I scarce know how I feel yet, except I wish it just exploded everything, instead of burning.

No more terrifying thoughts tonight. Let us grasp very firmly onto commonplace, comforting things.

So good night and good night.

My love to you,

Joan xxxxxx

## 11 AUGUST 1945

My darling Joan,

I flew down to Cairo on Friday and the ground staff met me with excited rumours of a Japanese surrender when I landed. So far it has not been accepted, but I have very high hopes. Wonderful thought that we may be together so soon. It will probably be a few months, even if peace comes. I expect that it will be difficult to get everyone home quickly. This may be that lovely Christmas that we have been dreaming of.

I have to go down to Cairo again tomorrow, and, if Japan accepts the terms, all aircraft may be grounded, so I shall be unable to get back for a few days.

With all my love and eager hopes,

Tony xxxxxx

## 13 AUGUST 1945

Dearest Joan,

There is still no reply from Japan, and we are all standing by expectantly as no doubt you all are at home. The suspense is far greater than before VE Day because then we knew that Germany was finished, but Japan can still fight on. How disappointed everyone will be if the negotiations fail.

I felt very bitter about government departments the other day. In May I was President of a court of inquiry investigating the death of a local civilian employee of the Air Ministry. The accident occurred while he was at work, and I exonerated him from any suspicion of carelessness. I recommended that a pension be paid to his widow, who had two children and had no other means of livelihood now that her husband was dead. The matter passed out of my hands, and now I find from a chance enquiry that so far no pension has been given. As there is no poor relief on this island, the woman and children are starving, being dependent on the generosity of neighbours.

The local section officer has sent off hastening signals, but no action has been taken. The case is probably in the 'Pending' tray of some minor official who is too busy to worry about compensation in the case of a local labourer. As the dependants are not working with the RAF, it will not come before an RAF tribunal should anything happen to them. How I would like to preside over such a court! It is a terrible thought that such incompetence, endangering human lives, can be concealed by the anonymity of service administration. So many urgent reforms are necessary that I hate to think of the spread of nationalisation.

I am sorry, my darling, to write of such grim subjects, but I know that you, too, are interested in social reforms and improving the lot of all peoples. We should be able to start a crusade with our enthusiasm!

Goodbye, dearest Joan,

Tony xxxxxx

## 15 AUGUST 1945

Dearest Tony,

Congratulations and God bless you on this Day of Days!

Much, much too excited to think of words to write. You will know how I feel.

My love and thoughts with you,

Joan xxxxx

## VJ DAY, 15 AUGUST 1945

Joan, my darling,

Today it is the great day for which we have been fighting and hoping so hard. Now that it has come I can hardly realise what it means – so many visions and plans of a wonderful future seem to be ready to spring to life.

Dearest, on this great day let us resolve that throughout our life together we will strive always for the cause of peace and to increase the happiness of everyone. War has been ended, but at what a cost – the flower of our youth left on the battlefield. Our dead would want only one memorial: a happy, safe and free England, the champion of the ordinary man of every land. The easy part of our fight has ended; the greater trial lies ahead. It is easy to unite the people and lead them in war when enthusiasm and a sense of common danger are uppermost in the minds of all. It is far more difficult to convince people that the same drive and enthusiasm are necessary to secure a successful peace.

How will ex-servicemen settle down to civilian life again? They have travelled far, known danger and the wonderful feeling of comradeship that danger brings. They have been trained to forget the ways of peace and to obey orders in the field which were against all their former principles. Death has become familiar and so less formidable. Yet another of our tasks will be to remould our fighters.

What a strange and disjointed letter you will think this – the first letter I have ever written to you in time of peace. It should be neat and logical, a model, but I feel so mixed up and illogical at the moment! I shall not settle down until I am home again and able to talk to you and find out that all these lovely things have come true. It *is* like a fairy story, and the ending will be: 'They lived happily ever after.'

Let me tell you something of my topsy-turvy day today. I got up at 6.30 so as to make an early take-off. At breakfast I was told that VJ Day had been declared and that all aircraft were grounded. I contacted the CO and was given special permission to carry on. I reached 'Alex' at 12 o'clock, and by the time I had managed to find a room in a hotel it was 2 o'clock. I decided it was too late to have lunch and went out to the Sporting Club to swim. I had dinner alone in a quiet little restaurant and returned to write to you. Two searchlights are forming a great 'V' in the sky outside my bedroom window, and it seems a satisfactory close to such an eventful day.

I have to stay here until Saturday morning and will probably return via Palestine. As I said in my last letter, I expect it will take some time to bring everyone home from overseas, but I feel sure it will not be too long and that we shall spend Christmas together. How lovely this first Christmas will seem and how much we have looked forward to it. The only present I want is to see your dear face and hold your hand. Nothing matters but being with you. No more shall I have to try to put my poor thoughts on paper; I shall be able to tell you all that is in my heart.

Goodbye, dear heart,

Tony xxxxxx

## 18 AUGUST 1945

Dearest Joan,

I am in Palestine at the moment. We were returning from Egypt and called here for the evening.

There is a swimming pool here, and, as you will have guessed, I immediately decided to swim. Alas, it was almost pure chlorine, and my eyes are still smarting! As soon as anyone dived they vanished, the water was so opaque. Still, it was quite cooling.

With my happy eager thoughts,
Tony xxxxxxxx

## 20 AUGUST 1945

Joan darling,

Your description of your picnic in a peaceful Surrey field sounded so lovely and seemed so real. You really do love Surrey, don't you, dearest? We will make our home there if it can possibly be arranged.

The atom bomb is indeed a terrible weapon and one that must be a closely guarded secret. How dreadful it would be if it fell into the hands of an unscrupulous enemy. The Security Council should be sufficient protection, though, for any nation committing an act of aggression against another could instantly be destroyed by the rest.

Yesterday I had a letter from a Flying Officer. I saw his brother shot down in January 1944. I met him and he asked me for details. I wrote a long report and posted it to him. He went home, and I have now received a letter from him in which he says his mother is still hoping that her elder son is safe and asking me if I can have any idea what could have happened to him. They have had no news, and all prisoners of war have been released. I am certain in my own mind that his brother was definitely lost, but it is so very difficult to say so. I will try to point out gently that there is no longer any hope. It seems so terrible that she should continue to wait and wait endlessly. I will tell the brother and leave him to break it gently to his mother.

How very lucky we have been, Joan dear. There are many families today who have little cause for celebration. Not only are there lost ones from the services, but the civilian casualties are very great also. I used to worry a lot, darling, when I thought that you might be returning to London, but now I can give thanks to God that He has kept you safe.

How wonderful the start of our life has been. Love born amidst the chaos and horror of war and preserved and strengthened although we have been far apart. How glorious it will be when we are together forever, to watch over and care for one another.

Goodbye and God keep you still safe, my darling,
Tony xxxxxxx

## 21 AUGUST 1945

My dearest Tony,

I am most concerned about the widow of whom you wrote, Tony. My first consideration was whether *I* could do anything to help – can I, Tony? I have since wondered if, were I in possession of full particulars of the case, if it were the direct concern of one of our government departments and, of course, the woman was agreeable, a personal visit to the official concerned at HQ might astound him out of his lethargy??

Is there anything I can send for the children – clothing, chocolate – Tony?

Of course, I realise you may not be acquainted with the family, or that they may have friends to care for them, but from your letter it seems that they are in great and desperate need. If it is possible to help, please tell me.

As for the Civil Service, the only way of shaking it is a Parliamentary Question. PQ files almost run around on their own legs, so great is their priority!

The war has come to a strange end, Tony. We are glad indeed, but with a sober gladness. The A-bomb is yet heavy in our hearts. Will the fear be lifted, this weapon end, instead of adding to, the horror of war?

But, of course, we are joyful and have been celebrating the fact that no more of our men will perish. I feel relief, the joy, like a physical thing, Tony.

And I have been celebrating. Away out all the hours to town, to dances and bonfires, with my cousins and many friends. They are all young and I as gay and crazy as any! To me the laughter, music, lights of London have been a wonderful tonic.

Wondering and wondering what the full statement on demobilisation promised this week will tell. Reductions in coal output, sugar and clothing seemed a poor beginning for the Labour government, but we must fairly acknowledge that such measures might have been necessary in any case.

But organisation of manpower seems to me a poor excuse for longer-term clothing rationing cuts. So swiftly were the spinners switched to war factories, surely they could be drafted back to their own trade equally swiftly? Negotiations over their working conditions are surely not so insuperable.

It would be so easy to go without to clothe and feed the stricken people in Europe, but it does seem hard, after so many years of privation and *organisation*, that the people of Britain should have to accept greater hardships in peace than in war, simply because of lack of organisation!

Enough of my funny old politics!

Good night, dear. Bless you and love,

A very yawny Joan xxxxxxxx

## 21 AUGUST 1945

Dearest Joan,

I went down to the town this morning, and, as I was sitting in the car waiting for my friend, an old man came up, begging. I gave him a few piastres − about sixpence − and he burst into tears. Then he bowed two or three times and walked away, turning to bow again every few paces. I felt quite ashamed to think that there were people to whom so little meant so much while I am so careless about money.

This afternoon we went over to Kyrenia to swim, and the lorry broke down at the foot of the hills, about two miles from the nearest village. Among other things, it needed water. A taxi stopped, and the driver offered help, eventually driving to the village and coming back with a can of water. When the lorry still would not start, he took off his coat and helped the driver overhaul the engine. When everything was all right once more he would have left without asking for any compensation for his trouble, had we not insisted. It was a very good example of the friendliness of the average Cypriot.

There is a small political element which agitates for the return of the island to Greece (though at no time has it ever belonged to Greece), but, as a government publication acutely observed, it is, in general, only unrest for its own sake, and no one would be more alarmed than the agitators if their requests were taken seriously. Greece could never spend the necessary amounts of money required to improve the amenities of the island, and there would be far less political freedom. Some of the articles in the press here are openly subversive. Then, too, about one-fifth of the population is Turkish and has no love for Greece.

There are many wild rumours about concerning demobilisation. There is, I think, to be a government statement sometime this week, and then all our hopes and fears will be settled. How eagerly I await it!!

I shall be leaving for the Delta again on Thursday and returning on the Saturday. How much I am travelling lately!

With all my love and thoughts,

Tony xxxxxx

## 22 AUGUST 1945

Dearest Joan,

I am off to the Delta early tomorrow morning – or rather this morning for I have been on duty and it is now past midnight. I just wanted to write you a short note in case it is difficult while I am away.

Among other things, I had to close the bar this evening, and, about an hour later, when the barman had gone to bed, another officer, a regular, asked me to instruct the barman to serve some more drinks. He was very indignant when I refused and said that it was very different from peacetime. I think that the barman's time off, especially at night, should be respected, the more so as he has done a hard day's work. So many people seem to regard the mess servants as machines without feelings.

Goodbye and God bless you, sweetheart,

Tony xxxxx

## 26 AUGUST 1945

Tony dearest,

We visited the aircraft exhibition in Oxford Street, and I paid special attention to the Beaufighter. I should dearly have liked to climb into it but suppose that just could not be allowed! A ladder propped most temptingly against the Lancaster had a notice 'Staff use only' propped on the topmost rung. Home again in much better spirits, I tried to describe the Beaufighter cannon to cousin Tony. I must have got the measurements a little mixed, because he asked me just where the plane fitted onto this gadget! I fear I haven't a mechanical mind, although it is quite probable that he teased just to muddle me.

Most everyone is disappointed at the demobilisation programme. Daddy is of the opinion that the government is afeared to bring the fighting men home in any body lest they show their dissatisfaction with the state of affairs, and they would be dissatisfied too forcibly. The policy seems to be to keep men in the services until there are houses, clothes and goods for them. Sound enough from one point of view, but surely the vigorous eager young people are best fitted to hustle and build and shape the peace for themselves?

We must be fair: the Labour government have a terrific task, but five years' emergency powers when only two were granted in the days of darkest peril?!

I seem always to be ending on a political note! But I must say goodbye, dear.

My love to you. I do so wish you could come home,

Joan xxxxxx

## 27 AUGUST 1945

Joan darling,

As regards the widow, dearest, I have offered financial assistance, but it has to be done in such a roundabout way so that it does not appear to be in any way official. The fellow workers of the husband are helping, and signals have been sent off requesting immediate instructions.

I have thought about a PQ but consider it possible that action may be taken before the question could be asked. If nothing has been done by the beginning of September, I will give you all particulars, and, even if something has been done, the delay should be deprecated. How inhuman the Service can be.

With my eager loving thoughts,

Tony xxxxxx

## 28 AUGUST 1945

My dearest Joan,

I am off to Alexandria again tomorrow. I spend almost more time down there than I do in Cyprus!

I have bought some raisins, sultanas, etc. and am posting them to you in the hope that they will arrive in time for any Christmas cake making. I am sending them in two parcels so that if one goes astray you will still get the other. I had to pack the sultanas in a cigar box, as it was the only container of strength that I could find. I hope that it will not spoil the flavour. They are well wrapped up in paper.

Goodbye and God bless you, darling,

Tony xxxxxx

## 30 August 1945

Dearest Joan,

Once more I am back from the Delta.

I found myself with an hour to spare in Alexandria and decided to stroll along the seafront. It is very broad, and the road is divided into two traffic lanes by a series of long 'islands'. In the centre of each of these is a large street lamp, and so there is a graceful necklace of lights following the sweep of the sea.

On the far side are brightly lit cafés with crowded tables on the pavement, so that people have to pick their way among them or else walk in the roadway. This is a perilous undertaking for there are streams of horse-drawn carriages with oil lamps, yellow taxis, great single-decker buses and private cars cascading in all directions with reckless abandon.

On this side couples are strolling slowly along, enjoying the fresh sea breeze. The sea itself looks very dark and menacing, and the lights glint on an occasional white cap. Further out, red and green lights are winking cheerfully, indicating the entrance to the harbour. All along are natives sitting by the parapet with braziers, roasting corn and peanuts. Others are walking along with incense-burners or else selling little necklets of jasmine.

For a while I sat on the low wall, watching the passing crowds. It was a gay scene and a babble of many languages. The modern, brightly lit buildings of a strange, ornate design added yet another note.

An amusing incident I wanted to tell you about: in the afternoon I was on a tram, standing near the driver. He was a short, tubby person who reminded me irresistibly of Tweedledum and Tweedledee! We stopped, and, just before we started again, another Egyptian got on, shouted violently and, in spite of the valiant attempt at resistance by the driver, pushed him on to the pavement where he stood sulkily. The newcomer then drove off! What a strange country Egypt is – the people seem only to play at being westernised.

Goodbye and God keep you, my darling,

Tony xxxxxx

## 31 AUGUST 1945

Joan darling,

I have just come back from a very pleasant day's outing. I left this morning at ten o'clock to visit some outlying units. We drove from Nicosia to Larnaca, where we had lunch on the seafront. I think that Larnaca is one of the nicest villages to visit for an afternoon – the front is so cheerful with trees and shrubs and the houses are so quaint.

Next we visited a small RAF detachment nearby. They were quite at home and kept chickens and even had two tame pigeons of which they were very proud. It always surprises me how well the British soldier can adapt himself to circumstances and make friends with the local people.

Next stop was Famagusta, and, our business completed, we went swimming on the silver beach. The time passed all too quickly, and we changed once more and returned to Nicosia.

Tomorrow I'm going to Paphos and then on to Troodos for the night. It will make another pleasant break. I have so little to do and am making the most of the opportunity of seeing the island.

Goodbye and God bless you, dear heart. All my thoughts are of seeing you again.

Tony xxxxxx

## TOLWORTH RISE, SURREY, 1 SEPTEMBER 1945

My dearest Tony,

First, thank you many times, sweetheart, for your lovely flowers. I wished you might have come with them – the flowers would have made a lovely wedding bouquet!

As the late owner moved out last week and the removers are unable to bring the bulk of our furniture until Monday, the house is furnished with just two beds, and three chairs and a table sent in by a very kind neighbour on hearing of our difficulties. This all sounds crazy, but these topsy-turvy days it is impossible to rely on transport or even the possession of a house when you buy one, and dates for transactions are more likely to be kept within weeks than hours. The shortage of manpower is so very acute.

RAF personnel are, according to my friend's husband, enjoying a great relaxation of regulations, the stations closing altogether at weekends. Would it not be wonderful if you were stationed in England, Tony?

Still chattering and wondering! Time for tea and arranging my flowers.

All my love. God bless you, dear,

Joan xxxxxx

## 3 SEPTEMBER 1945

Joan darling,

The aircraft exhibition must have been very interesting, and I am very pleased that you saw a Beaufighter. It is a lovely aircraft, my favourite of all British or American planes! Perhaps, though, I am prejudiced! The cannon, by the way, are four 20 millimetre and are about 12 ft long. We carry 250 rounds for each.

Goodbye for a little while, darling. Please be happy and don't worry.

With all my love,

Tony xxxxxx

## FRIDAY EVENING

Dearest Tony,

I have been so busy I do not even know the date! My nursing and housekeeping duties tire me so completely that as soon as I rest I fall asleep!! My muscles are unaccustomed to strenuous work.

When I am tired I often recall your long flying hours and struggles with the elements in the desert. You were so very tired then. How much you have travelled and done since then, Tony, and how well and full of energy you seem again.

I wish, too, that I might be with you. What fun we could have, dearest. A houseboat on the Nile seems very romantic, and I am longing to hear about it. Maybe I can imagine I am Cleopatra, floating slowly upriver in the soft evening, with you my Anthony!

Goodbye and God bless you.

My love,

Joan xxxxxx

## 5 September 1945

Dearest Joan,

I have another job promised me now: an administrative post at HQ ME. So far it is only a promise – there is nothing definite. I am growing weary of waiting about for the powers that be to make up their minds. Still, as you say, I shall have left the RAF by spring and will be commencing a new life with you beside me to plan and share it. How lovely everything will be.

With my ever-loving thoughts,

Tony xxxxxx

## 6 September 1945

Joan darling,

I have been given a new job while I am awaiting posting. I am now Station Administrative Officer. It is very interesting and carries an enormous list of duties. Among others are: Supervision of the Station Adjutant; President of the Airmen's Messing Committee, President of the Fire Committee, Entertainments Officer; Officer in charge of Cinema and Welfare; Officer in charge of all Non-public Funds, Officer in charge of Works Services; and Commanding Officer of the SHQ Unit. A great advantage is that I now have a car of my own: a creamy Ford.

I welcome this job because it means that I shall have some work to do and time will pass so much more quickly.

I have had to cancel my trip to Alexandria tomorrow; I am now chained to an office! I shall have plenty of opportunity for flying afterwards, I expect.

Goodbye and God bless you, dear heart.

With all my love,

Tony xxxxxx

## 8 September 1945

My dearest Joan,

I am kept quite busy nowadays, and it is a welcome change.

There was an ENSA concert last night. It was quite good, far better than the average show. Fortunately I did not have to make a speech of thanks, although I was deputising for the CO. Before the applause had died away, the band struck up 'The King'.

A man was brought before me this morning, charged with being absent without leave. He was a Rhodesian, and his wife, who is living on the island, was being repatriated to Rhodesia. He was given a 48-hour pass to help her pack, and, as she could not get ready in time, he stayed beyond his leave to complete the task. I was very sympathetic, remembering my own troubles with packing, and dismissed the case!

I saw the new moon tonight and wished very hard – you will guess what for. May we be together again very soon; waiting seems so long.

Goodbye and God bless you, sweetheart,

Tony xxxxxx

## 9 SEPTEMBER 1945

Dearest Tony,

I am glad the widow is receiving help from her husband's friends, but it is disgraceful that she has not yet received her pension. What a pity you did not hear earlier of her plight and write to your MP. It often helps future cases as well, I think, if these cases are publicised – by keeping government departments on their toes. How are you planning to help them, Tony? Are they English people?

It is cold sitting up in bed tonight – winter cannot be very far away! So I am going to curl up under the clothes and go early to sleep.

Good night, sweetheart.

My love and dreams,

Joan xxxxxx

## 10 SEPTEMBER 1945

Dearest Joan,

I thought you might like to have a description of my new office. It is in a stone building, creamy coloured, with a sloping corrugated-iron roof. Four steps lead up to the corrugated-iron door. How metallic it all sounds! On the left is another door, leading into the Group Captain's office. There is a shelf along the wall beyond, and on it are one or two trophies – cups, a silver map of Cyprus mounted on a polished stand.

On the desk are a telephone and a row of four buttons. These are for the flight lieutenant admin, the station warrant officer, the runner and the orderly room – the latter having a complicated code to indicate the individual required.

The other wall is covered by a green baize noticeboard, on which are pinned large photographs of lovely English scenes. They make me feel quite homesick. On this side there is another door leading to an office with another desk and a safe. This is for anyone who is doing anything for me.

Goodbye, my darling, I hope that soon all the things of which I write will be but a memory for us to look back on.

With every eager, loving thought,

Tony xxxxxx

## 11 SEPTEMBER 1945

Joan darling,

At last I am posted to Air Headquarters at 'Alex', but I expect that I have to report there merely for instructions.

In the meantime I am carrying on with my duties and will hand over at the last minute. One will continue, even after I leave. The AOC invited the CO to a party on Saturday – Battle of Britain Day. As the CO is unable to leave he has asked me to represent him.

I am sorry to leave Cyprus and set out on my travels again. It means starting afresh in a strange place, knowing few, if any, people and settling down once more. The move I am really awaiting is that happy one which will bring me to you and the wonderful realisation of all our hopes and dreams.

Goodbye and God keep you, my darling.

Tony xxxxxx

## 12 SEPTEMBER 1945

Dearest Joan,

I have had an extremely busy day today, making preparations for our Battle of Britain celebration. The mess is to be floodlit, a Spitfire positioned near it, the inside of the mess to be repainted, the campsite cleaned, the swimming pool cleaned, the parade to be arranged and flags and saluting base obtained. These are few of the odds and ends dealt with by the 'SAdO'!!

HE The Governor is coming to the party on Saturday and to take the salute on the parade on Sunday, so everything must be spick and span. The parade should go very well; a band has been arranged and there will be a fly-past of fighters. I shall not be here to see the fruits of my labour!

With every loving thought from your impatient, wondering,

Tony xxxxxx

## 13 SEPTEMBER 1945

Dearest Joan,

I am off at eight o'clock tomorrow morning.

I promised that I would let you have the details of the widow who was awaiting compensation and checked all the information this afternoon. Here it is:

The workman was Michael P. Hallis of AFANIA, Cyprus. His age was 36, and he was married.

He had been employed by WD from 16 July 1943 to 27 April 1945. He left three dependants: his wife, Despina, a child aged six months and his mother-in-law. They were entirely dependent on his earnings and have no other means of support.

Michael Hallis was on duty at the time of the accident and was in no way to blame. His clothes caught fire while he was attending to a tar boiler at Tymbou aerodrome, and, although he was rushed to hospital, he died.

The findings of the court of inquiry were partly as follows:

'The Court finds that the accident resulting in the death of Michael P. Hallis was due to circumstances which could not have been reasonably anticipated by anyone; that no reasonable precautions had been neglected and that no allocation of responsibilities can be made.'

The remarks by the SAdO were as follows:

'I concur in the findings of the court and recommend that compensation be paid to the dependant of the deceased according to scale.'

The remarks of the Station Commander were:
'I concur.'

The above entries were dated 15 May 1945. The subsequent history of the case is as follows:

21 August. AMWD Nicosia to RAF Nicosia.
'. . . still no authority to pay pension. Unable to grant ex gratia payment on own authority, referring matter to Superintendent Engineer and requesting a hastening signal to Air Ministry.'

7 September. Letter from Nicosia to AHQ Levant.
Copy to AHQEM
'Request hastening action.'

That, then, dearest, is the story to date. All blame seems to rest with Air Ministry since hastening letters and signals have been sent to them by Air Headquarters. The pension has been approved by everyone up to the AOC, and Air Ministry's consent is really automatic.

I do hope that the responsibility can be fastened on the right person. It is terrible that such a long delay should be allowed.

Sorry that this is such a dull letter, darling. I will make up for it tomorrow evening and may have some news by then.

Goodbye and God bless you, sweetheart.

My ever-loving thoughts,

Tony xxxxxx

# 7

## INTRODUCTION TO THE LAW

I was appointed to a post in Headquarters, with responsibility for discipline.

### 14 SEPTEMBER 1945

Joan darling,

An extremely busy day again today! I awoke early to hear the liquid tinkle of sheep bells from the other side of the valley. Arising promptly, for once, I was in time to see the sun rising over Cyprus for the last time. A hasty breakfast and completion of packing, and I was in the air by eight o'clock.

On arrival at HQ I was informed that I was posted for staff duties and told to find accommodation. Fortunately, I met someone who had been posted from Nicosia a month previously, and he told me that there was room at the house where he was staying.

The people are Syrians. The lady – Mrs Halaby – married an Englishman and lived in England for many years. Her husband died, and she came out here. I am sharing a room with my friend, and everything seems quite fine. The room is quite spacious, with beige walls and a figured carpet. The furniture consists of two beds with bedside tables; three chairs; two sideboards, one of which is already covered with my books and on which I am writing; a wardrobe and a dressing-table. It is a corner room, and there are windows on two of the walls.

I have all my meals here. The one I have had so far seemed quite good.

With every loving thought from your rather unsettled,

Tony xxxxxx

## 16 SEPTEMBER 1945

Dearest Joan,

The cocktail party last night was quite a success, although very formal with so many high-ranking officers present. It was held in the garden outside Air Headquarters and was very pleasantly arranged. The lighting was coloured lamps, and there was a bright moon. Fortunately, it was quite cool – we had to wear full KD uniform, tunics, etc.!

This morning there was a big parade at the Sporting Club and 120 aircraft took part in a fly-past. They were all types, ranging from Liberators and Lancasters to Spitfires and Thunderbolts.

Tomorrow I start work in earnest and will be quite glad to have something to keep me occupied. On Tuesday I am flying to Benina, near Benghazi, and will be coming back on Thursday. It will be a change to see the Western Desert again.

When my room was arranged according to my liking, Mrs Halaby came in to look at it and, catching sight of your photograph, endeared herself to me forever by exclaiming, 'Oh, what a pretty girl.'

This letter is being continually interrupted as I go out onto the balcony to watch the formations of aircraft still flying past overhead. Some of the flying is really excellent.

I will try to write while I am away, dearest, but as we shall be moving about a lot it may be difficult. I know you will understand.

Goodbye and God bless you, my darling,

Tony xxxxxx

## 16 SEPTEMBER 1945

My dearest Tony,

A car – you must feel very important! Maybe it won't be long before we can drive out into the cool Surrey evening from London's dusty summertime. Or bundle cosily into the car after dinner on winter evenings, to go to the theatre or dance. And we'll have friends to visit, to share picnics on the river, to be happy again, with no great shadow over us and all the land.

I would be pleased, Tony, for you to send some soap. We have quite a good little stock saved from St Annes, but there is insufficient in many places to meet the ration of three tablets a month. With London's hard water and a tablet given to some less fortunate, occasionally, our store will soon be used!

Thank you, dear, for all your letters, your patience, your thoughtfulness.

My love and blessings to you,

Joan xxxxxx

## 19 September 1945

My dearest Tony,

I received your letter about Mrs Hallis and trust you will agree with my hastening to write to my MP, Major Boyd-Carpenter, and to D.N. Pritt, the 'Forces MP', who, I expect you know, interests himself particularly in pensions and so on.

There are two points about which I wondered, Tony.

1. The nationality of Michael and Mrs Hallis.

2. Whether it was not possible to find employment for Mrs Hallis, her mother caring for the baby.

Tony, dear, writing these documents has taken most all the evening (besides a little time for enquiries borrowed from the Ministry during the day!) and it is already past my special bedtime – so you won't mind if I so soon say goodbye. I take quite an hour to get into bed from saying good nights, you see!

My love to you, and hoping I have helped a little,

Joan xxxxxx

## 20 September 1945

Dearest Joan,

Back again after a tour of inspection of nearly 1,500 miles! There was a strange mixture of news awaiting me. First, and most welcome, was a letter from you forwarded on from Cyprus. I was especially glad as it means that letters will be following regularly now, after the break due to my moving. Next, and unwelcome, was the news that I had been posted to HQ RAF ME. It is to a legal branch, and I am resisting it, as I am quite nicely settled here. I shall know definitely about it tomorrow. My present work is more interesting and keeps me in touch with flying.

From Alex I went to Mersa Matruh, where we had lunch, and then set out for El Adem, near Tobruk. Tobruk is unrecognisable now: everything has been rebuilt and tidied up. Last time I was there all buildings except two were out of bounds, being mined and in a state of collapse. This time we had dinner in a luxurious officers' club overlooking the harbour – a club as well appointed as any I have seen in the Middle East. There are numerous canteens and bars for the men, and the streets are clear and the roads smooth.

Our next stop was Benghazi. Here, again, there was a startling transformation. The buildings were not so new and shining as those of Tobruk, but they were in excellent condition and the town was very much alive, with a considerable civilian population back once more.

On the way back we flew over Gambut, near Bardia. How many memories it brought back of carefree days with the squadron, of sandstorms and rain, and of very many friends.

The years out here have been very full ones. I thought only this morning how rapidly the time is flying by. Soon it will have swept all our sorrow of parting away and brought us near together again. Our happiness then will be ample compensation.

With every loving thought from your very sleepy,

Tony xxxxxx

## 21 SEPTEMBER 1945

Tony darling,

My mother was knocked down by a motor van yesterday morning. An X-ray disclosed no serious injury, but she is bruised, cut and severely shaken. She may be leaving the hospital today or tomorrow but will be laid up for about two weeks.

So it seems that once again I must undertake my housekeeping job – but thankfully, of course, that Mother is no worse.

I have done most of the housework this morning, but many duties await attention – lunch, shopping, a sweet for tonight's dinner – and during the afternoon I hope to see Mummy. So I will write you again as soon as I have more time to think, sweetheart.

I do so wish I had your company,

Joan xxxxxx

## 22 SEPTEMBER 1945

My dearest Tony,

I wonder what you are thinking with such a 'faraway' look in your frame on the shelf?

My thoughts have turned from the worried ones of a nurse-housewife's day to a drowsy contentment, snuggling into bed with a hot bottle and a cup of coffee made with *real* milk. I wish there were a coal fire crackling and dancing in the hearth – but you will be imagining winter snows!! It is not so cold yet, but the evenings are chilly, and you know how cosy I like to be!

Mother was brought home yesterday afternoon, Tony. She was scarcely fit to be moved, but no doubt her bed was needed urgently. Hospitals are, unfortunately, as understaffed as everything else. She is severely bruised, and cannot sit up yet, but feels less shaken today. Doctor says it is fortunate Mummy is well covered and not like me, for I would have broken to bits!

Two very pleasant and so far satisfactory letters from the Commons today, Tony.

D.N. Pritt wrote that, although nowadays he has to limit the number of cases he takes up, and tries to limit them to people in his own constituency, he thought he could stretch a point for someone from Cyprus – and so he has taken up the case of Mrs Hallis with the Air Ministry, urging them to do something at once!

And, in a dreadful scrawl, John Boyd-Carpenter thanked me for my letter. He said he knows from his own experience that only too often great hardship can be caused by wholly unnecessary delay in dealing with cases such as these. He says that he is, therefore, only too glad to send particulars of it to the Air Minister with the request that he tells his department to get a move on (!). He said he was very grateful to me for letting him know about this. I do hope we hear of an early and happy conclusion to this affair, Tony. You will perhaps hear from someone at Nicosia? I should like to thank the MPs too, if their efforts succeed. Mm, I hope the Air Minister doesn't remark to either that I wrote both – they might not be too pleased, particularly as their politics are so opposite!!

Once more sandman's will is stronger than mine, so I shall have to say good night, Tony dear.

My love to you,
    Joan xxxxxx


Sunday morning – not officially awake yet!

    I wonder if, next time I see you, you will be a civilian, Tony? It will seem a little strange to me to see you in civilian clothes, and shall you feel a little strange too? I wonder what is your choice, particularly in ties?!

    We haven't had much time to talk about us lately, with so much unsettling. Do you still feel the same about me, Tony? Wonder when we shall be married and whom we shall invite, if we will have a formal wedding? We have so many friends! And please, Tony, will you wear uniform? Because somehow I have always imagined marrying a flyer. I am almost superstitious about it! It's a funny feeling.

    Love and thoughts for you,
    Joan xxxxxx


## 24 SEPTEMBER 1945

Dearest Joan,

I arrived at HQ ME this morning and went to see my new chief. He told me that I was to stay at HQ ME for a few days and then go on to 206 Group, which is quite near. I am staying on the houseboat I mentioned. It is very spacious with two decks of cabins. I am in a very coveted cabin on the upper deck. It was given to me as I am only staying a short while and it is needed for someone else later on.

    The boat is painted white and is called 'Egypt'. It belongs to Thomas Cook and Sons and used to take tourists up the Nile to Luxor and Aswan. Now it is firmly anchored and is used to accommodate officers from HQ.

    The food is quite good, and the dining saloon is a pleasant, well-lit room extending the width of the ship. My cabin is small but quite well equipped. There is a bed with mosquito net, a wardrobe, two small tables and a washbasin with hot and cold water. My window overlooks the riverbank, and it is a fresh, green scene with trees and grass.

    A bus takes us to and from the office – so you will see that everything is quite well organised.

I will write you a short note every day telling you my trials and experiences until I am properly settled down again.

Goodbye and God keep you, dear heart.

Tony xxxxxx

## 30 SEPTEMBER 1945

Dearest Joan,

Another month has ended, and the year is drawing slowly to a close. Soon I shall have been away two years. When last I saw you, little did I think that it would be so long before I saw you again or that so much would happen in the meantime. Has waiting seemed very long and weary to you, dear? I know that it is far harder for you than for me, for I have been travelling about and have had little time for reflection. With further news of demobilisation on Monday or Tuesday the outlook may brighten.

It is Sunday today, and this morning, as I was sitting on the deck reading, I happened to glance down the river and saw a lovely sight. As far as I could see were dhows with great white triangular sails – they looked like a fleet of swans. They drew nearer, and I could hear the water splashing softly against their broad bows. The design today is the same as it was 5,000 years ago. I have seen identical representations on ancient tombs. Slowly, majestically, they passed, scornful of the poor modern vessel with its noisy engine to drive it, and then swept away into the distance.

It is a novel experience, living on a boat, and I shall be quite sorry to leave. The increased space will, I expect, be ample recompense!

I am so longing to receive a letter from you again. Oh, how I wish and wish that we could be together again, able to tell all our thoughts instead of writing and waiting. May it be very soon, my darling.

Goodbye and God keep you, dear heart.

Tony xxxxxx

## 2 OCTOBER 1945

My dearest Tony,

Thank you very much for the sultanas; they arrived in perfect condition and will keep beautifully for the Christmas cake. Tony, I have lots to tell you whenever I can organise some off-duty hours for nurse Joan!

All my love and longing to see you – when, when, when?
Joan xxxxxx

## 4 OCTOBER 1945

Tony dearest,
Yesterday I understood why hospital visiting hours are so strict. I seemed to be preparing trays for teas and suppers from early afternoon until midnight! We had so many visitors.

Sometimes I think that I should like to live all alone, so I could get everything sorted out and do things just when I wished. But I guess I should get awfully lonely!

My love and thoughts,
Joan xxxxxx

## 7 OCTOBER 1945

My dearest Tony,
I have given all my family breakfast in bed, so now the house will be still and quiet for at least an hour while they eat and read the papers – and I can write you. Did ye ken how cunning I could be?!

Thank you for your letter, and all 320 of them. Yes, dear, nearly two years since we said gaily, 'See you soon!' It has seemed a long time to me, Tony. Not the first year so much, but the second seems endless. Perhaps because it has been such a weary, worrying time at home, with illness, food problems, queues. And, perhaps selfish of me, I have felt so restless, longed to get away – to the seemingly carefree existence of a girl in uniform.

But most people are restless, grumbling, these days. Mother assures me I shall be full of happiness again when there is you and holidays and a normal life. So hasten home, that we may make real plans – beautiful, shiny carrots! I wish it need not be another year away.

Oh, Tony, how lovely a scene those dhows sailing slowly along the river! You have seen many beautiful things, and I long to share them.

I went to Kingston yesterday afternoon and bought a whole tin of ice-cream wafers! These are unrationed and, spread layer upon layer with chocolate filling, will make delicious biscuits for tea parties. It is impossible to spare rations at all for visitors now, and cakes are at the other end of queues!

My love and thoughts for you and all our hopes.

Joan xxxxxx

## 9 OCTOBER 1945

Joan darling,

Thank you, dear, for writing letters so promptly to the MPs concerned. I feel sure they will do a lot of good.

As regards the two points you mention. The nationality: since Michael Hallis was born before 1914 he was an Ottoman subject, although he had always lived on Cyprus. As regards the question of employment. I fear there is no chance at all. Mrs Hallis is only a typical peasant with no training. Some of the women do manual labour on the roads and fields, but there are already too many available. A PQ from two members should, however, have an immediate effect, and I hope that it will eliminate delay in future cases.

I, too, feel sad about the release news. I had such high hopes. Never mind, my darling, time will pass very quickly. How eagerly I am looking forward to our meeting.

Goodbye and God keep you, dear one.

Tony xxxxxx

## 11 OCTOBER 1945

Joan darling,

Among other duties, now I have to approve marriages of airmen and airwomen – often it is no easy task when they want to marry a 'local' who would find it impossible to fit into English life. Often they can only just make themselves understood, and in one case neither could speak a word of the other's language.

Another duty, not quite so pleasant, is that of prosecutor. I can be called on by the Judge Advocate General to prosecute at any court martial, although by reason of my duties I cannot be a member of the court or defend. I should hate to be responsible for sending a man to prison. Do you remember my remarks about imprisonment? But I never thought that I should be placed in such a position. Still, the interests of the people as a whole must be safeguarded against individuals. I do not relish the task, though.

Goodbye and God bless you, dear heart.
With all my eager, loving thoughts,
Tony xxxxxx

## 15 OCTOBER 1945

My dearest Joan,
Thank you for all the trouble you have taken to copy letters and
forward them so promptly. I feel very guilty, especially as I know
how busy you are. I agree that Mrs Hallis' pension is very small
and hope that it will be increased when Air Ministry eventually
find out that Mrs Hallis and her family have no other means of
support. Of course, money in Cyprus goes further than in England,
and a family can live on about a shilling a day.
　　Thank you again, dearest, for your letters and dear thoughts.
Goodbye and God bless.
With all my love,
Tony xxxxxx

## 16 OCTOBER 1945

My dearest Tony,
Thank you for your letters. I do like them very much.
　　Thank you, too, for the parcel, which my uncle and auntie brought
along this evening. Dried fruit is on 'points' and almonds a rare luxury,
so these are very welcome, Tony.
　　Mr Pritt has written me again, sending, as he writes, a 'shabby excuse'
from the Air Ministry. They plead postal delays and say that Mrs
Hallis is receiving her pension from 17 September. Good night. My
love to you,
　　Joan xxxxxx

## 18 OCTOBER 1945

Dearest Joan,
You ask if I still feel the same about you, darling. No. When I left
England I thought I loved you as much as I possibly could, but since
then, with every letter you have written, I have found something
fresh about you to love. Then, I really knew very little about you,
but now our every hope and thought of all our lives are intertwined

until they form but one, which we share. I can never properly tell you what you mean to me until I can see you again and hold you in my arms. Oh, what a glorious day.

Yes, Joan, I can wear uniform at our wedding. We shall have ample time to plan everything before my leave ends. I, too, would like to be in uniform, as it was in uniform that I met you and in uniform that I have always seen you.

With every eager hope and loving thought,

Tony xxxxxx

## 19 OCTOBER 1945

Tony darling,

At last I am on top of the housekeeping, instead of it on top of me! Mother is really recovering now and the house 'settling' after removal; a laundry has been persuaded to call and a man to deliver potatoes. And all this makes so great a difference.

Daddy, dear, is willing enough, but seems exasperatingly unintelligent about housework! Never mind, I will remember your advice and teach you to be really helpful.

I was offered a new job yesterday at the nearby office of a big building firm. I would like a change, but there are obstacles in changing now, and wrestling with the British government is no easy task!

My love to you,

Joan xxxxxx

## 21 OCTOBER 1945

Dearest Tony,

Good news that the ounce cut in our cooking fat and cheese rations is to be restored. Visions of an occasional apple pie!

Dissatisfaction increases as men on leave bear news of well-stocked larders on the continent. My Uncle Peter was furious on his last visit home, since wherever he travels – Belgium, Holland, Germany – the people have plenty of food compared with Britain. It is certainly hard to know what to believe. Is it possible that the officials who ask us to be patient, while the starving people of Europe are fed, are being 'hoodwinked' and the ordinary soldier, who makes friends and visits continental homes, is a better judge of the comparison?

I was away to Kingston shopping yesterday afternoon. The markets fascinate me, Tony. They used to, especially when I was a child, the stalls piled high under the dancing, spluttering flare lights. And I always wanted to buy the tiny, wee tomatoes that shops disdained to sell! Yesterday it seemed much more fun buying 'bargains' of lettuce and cauliflower, held out by merchants who chanted the praises of their wares, than to purchase greengrocery in a dull shop.

My love, dear,

Joan xxxxxxx

## 24 OCTOBER 1945

My dearest Tony,

Your optimism about marrying before your leave is over is good, dear, but please do not count too much on it. The home problem is so terribly acute, Tony. Perhaps we shall be fortunate – we have lots of friends to help us search. And if you can get a car, and don't mind a long drive in the morning, we can live miles out of London. And maybe I *will* carry on a job for while – it would be fun whizzing off in the car together. Some evenings we could stay in town, then, or visit friends and most often chatter our way home again because there will probably be things to 'fix'.

You see, I have trailed us out into the country again! But it might prove more practicable than a flat in London, where every room is in demand, and I believe you would think it much nicer? What *do* you think, Tony?

Joan, with love xxxxxx

## 28 OCTOBER 1945

Dearest Joan,

I don't believe I told you about the catering arrangements at the place where I am now staying. We have breakfast here but go to the house next door for all other meals.

At this other house there are two lovely children, John, aged ten, and Jill, aged nine. They both speak English and French fluently and both play the piano extremely well. I love to sit and watch little Jill at the grand piano, concentrating on some difficult piece. They are far from the popular conception of child prodigies, however. I spent this afternoon romping in the garden and playing ball with Jill. John, too, is full of mischief! They must take after their mother, who is a brilliant pianist – she is playing now, and I have just torn myself away.

Good night, my darling, and all the love of your eager, impatient,

Tony xxxxxxxx

## 2 NOVEMBER 1945

Dearest Joan,

The university opened a few weeks back, and the police had to draft in strong reinforcements and bring up armoured cars because they feared a demonstration by the students. Cairo was put out of bounds to all British forces.

Now, again, there has been trouble. Some organisation decided to call a general strike in sympathy with the Arabs in Palestine, and bands of youths went round all the shops telling the shopkeepers that they must close or have their shops broken up. The shopkeepers protested but said that, as the police could not protect all of them, they would have to obey. So once more all Cairo was put out of bounds to the services. The loss of trade must be enormous.

Oh, how I long to be back in England, which, with all its faults, manages to run peacefully even with the nationwide dock strike. The army is certainly not mobilised when a new varsity term begins!

With every loving thought from your puzzled, wondering,

Tony xxxxxxxx

## 4 NOVEMBER 1945

My dearest Tony,

Our grocer is extremely optimistic about rationing being removed from dairy produce in the spring. It seems only a matter of shipping, since Denmark has ample produce for export. But it seems too wonderful to be true to be able to go to a shop and buy half a pound of butter, a dozen eggs! Best not think about it until it *is* true.

My love and thoughts to you,

Joan xxxxxx

## 4 NOVEMBER 1945

My dearest Joan,

Unrest in Cairo continues. Yesterday, demonstrators went through the city in mobs breaking every window they came to (fortunately most of the shops and houses have shutters). It was all part of the pro-Arab, anti-Jewish campaign, but the silly part was that all the property destroyed belonged to Arabs! The shops were shut for two days and must have lost a tremendous amount of business.

A very influential Frenchman told me that all foreign residents in Egypt hope that the British will not leave the country. If they do, he said, he fears there would be widespread disorder. Egypt is so young in democracy, the novelty seems to intoxicate the students and common people. I must say, though, in all fairness, that the better-class Egyptian deplores these riots and the police are very active in trying to quell them.

You are right, darling, I do miss flying. I miss especially the good feeling and comradeship of a squadron. No, I do not want to fly when I leave the RAF, except for pleasure. After operations all other flying seems dull and rather uninteresting. It has been a grand experience, and I feel very grateful for it. Often I read through my logbook and live through those days again. Every memory is as vivid as if the incident occurred yesterday.

With every loving thought,
Tony xxxxxx

## 8 NOVEMBER 1945

Dearest Tony,

Thank you for a parcel today, dear – but not exactly the parcel you sent! Having been damaged in transit and repacked, it arrived plus two very patched and darned pairs of pants!! We should really thank the GPO for all the merriment this unusual gift caused my family.

Now I am going to brush my hair and snuggle down. Good night dearest.

My love to you,
Joan xxxxxx

## 8 NOVEMBER 1945

My dearest Joan,

On Tuesday I had to attend a court martial which lasted all day, and, as a result, Wednesday was extremely busy, as all the files had piled up in my 'In' tray. I have five trays: 'In', 'Out', 'Immediate and Signature', 'Policy' and 'Marriage Applications'. There is no room for any more, so files waiting for letters to be dictated rest on the wastepaper basket! I often feel like pushing them in.

At least half an hour each evening, now, I sit and listen to Mrs Chalom playing the piano. Usually she plays one of Beethoven's piano concertos.

You will be highly amused to hear I may be moving again – this time only to the Chaloms' house, the one where I have my meals. My friend was posted, and I am alone in the room and would prefer in any case to live and have my meals in the same house. No, dearest, I shall most certainly not develop a moving complex. I hate packing too much! Each time I move my packing gets more and more complicated. I begin to despair.

Goodbye and God bless you, sweetheart.

Happy dreams and all my love,

Tony xxxxxx

## 11 NOVEMBER 1945

My dearest Tony,

Many things which have been almost unobtainable suddenly reappear on the market. In small towns this means long orderly queues, which suburban housewives form automatically, and in West End stores a jostling crowd, all grabbing at kettles, saucepans, hairgrips. I much prefer the latter, but maybe I was born without the womanly amount of patience! Most men denounce queuing as absurd, but it has not been proved to what lengths (of queues?!) they might go if women refuse to stand. Men get awfully *hungry*!!

Time to put away my thoughts and sleep. Somewhere this letter was interrupted by bedtime, but my thoughts ran on so I forgot to mark it.

I wonder what you are thinking about? I believe it is as impossible for you as for me not to think, wherever we may be.

Good night, dear. May all your heart's dreams be made reality.
Joan xxxxxx

## 11 NOVEMBER 1945

Joan darling,

Today is our very own anniversary once more, dearest. Do you remember that evening two years ago when we went to the theatre and then drove home along the seafront? How long ago it seems, and yet how clear the picture remains. Little did we dream what great events would take place and what the future held in store for us before we met again.

Only a few more months remain now, darling, and then parting will be a thing of the past and we can take up the threads of our life and weave it into a lovely pattern for the future.

The mists are beginning to clear, and we can get glimpses of our dreamland, which before seemed an elusive mirage but which is now so very close. How wonderful to explore its treasures and beauties together and even to add to them by our hope, faith and love.

The years of parting have proved our love strong, my darling. Strong enough to endure even when lasting happiness seemed almost unattainable. Let us make certain that nothing will ever try to dull its brightness. Surely we have earned our right to a glorious golden future.

With every loving thought from your happy, eager,
Tony xxxxxx

## 13 NOVEMBER 1945

Dearest Joan,

I feel very tired this evening but want to write you before I go to bed.

I listened to the Armistice Day service on the radio and thought of you during the two minutes' silence. Oh how lucky we have been, dearest, to have each other when others have known so much sorrow – and how good it is to be alive. It is all over now so I can tell you: when I first joined the RAF, I never expected to survive; so many of my friends with whom I had trained were lost. Then, as time went on, I grew more hopeful, and after I met you I was certain that nothing could happen to me as I had so much to live for. Now I feel my life must really mean something since I have been allowed to come through safe and sound. With you beside me to help and encourage, darling, we may really be able to do something to show our gratitude.

In the meantime, all lovely dreams and happy thoughts from your very sleepy,

Tony xxxxxx

## 16 NOVEMBER 1945

Dearest Tony,

Here is my day.

Waking just before the alarm at 6.30, as if to outwit that objectionable bell, I snuggle tightly under the bedclothes again to *think* about getting up, for 20 more minutes! Not until I am up do I really waken, and my thoughts busy themselves with the day to come: will there be any mail for me?, what shall I wear?, read in the train?, and so on.

And then I am on my way to the station. The morning is beautiful, now: a white frost, elm trees traced against a misty sunrise. I think what a lovely ball-dress the sky would make: panniers of pink brocade glimpsing through silver brocade. But I am still lingering in eighteenth-century France! It is 1945, England, and my toes are very cold!

At the station, people are rubbing their hands. If you were here you would chafe my freezing fingers till they glowed.

Then, today, a boy brushed my season from my hand in the scramble for the Underground at Waterloo. Searching for it when the platform was clear, I found an old railway man had picked it up. Offering him a little reward, I was answered with a chuckle and 'give it to Jim 'ere, Miss, I'm not so poor as 'ee is.' Turning to 'Jim', I beheld an inspector! And we all three had a merry laugh together.

How different the disagreeable gentleman in the Tube tonight. The trains are particularly crowded on Fridays with the troops travelling on leave. There he sat, while crowds pressed frantically into the train, making testy remarks because a lady pushed against his shoulder!

But there is the in-between of today about which to tell you.

Lunchtime, Pauline and I hurried to 'Kettles' in New Oxford Street to buy Christmas wrappings. These are yet scarce, and customers stood three deep all along the counter. Our wait was rewarded, though, with coloured and silver papers, cellophane ribbons and wee boxes.

Pauline's husband made his first flight to India last week and was delayed four days. Eventually, the plane loaded with mail had to be left in France, the crew coming home passenger-wise. Peter was able to bring a carpet (so cheap in India and so priceless here), slippers and shoes for Pauline, and quantities of foodstuffs. No wonder so many flyers are eager to join Transport Command!

Yes, I remember the evening we loved so much.

Thinking about it, I will say good night, Tony.

My love to you,

Joan xxxxxxxx

## 22 NOVEMBER 1945

Joan darling,

Today I moved and spent part of the afternoon settling in. The house is not so modern as the other one, but the atmosphere is much more friendly. There I could never sit in the lounge but had to spend my time in my room. Here, even when I only had meals here, I was always made welcome and even invited to tea in the nursery by the children!

Now, too, I can lie in bed and listen to the piano being played downstairs. I almost know Beethoven's 'Third' and 'Fifth' piano concertos by heart, and they seem lovelier each time I hear them.

Good night and lovely dreams, my darling.

Your drowsy, yawny,

Tony xxxxxx

## 25 NOVEMBER 1945

Dearest Joan,

Yesterday evening I was forcibly carried off to a party by Mr and Mrs Chalom. It was very enjoyable, although I did not fully appreciate it as everyone was French and very excited, and I could only follow about one word in five! It finished at quarter past ten, so I did not have too late a night.

Life at the office is rather busy these days. Normally there are three of us, but now one has gone away on a six-week course and the other has gone to Khartoum for a week – so now I have three 'In' trays and two telephones, which always ring simultaneously!! Don't worry, though, dear. I am not overworking.

Since I wrote the last sentence I have been to yet another party. This time a children's party for Jill's birthday. There were about 20 children, so you can imagine the noise! There was one lovely little boy – three years old – who spoke very gravely in French, English and Arabic. I asked him if he would like some milk and he replied 'No, thank you, I prefer tea'! His father is headmaster of the English school in Cairo, so that may explain it.

Reverting to the children's party for the moment – Mrs Chalom was going to play the piano and asked for requests. The reply from the children (average age about nine) was astonishing: a unanimous request for Chopin's *Polonaise*! Afterwards they all played, and most of them extremely well.

Excuse me, darling, I am drowsing off. I should go to bed.

All my love and happy dreams,

Tony xxxxxx

## 27 NOVEMBER 1945

Joan darling,

I am feeling rather pleased at the moment: a man was court martialled a little while ago and sentenced to six months' imprisonment, and I managed to get the AOC to reduce it to three months. He will be able to reduce it still further if the man's conduct is good, so the sentence is now quite light. Reviewing is far nicer than trying to obtain a conviction.

I forget whether I mentioned it before, but one of the judges asked me to go to the opera with him next Sunday. A local company is giving ten Italian operas, and he suggested that if they were good it would be well worth going and that if they were bad it might be incredibly funny! I hope they will be good.

I am sleeping very much better these days; perhaps it is because I feel very tired in the evenings. It is satisfactory, though, to know that you are tired because you have managed to finish all your work. I rather enjoy having to work furiously!

Goodbye and God bless you, sweetheart.
Lovely dreams and all my love,
Tony xxxxxx

## 1 DECEMBER 1945

My dearest Joan,
A happy new month to you. Looking through my record of letters,
I find that it is just two years since I wrote you my first letter from
overseas. How strange everything seemed then. And now the journey
is drawing to a close, and soon I shall be back. Each year we have
said 'surely this year', but now it will be true.

With every loving thought from your very impatient,
Tony xxxxxx

## 3 DECEMBER 1945

Joan darling,
I did not go to the opera yesterday after all. We heard very bad reports
of it, and the Judge had to leave for Iraq early next morning, so we
decided to have a quiet dinner and talk. He was very interesting – he
writes articles for the *Spectator* and *Transatlantic* – and we talked until
after 11 o'clock. I was very sorry for him – his aircraft was leaving
at three in the morning! We shall be meeting again next week when
he returns and plan to go to the promised Shakespearean season (if
it materialises).

This afternoon I went along to the English School with Mrs
Chalom and Jill and John. The different 'Houses' were giving plays,
rather like an English 'Speech Day'. I enjoyed them very much,
especially a rather original arrangement of *The Merchant of Venice*.
The school is very large and modern, and the hall had a perfectly
equipped stage and an amplifier system!

Some of Mrs Chalom's pupils played during an interval – four
pupils on two pianos – a 'Polish Dance' by Scharwenka. It was
excellent.

Oh dear, how busy life seems nowadays. I never manage to have
those quiet days I enjoyed so much in the desert, when life was simple.
I think living in the country would be a wonderful idea!

I am grateful, though, for being occupied speeds the time of our
parting and I have no time to think too much of 'might-have-been'.

Have my letters changed much, darling? I often feel they are getting very scrappy and that I am neglecting you. Tell me truly, please, dear. I know, though, that you understand – you always do.

    With all the love of your very repentant,

    Tony xxxxxx

## 4 DECEMBER 1945

My dearest Tony,

I think I knew how you felt about the war. That is all I can say, dear. I understand.

    The children's party must have been an experience for you. Did you enjoy it? I like children's parties very much but always feel completely exhausted after!

    Good night, Tony.

    My love,

    Joan xxxxxx

## 11 DECEMBER 1945

My dearest Tony,

Yes, dear, I understand if your letters are less frequent or concerned only with your present life. Your letters from the desert were beautiful, Tony. You seemed to live then in a wonderful world of your own.

    With all my love,

    Joan xxxxxxx

## 13 DECEMBER 1945

Joan darling,

Thank you for the lovely Christmas card and all your good wishes. You are very sweet and very dear to me.

    On my way back to work this evening I met the children, who were just getting off the school bus. They have rather a good idea out here. Most of the children live at home, and a number of special buses call round and collect them.

    May your Christmas be all that your heart desires, and may every happiness and good wish be yours.

    With all the love of your dreaming, hoping,

    Tony xxxxxx

## 15 DECEMBER 1945

Dearest Tony,

About three bands of carollers come each evening. Last evening pleased me most: a pretty, clear wee voice (and two others not awfully in tune!) singing 'O Holy Night'. The two little boys had their backs half turned to take their pennies and run off to the next house, but an earnest child with long dark lashes said, surprised but most politely, 'yes, certainly', when I asked her to sing the song again. Funny, I keep thinking of that little girl's face. It probably was not remarkable, but it looked intensely beautiful, upturned in the darkness.

Good night and happy dreams this Christmastide. Love to you,
Joan xxxxxx
Happy Christmas

## 16 DECEMBER 1945

Joan darling,

It will be Christmas by the time this letter reaches you, and I shall be thinking of you more than ever. What a happy feast Christmas is, and how much happier it will be next year when we are together.

I have been thinking today of past Christmases during the war. 1939 I was lucky enough to be at home, 1940 I was stationed in Wiltshire, 1941 near Wolverhampton, 1942 again at home, 1943 at Gambut, near Tobruk, 1944 at Shallufa and now 1945 at Heliopolis.

I am very amused at the RAF's educational vocational training. At HQ it consists of a series of lectures given by anyone who will volunteer. I am always too busy to go, but the other day my colleague had to attend. It was a lecture on local law in England given by an airman who, through no fault of his own, was not particularly well educated. Apparently he made numerous mistakes and my friend – who is a solicitor – was furious!! He said, very indignantly, that he thought that they would make doctors attend lectures on first aid given by a layman!

An annoying point is that regular officers are not required to go. As one of them said, the RAF realised it was hopeless to try to educate them! Seriously, though, the lectures take place during office hours, and we are far too busy to waste time. We have been told to take our work home if we cannot finish it. Fortunately, my name has been left off the list for EVT, and I am most certainly not going to ask anyone why.

A very Merry, Merry Christmas to you, my darling; may your every wish and dream come true.

All my love,

Tony xxxxxx

## 21 DECEMBER 1945

My dearest Joan,

The days are racing by, and it is nearly Christmas. How quickly the year has flown.

Something I notice every morning: a little Arab girl of a fairly well-off family walks along the road to meet the school bus. There is the usual case of books etc., but she does not carry it herself: a tiny, barefooted servant girl carries it for her! What a wide gulf there is between the social classes in Egypt!

Goodbye and God bless, sweetheart.

All love and dreams of your very drowsy,

Tony xxxxxxx

## 22 DECEMBER 1945

Dearest Tony,

I went shopping today in the West End but did not buy very much. I love roaming through the stalls, along streets ringing with the cries of hawkers – their barrows piled high with holly, toys, crackers, paper chains and those mangy fur animals which dance on the end of a string. (These fascinated me as a child, but I can better understand now why Mother was always horrified at the suggestion of my possessing one!)

It was very like a pre-war Christmas in London, except that the crowds were little burdened with parcels – most things are too expensive. I felt a little lonely wandering around alone; there seem so many young couples excitedly enjoying Christmas leave.

London is full of troops on leave, scattering then to their homes. They waved telegrams – 'ARRIVED', written in enormous letters

– in the PO! Boat train arrivals are posted at Waterloo again. And it all seems exciting.

I am actually beginning to believe in demobilisation! The number of young men on the 8.04 increases. Occasionally one is stunned by eager, courteous service in a shop, from a joyful young ex-serviceman.

The control of women is ending, except for Essential Works. I still come under this order, but should be released early in 1946, I think. I certainly did not believe I would spend seven years in such monotonous work! I wonder, have I helped a potato to grow, a kipper to reach a breakfast table?

Maybe there will be oranges and bananas.

Oh yes, hail to you, 1946! I greet you with open arms.

A happy year to you, Tony dearest.

My love,

Joan xxxxx

## 22 DECEMBER 1945

Joan darling,

The children are getting more and more excited as time goes on. There is a party today – which I have been invited to attend – and yesterday everyone was busy hanging up decorations and preparing the Christmas tree. I have bought books for the children for Christmas and brooches for Mrs Chalom, Ninnette, the governess, and Daisy, Mr Chalom's sister. For Mr Chalom I chose a wallet.

There is no further news of my move. It may not come off, and, then again, it may only be to another headquarters in the Cairo area. I hope so, because I really don't want to move away – everyone is so kind here. I should know definitely within the next fortnight or so.

The weather is better at the moment; it is far nicer outside than it is indoors. There is absolutely no means of heating, not even oil stoves. How often I dream of you curled up in an armchair in front of a blazing fire, drowsily purring.

Goodbye and God keep you,

Tony xxxxxx

## 25 December 1945

My darling Joan,
A very happy, Merry Christmas to you. It is nine o'clock now by your time, and I wonder what you are doing. Perhaps just coming down to breakfast or perhaps already curled up in front of the fire looking at presents.

How lovely Christmas is in England with carols and fires and holly and decorations and, most of all, those you love. Out here it is sunny, with not a cloud in the sky. Most of the people are Moslem and are not celebrating, and, for those who do, it is not so much a family feast as at home. People are very kind, but they are all comparative strangers and have their own circle of friends, and I always feel that I am intruding.

This letter was just interrupted by lunchtime. Lunch was excellent, and the pudding was really on fire! The children were very excited. They have very nice presents. John had a Hornby train set and Jill a beautiful set of doll's furniture. Both given by an extremely wealthy Egyptian friend. I thought they would be unobtainable nowadays. With enough money, though, one can get anything in Egypt.

This morning I took the children to the Cairo Zoo. It is very pleasant, and we threw bread to the birds and animals, and the keeper threw fish for the solitary seal. I felt very sorry for the lions in their tiny cages.

I have a scheme on foot to go to India. A friend of mine in another group has a court martial shortly in Delhi and asked me if I would like to defend. I certainly would, and he has promised to try to arrange it. It would mean about a week away, and he can get me a special aircraft both ways! How wonderful the RAF is!!!

Goodbye and God keep you, my darling.

With all my love and every eager, wondering thought,

Tony xxxxxx

## 28 December 1945

Joan darling,
When I went back to work this morning there was a lovely long letter from you waiting for me.

I, too, felt lonely, dearest, wandering around the shops on my own. Oh, how wonderful next Christmas will be.

The Christmas paper you like so much was used to counter enemy radar devices. When an aircraft was picked up by the enemy it dropped pieces of this paper, and the ground stations became confused and unable to decide which was the aircraft and which the decoy paper.

I am glad you gave my address to your friends and will be very pleased to meet them. I hope they will not be bored, for I shall probably do nothing but ask them questions about you! You need not worry about my falling in love with Gwen, darling; I could not, for I lost my heart over two years ago and it is in very safe keeping. It will never belong to anyone else.

By the way, dear, I may have occasion to send a cable in the next month or so. It will not be about my homecoming so please don't be disappointed. Now then, there is another wonder for you – a fifth wonder that perhaps may never happen. I am not fair to you, am I?!!

Goodbye and God bless you always, sweetheart.

With all the love of your naughty, teasing,

Tony xxxxxx

## 31 DECEMBER 1945

My darling Joan,

1945 is fast drawing to a close, and we await the dawn of a New Year with eager, hopeful hearts. How much it has in store for us, and how well we must use it to make up for the precious time we have lost.

This is the first New Year of the peace, and surely now the nations will make a fresh start to build up our weary, war-torn world. We, the people, must see that they do – for it is our lives and happiness that are at stake.

1945 was a year of wild rejoicing as victory after victory rewarded our efforts and nation after nation yielded to our power. 1946 also will be a year of rejoicing, but rejoicing of a quieter, more purposeful character. We shall rejoice first of all in reunion and then in the laying of the foundation of our life together. How much we have to do, and how much we have to be thankful for.

I am so grateful for your love, my darling. It has meant, means, and always will mean so much to me. I can only say thank you, dearest, for everything you are.

It is midnight now, and the old year passes.

A gloriously Happy New Year to you, Joan darling; may all your dreams, hopes and wishes come true.

Goodbye and God bless you always, sweetheart.

With the ever-loving thoughts of your eager, impatient,

Tony xxxxxx

# 8

# THE FINAL CHALLENGE

I became responsible for personnel and discipline throughout Iraq and Persia Command.

## 3 JANUARY 1946

My dearest Tony,

It would be wonderful for you to go to India. I wonder if that will be possible now? It is a pity you have to move again and from such pleasant people, but I know you will soon make new friends. And so soon you will be moving again – home.

It is cold here. Jack Frost has painted wonderful fantasies on the windowpanes, and the morning paths are iced. The passengers at the station on foggy Monday morning reminded me of a school of sea lions, coughing and flapping their arms! My sense of humour begins to fail, though, as the wait for 'lost' trains grows long. I envy your flying boots these mornings!

Our party was great fun, Tony. We played foolish games, forfeits, crazy races and then cards – the enthusiasts until 2.30 a.m.! I arranged a buffet supper with tiny trays of violets to match our new china. There were wonderful jellies set with apricots – thanks to you, dear – and a big cake iced with 'Happy New Year' and decorated with a posy of tiny silk flowers.

The salmon was delicious, Tony, and, while I am reminded of your shopping, Mother's great thanks for the soap: it arrived on Christmas Eve!

Love and all good wishes,

Joan xxxxx

## 3 JANUARY 1946

My darling Joan,

I am now at Habbaniya, about 60 miles from Baghdad. I am staying here until Saturday or Sunday and then returning to Cairo. It will take me about a week to hand over, and then I shall come back here for good. Until March that is!

The station is in the middle of the desert, but it is most luxurious. I have three rooms: an enormous bedroom, with central heating, fans, etc.; a dressing room with running hot and cold water; and a room for storage and for the use of my batman for cleaning etc.!! I am in the AOC's staff mess, and it is beautifully furnished and the food is excellent. I will wait until my return from Cairo before describing everything properly, but I feel I shall like it very much. I am very sorry to leave my friends at Heliopolis. Still, Cairo is only four hours' flying time away, and I may be able to get over sometime.

Goodbye and God bless, my darling. With all the love of your very excited,

Tony xxxx

## 4 JANUARY 1946

My dearest Joan,

There is a big party tonight in the mess: a Christmas party, somewhat belated. The rooms have all been decorated with greenery and coloured streamers and balloons. It is planned to go on until two o'clock! But I have a lot of work to do tomorrow morning. I shall be leaving on Sunday and want everything to be straight.

My new chief seems very nice indeed, and indeed everyone is most friendly. As I said in my letter yesterday, I feel sure I shall like it.

I can sleep a little longer in the mornings now. Work does not start until eight o'clock, and I live only a hundred yards or so from my office. The batman brings me tea at seven o'clock, and I get up very leisurely, stroll over to the mess for breakfast and have ample time to get to the office.

One big job I foresee ahead: the filing system is in a state of chaos, and I shall have at least a month's work straightening it out. Still, it will be something worthwhile to do – work will become so much easier.

Goodbye and God bless, dear heart. With lovely dreams and the fulfilment of all your hopes.

All my love,

Tony xxxxxx

## 10 JANUARY 1946

My dearest Tony,

By now you will be settled in your luxurious new quarters. I am glad you are going to be happy there. But you say you are growing conceited and spoiled!! However shall I get *my* tea in bed?!

Tony, are you really leaving Iraq in March, for home? Oh, Tony, I wonder how you will travel, where you will land. Wonder, wonder, wonder!

Time to say good night and God bless you.

My love,

Joan xxxxxxx

## 12 JANUARY 1946

Joan darling,

At last I have a few minutes to spare. I have been busy all day trying to catch up with the week's work!

First of all, to tell you the story of my moves. As you know, I left Cairo on Thursday morning to come here. I was called at about three o'clock and, after a hasty breakfast, rushed down to the aerodrome. We took off, and I slept for a little while. Soon I woke up and then sat and watched the sun rising beyond the hills of the Transjordan. We were well above the clouds, and it was like sailing on a sea of golden billows with the mountain tops like reefs rising out of them. The beauty soon passed, and we settled down to flying over more than 500 miles of unbroken desert. Then the river Euphrates glistened in the distance, and we were soon circling Habbaniya. I met the person I was relieving and then was shown my room.

It is very large with cream walls and green woodwork and doors. The floor is of polished red tiles. On either side are radiators – the temperature falls to freezing level at nights – and overhead is a great electric fan. This is for the summer when the temperature is 120 degrees F in the shade and over 150 degrees F in the sun!

The doors are flush fitting, and on one side is a single window and on the other a window and glass doors which open on to the veranda.

In one corner is a highly polished, compact chest of drawers and, next to it, a bookcase. On the other side is my bed and, next to it, a big desk with a reading lamp. My books and papers are almost lost on it! To complete the furnishings of the bedroom, there are two easy chairs and a large rug.

One door leads to my dressing room. In this there is a washbasin with running hot and cold water, another radiator and fan. Then, too, there is a big wardrobe and a dressing table.

The last room is a box room, with shelves and the things the bearer uses for cleaning. It is rather bleak and, at the moment, very cold.

This, then, is my home for the next few weeks, and I'm sure you will agree that for the desert it is extremely comfortable. What a change from Gambut and Tobruk!

The next thing to describe: the mess itself.

This is a square building. It consists of a large central lounge with rooms opening from it. There are other rooms upstairs, and a balcony runs round inside as well as another outside. Here, again, the walls are cream and the woodwork green. The floor is of red tiles, and there are numerous rugs. Around this lounge are big easy chairs and sofas.

To the right are two small lounges. In the first of these is a fire! The other attractions are a radio and the gramophone and, of course, more easy chairs. The second houses a table-tennis table.

Last of the 'public rooms' of the mess is the dining room. This is half-panelled in dark oak, and the tables are, I think, also oak, highly polished and rather lighter than the walls. There are two large tables, and on each are three lamps. These are most intriguing, with shades made out of maps. At the far end of this room is a dark leather screen.

In the meantime, dearest, thank you once more for your thoughts and wishes.

Goodbye and God bless, sweetheart.

All my love,

Tony xxxxxx


## 17 JANUARY 1946

My dearest Joan,

There is a long court martial going on at the moment, and I have had to entertain the Judge. Fortunately, I managed to slip away this evening; he is going to the cinema with one of the members of the court, and I excused myself.

I promised I would describe my office. It is fairly small and quite cosy. My desk – a big roll-top – is across one corner with a large double window on my left. Under this window is an ultra-modern metal table with all my reference books. These have such lurid titles as *Criminal Pleading and Evidence, Law of Evidence, Judges' Rules and Precedents, Manual of Air Force Law*. It must look very imposing to the casual visitor! Then, too, I now have six trays! My telephone is at the left of the desk together with a bell push.

On the wall opposite are some bookshelves with manuals less frequently referred to, and under the shelves is another long table with outstanding cases and courts on it. There is another window and two doors and, of course, the usual fans and radiators. The walls are cream and the metalwork of the doors, windows, etc., green. I have just had a noticeboard put on the wall beside me, and I also have a large map of the Persian Gulf.

In fact the only thing wrong with my office at the moment is the presence of numerous files – many bequeathed by my predecessor, but a lot which have arrived since he left. I am working through them gradually, though, and by the time I leave Habbaniya my trays should be quite empty! The easiest way to get rid of them, if I am particularly busy, is to minute them to someone else for comment, and, by the time he sends them back, I am a little freer!

Goodbye and God bless you, dear heart. I shall be seeing you very soon now. What a wonderful day that will be.

All the love and eager thoughts of your happy, impatient,

Tony xxxxxx

## 19 JANUARY 1946

My dearest Joan,

Perhaps you may like to hear a little more about Habbaniya. It is very big, and I have not explored very much so far.

The Air Headquarters building is oblong with two square courtyards in the centre of it. These are lined with small trees and are quite grassy. If it were not for the mud and the rather contrasting building it could almost be the cloisters of some old abbey.

We have a garden attached to our mess, and it is very pleasant indeed to sit in the sun and imagine that you are back in England – for it really seems like a little piece of England with the grass and flowers and tall trees.

Soon we shall not have to rely on letters, my darling, but will be able to tell all our thoughts and our hearts' desires.

All my love and lovely dreams,

Tony xxxxxxxx

## 22 January 1946

Tony dear,

Now we may soon be roving again! Daddy is hoping to get a new house from an acquaintance who is building under private licence. You cannot appreciate what a miracle this is, Tony, and a great secret. There are thousands of people clamouring, so we shall be very fortunate.

There is no relief in sight for the housing problem. Some friends rent a room in Vera's house but have to move out when their son comes home on leave because there is no room for him at Vera's. Yet their case is not considered 'urgent' enough for them even to be put on the Council's housing waiting list! So, you see, even prefabs become dream castles to Englishmen today. But, you know, we are grown far too patient in this country. And now reliant on the state. No, it would seem much more sensible for me to seek a builder to build my house than a government department. And if one hasn't influence, there is always persistence!

And are you really coming home in spring, Tony? Is it possible that it is only weeks and not even whole months?! I did not quite believe it until practical Mummy said that you would sleep in the wee room and that I must have a new dress!

What plans, Tony? Will it be possible to meet you?

Oh, and I have gathered that it is extremely advisable to get demobilisation clothes. These are apparently superior to those offered in shops at present, and tailors' orders for civilian customers are often whisked away for 'demobs' anyway! Shoes are always a subject for many weary queues.

I just have to leave the fire sometime! Good night, my dear.

God bless you and speed you,

Joan xxxxxx

## 22 JANUARY 1946

Joan darling,

Just as I thought my work was becoming a little clearer, I have had more thrust upon me. My chief, Wing Commander Desmond Garvin, is long overdue for repatriation. Now the AOC says that he need wait no longer but can hand over to me, and Air Ministry are to be requested to send someone out from England. So I must now do his work as well as my own.

To add to my troubles, I was elected Messing Officer at a mess meeting yesterday. How quickly the time will pass!!

No matter how spoiled I get, you shall still have your cup of tea in bed, dearest!! It will spoil me still more, since all I want to do is to do things for you. Nothing else will make me really happy.

With all the love of your eager, hopeful,

Tony xxxxxx

## 25 JANUARY 1946

Joan darling,

I am hoping to go to Baghdad on Sunday and will look for a rug. I have seen some, and they are really lovely. The dealers do not want you to buy them straight away but prefer you to take them away and have them in your room for a few months so that they get a more mellow appearance. I shall choose very carefully!

There is a pack of jackals outside howling at the moment; they rush through the camp from time to time looking for food. I get very annoyed when they wake me up about three o'clock in the morning!

Goodbye and God bless you, dear heart. Our long and patient wait is nearly over now, and parting will soon be but a memory.

All my love and happy thoughts,

Tony xxxxxx

## 27 JANUARY 1946

Dearest Tony,

You won't let success spoil you ever, will you, Tony? Your thoughtfulness and kindness are the most important things in the world, and to me.

A favourite colleague is back in our section, cheerfully bewildered with everything!

1946 will awaken a lot of Sleeping Princesses, and Princes, too, from a long, bad dream. Only we shall feel sad still for all the ones who have missed the wakening.

Goodbye for a little while, dear. My love to you.

Joan xxxxxxx

## 27 JANUARY 1946

My dearest Joan

I did not go to Baghdad over the weekend after all; the AOC wanted to see me during the morning, and I was summoned urgently again just as I had changed for tennis. It was difficult to settle down to serious work in white shorts and an open-neck shirt!

It is after 11 o'clock now, and I must try to keep my resolution to go to bed early.

With all my thoughts and lovely dreams,

Tony xxxxxxx

## 28 JANUARY 1946

My darling Joan,

So you may be moving again. You are wandering about almost as much as I am – we shall make a fine pair. Perhaps your thought of a caravan may be a good one! I hope I shall be home to help you move. I hope, too, that I shall be back in the spring. How lovely an English spring can be and, oh, how I long to see the English countryside.

I am so busy now. There is a lot of work to do, but I could manage were it not for the constant telephone calls. A station commander ringing up to ask for an engineer officer; the Camp Commandant reporting a fire; an airman wanting permission to take a pet dog back to England; the AOC asking for a summary of the personnel situation in the Command; an application for a permanent commission: these are a few of the queries I have had today. These are on top of my normal work! The days are flying past, though I can hardly believe that January is nearly finished. It seems that I am rushing through the pages of the novel, eager to come to the happy ending.

With all the love and every thought of your happy, excited,
Tony xxxxxx

## 30 JANUARY 1946

Dearest Joan,

Today has been dull and rainy, and there has even been a fog. Habbaniya seemed really like England.

At present I am very annoyed about the mutiny at RAF stations. There is no justification for them; the men have proper channels through which they can air grievances and which in these cases were not used. Demobilisation is the same for all services, and I think that generally the officers have more grounds for complaint than the men. Especially I am angry because it spoils the good name of the RAF among the other services. It is too bad after the war record which we won. What is the general reaction in England, dearest? The Prime Minister said in a statement to the House that these breaches of discipline would not be tolerated.

I shall not be able to discuss such grave things when I return, my darling. We shall have so much time to make up for, and there is so much to be done.

Until that happy, happy day, sweetheart.

Your eager, dreaming,

Tony xxxxxxx

## 1 FEBRUARY 1946

Joan darling,

When I finished work yesterday evening there were only two files left in my 'In' tray. I hate to come in first thing in the morning and find that it has overflowed on to my desk and into the other trays.

My clerks are very good, though, and work late every night without being asked. I was pleased to be able to promote two of them to corporal yesterday.

I must be strong-willed and not think of you too often, otherwise my work will be lost in daydreams.

Goodbye and God keep you, dear heart.

Tony xxxxxx

## 4 FEBRUARY 1946

My dearest Tony,

You *would* have a terrible time staggering home with a full-sized carpet! Perhaps the customs officials could be persuaded that it was a 'personal belonging' – a magic carpet. That on it you travelled through troubles and delays, thousands and thousands of miles to your wonderful 'Emerald City': the green countryside of England.

I wonder what colours your rug will be? Visibly or not, there will be woven in it the blues of many seas and rivers, the desert, brilliant hues of sudden flowers, grey sometimes for weariness, and gold of the sun you sought!

I am dreaming!

Good night and God bless you,

Joan xxxxxx

## 5 FEBRUARY 1946

My dearest Joan,

The batman does not sleep in the little room, dear, he only uses it for cleaning etc. All the Assyrians and Iraqis live in a township of their own on the camp, together with their families. The batmen come over to the mess in the morning, bring tea etc., and then each waits on his own officer at meals. Then in the evening they go back home – a matter of half a mile or so. Their camp is quite nice. It has a hospital, schools, a community centre and large playing fields. The girls' school is giving an exhibition of art and crafts next week; I will see if I can get some curio to send you.

I have now moved into my ex-chief's office and, since I also have my own work to do, brought four of my own trays. I now have ten!! And also an array of six bells! As there is not sufficient room on the top of the desk, I have a table on either side in a horseshoe shape. When I am interviewing anyone I can just lean back and vanish behind my barricade!

Don't worry lest I should change, my darling. I never take it seriously; I always feel that I am masquerading. I cannot believe that people are nervous about coming to see me. It is funny: I can do quite a lot for them but nothing for myself. I sent someone home to England by air this morning because his brother was ill, but I have to ask permission from the AOC to have an afternoon off to go to Baghdad!

I have a great opportunity at the moment. A nearby headquarters has asked me to defend at a court martial. It would be a lovely change. I am so tired of administering the law it would give me a mischievous delight to be helping someone avoid its penalties! It is very, very unprofessional of me, but even if he is guilty I shall fight to get him off. It is only a service offence, not a civil crime. How horrified my friend the Judge would be to hear me say that!

The future is very real, dear heart. And how near it is. I am almost frightened; I have done so little to deserve such great happiness. Oh how impatient I am growing, far more so than when I knew that parting was for a long time yet.

God keep you safe always, Joan darling. Goodbye, and all the happy loving thoughts of your very eager,

Tony xxxxxx

## 7 FEBRUARY 1946

Tony dearest,

Now a subject I knew would be near your heart: the RAF strikes. Although it may seem contrary for me to counter your condemnation, since obviously you are far better informed, I am going to tell you my opinions.

Strikes seemed wrong to me now there are other powerful methods of negotiation, because their power seems limitless and very harmful. I resigned from our CS association because I disagree with its policy of affiliation to the TUC. I visualise a PO strike distressing the whole country, for instance.

That, not very briefly, is to explain that I'm not condoning the strikes when I make excuses for the airmen!

They have given their best, dearest, through a long, hard war, dreaming always of longed-for things 'when the war is over'. We all knew, of course, that it would not be just like that, but the long, hard peace has come as a shock and disappointment.

So I imagine these men's grievances, many things long fretted about, to which demob has come to mean the solution: home troubles reaching them, loved ones they long to see (and who write most impatiently of seeing them!), news of America's speedy demobilisation.

The small world they fought to preserve, in which their interests lie (internationalists seem few), seeming only a matter of a 'red tape' away.

A series of successful strikes at home and in the US Army, the RAF cause is no less justifiable.

The Defence, having won its case with a smile, ventures to reassure the Beloved Prosecution on the point of honour of the Royal Air Force. Sympathy with the cause of demobilisation and appreciation of fine service overrides criticism of this action.

But again our burning question is *who* gets the food. We give it gladly to feed hungry people but want a great deal of assurance that it won't find its way into black markets on the continent to feed rich restaurant patrons! It is impossible to judge from hearsay, but observers say that, as in England, expensive restaurants serve food – steaks, poultry and so on – that the British housewives never see.

Oh, Tony, what a dreadful letter full of politics! And so soon you will be troubled with deciding whether your conscience allows you to buy those coupons or eggs on the black market, whether to queue for fish or go without! Even the Brains Trust concerns itself with these problems which Aristotle failed to solve!!

Hurry home, so I can ask you all the questions and tell you all the things in the world. And be quiet with you. One has to talk all the time in a letter.

Good night and God bless you,

Joan xxxxxx

## 7 FEBRUARY 1946

Joan darling,

Tonight is a guest night, and we are all dining in. I don't feel a bit like a party, but I shall have to go. Not many guests are coming so there will be enough food to go round. The other day some unexpected guests arrived, and I was watching the meat very anxiously to see if there would be enough. I am becoming quite a good housewife!

I was shocked to see in the paper that rations in England are to be cut still more and that bread may be rationed. What terrible effects this war has had. I wonder if anyone will ever be so foolish as to start another. Unfortunately people do not seem to learn from the mistakes of the past.

Goodbye and God bless, sweetheart.
Tony xxxxxx

## 9 February 1946

Joan, my darling,

I went along to the exhibition at the girls' school in the Civil Cantonment. It was quite interesting: there were two women weaving a carpet. I purchased a little lace mat for you. It is very similar to the work done in Cyprus; I wonder how it spread across from here, across Syria and over 350 miles of desert.

The girls' school is built of mud bricks but is quite clean, although a little dark inside. There were drawings by the children and some paintings by the older girls. The craftwork seems to compare favourably with English schools; the mat I am sending was made in Class 5.

With all the love and happy dreams of your so impatient,
Tony xxxxxx

## 12 February 1946

My dearest Joan,

Please forgive this very short note. I am very tired and have a lot of work to do yet. It is all in connection with the cases I am defending. You see, I have to do it all in my spare time, and the fact that I spend a few more hours on it may make the difference between an acquittal and a term of imprisonment for the two boys – they are only just over 20. I do not believe they are guilty. I know you will understand, darling.

With every loving thought from your very sleepy,
Tony xxxxxx

## 17 February 1946

Joan darling,

At last the court martial is over and I can relax a little. It continued until six o'clock yesterday evening. I was quite pleased with the result. There were four charges: creating a disturbance, attempted assault and two charges of wilfully disobeying an order given by an officer. The finding was 'not guilty' on the first and second charges and on the third and fourth 'guilty of failing to obey, but not wilfully'. I don't think I shall defend again while I have so much work to do; it is far more of a strain than prosecuting.

First for the reply of the 'Prosecution' on the strikes. Demobilisation is a 'personnel' matter, and so I am responsible for its smooth working throughout this Command. So far, although the Persian Gulf stations are supposed to be the worst in the RAF (Shaibah and Sharjah, for instance), there has been no trouble here. A lot of the trouble is failure to realise just what is happening and what the reduction in numbers really means. This is explained in a series of signals from Air Ministry called 'demob forms', and these are circulated and explained carefully. I must confess that it is the personal responsibility of the officers to keep their men informed and to answer their questions and that in nearly all the affected areas this cannot have been done. An oath of allegiance is a very binding thing, though, and should not be broken.

Goodbye and God keep you always, dear heart.

With all the eager, happy thoughts of your very loving,

Tony xxxxxx

## 19 FEBRUARY 1946

Dearest Tony,

Oh, Tony, I can scarcely imagine you as an anxious and harried housewife. A man in his time does indeed play many parts! Housekeeping is an anxious job now, but I can just remember before the war that it was rather fun.

And the Health Bill brings a storm of protest today from socialist as well as opposition MPs. A clause was to give power of prosecution, with possibility of a £10-*a-day* fine and loss of sick benefit, against a worker refusing any treatment recommended by a doctor. Thus one must submit to operation, injection, experiment, with appeal only to an official tribunal! The clause has had to be dropped.

Tony, I relate to you the temper and grumbles of home to give you a picture of everyday happenings, wrongs, grumbles which then get righted, and not for you to be distressed.

Four thousand miles' journey seems a desolate distance away, and I am wishing and wishing to know when you will be travelling it this way.

It has cheered me writing to you. It is a very comfortable feeling to share ones troubles!

Good night, darling; please run all the way home!

My love,

Joan xxxxxxx

## 20 February 1946

Dearest Joan,

I am going down to Shaibah on a staff visit on Saturday and returning on Sunday. The CO there is very anxious to get some more men, and I want to see how badly off he really is. I cannot believe all the desperate tales I hear over the telephone nowadays!

I spoke to the C in C's HQ this evening, and they said that so far they could not find anyone either for SPSO or P1 but that they are still asking Air Ministry to send someone from England. I shall leave in April whether anyone comes or not!

Goodbye and God bless, dear heart. At last we have a definite date to look forward to and for which we can plan.

All love and dreams of your very eager,

Tony xxxxx

## 22 February 1946

Joan darling,

I intended to write you a letter last night, but the Air Attaché from Tehran – Air Commodore Runciman – arrived, and we all stayed talking until after midnight!

I have returned my rug after all. There were one or two faults in it. I plan to visit the merchant Karshi, in Baghdad. He is very honest and is reported to have a wonderful collection. A friend of mine has bought four rugs from him so far! They are fascinating things, and I am beginning to learn a little about them. I hope to choose a really beautiful one for you.

Goodbye and God keep you, my darling,

Tony xxxxxx

## 24 FEBRUARY 1946

My dearest Joan,

The journey to Shaibah and back was quite uneventful. The Euphrates and Tigris rivers are very flooded, and many little villages are isolated. How different from the dry, sun-scorched plains of the summer!

I bought two carpets in Baghdad today. One is a Bukhara – from Russia – and the other is a Baluchistan. Both are quite quiet, for many of the gay designs would not harmonise with English surroundings – even out here they seem vivid.

Baghdad is the usual eastern town: not at all romantic but rather shabby and not too clean.

God bless, and every eager, loving thought, from your most impatient,

Tony xxxxxx

## 27 FEBRUARY 1946

Joan darling,

The sun is shining, but it is quite cold and there is a boisterous wind. There are lovely blossoms on the trees, and the gardens grow more colourful each day. We have bowls of violets and anemones in the mess and can almost imagine that we have been wafted to England on a magic carpet. I shall be coming home to almost the same scenes.

Although I cannot leave, I was posted, with effect from today, to England. So all I have to do is to find two people to take over my jobs; that, by the way, is not so simple as it sounds. I have tried every wing commander I know, but all have managed to evade me!

HQ Mediterranean and Middle East are not at all helpful, and I am going to ask the AOC to bring pressure to bear on them. It might have some effect.

Be patient just a little while longer, my darling; the days will soon fly by.

All the loving thoughts of your happy, excited,

Tony xxxxxx

## 1 MARCH 1946

Dearest,

Oh, Tony, I am disappointed and angry, too, at the postponement of
your homecoming. Would it be no use your getting mad, too? Could
someone not be found sooner than later to take your place?

Forgive me if I seem unreasonable, but it is wearying when carrots
keep popping out of reach as you come abreast of them. It makes even
a patient 'mokey' stamp her foot!

Good night, darling.

Love and love to you,

Joan xxxxxx

## 1 MARCH 1946

Joan, my darling,

I spoke to my chief at Middle East, and he said that there was
someone he could send to take over the legal side from me. All I
want now is a wing commander!

All love of your happy but bewildered,

Tony xxxxxx

## 5 MARCH 1946

Joan darling,

Just a few very sleepy lines to let you know that our address has been
altered to Royal Air Force in Iraq, as we have left Persia.

There was a long conference this morning, and when I got back
to my office my trays were crowded. So I have had to work quite a
lot of overtime.

There is still no news of my relief, but I don't think it can be very
much longer now and am in highest hopes!

All my love and happy dreams,

Tony xxxxxx

## 7 MARCH 1946

Joan darling,

I went into Baghdad again today and exchanged my Baluchistan
for another, rather similar but with a much richer red. It glows
beautifully. I am growing very fond of Persian rugs and can now

begin to recognise the district in which they were made!

We had a guest night last night, and unfortunately I had to stay up late until all the guests left. It was nearly one o'clock before I got to bed, and I was feeling very tired. I shall have a really early night tonight.

There have been one or two disturbances in Baghdad recently – but of a very harmless nature. As always it was by students, and the Iraqi government soon restored order by threatening to fail all their examinations for three years!! No one takes them very seriously.

I have to go into Baghdad again tomorrow for a conference at the embassy. I don't want to go; my work mounts up so while I am away. Still it is only for a very short time now, and I will soon be able to relax.

Goodbye and God keep you, dear heart.

Tony xxxxxx

## 10 March 1946

Joan, my darling,

Just a very brief little note to say that I have not forgotten you. It is very late, and I have had to work all day: something I object to doing on a Sunday!

I attended three conferences at the embassy in three days and have had to write a long report summarising the situation, besides catching up with the work that accumulated whilst I was away. Oh, how glad I shall be when I can relax for a little while. I think I have had more office work to do in the last three months than throughout the rest of the war!

With all my love and every thought,

Tony xxxxxx

## 13 March 1946

Joan darling,

I have had a signal from Air Ministry – which I have to action as Senior Personnel Staff Officer! – saying that I may not be held beyond 30 April 1946. So that, at any rate, is the final day. There is just the smallest possibility that it may be earlier. There are very big changes afoot, and I hope to net a wing commander and a squadron leader out of them!

All my eager, loving thoughts,
Tony xxxxxx

## 14 MARCH 1946

Tony dearest,

I mentioned your delay to Daddy, and he suggested a word this end would find a replacement most speedily. The ministers seemed very sensitive about the efficiency of their demobilisation organisations. W/C Carpenter would no doubt love to attack the Air Minister's modest programme! Of course, I would not write him without your permission, and perhaps you will have appealed if you think it necessary.

I know I am a dreadful worry about this, but I cannot help feeling that, since the wing commander was awaited long before you took over, you might go on waiting and waiting. My 'fierceness' is increased by the men killing time at home! Yvonne's fiancé, doing nothing between weekends at home, is being demobbed after only two years' service from his commission in the Fleet Air Arm. So demob doesn't seem fair, and you so deserve to come home – and I so want you to.

My daddy worries and worries about the dishonesty in the country. Every little citizen is a criminal in the eyes of the law over some rationing offence! A half-pint of milk from a neighbour, 'backyard-poultry' eggs exchanged for margarine, those coupons from a serviceman: all punishable crimes indeed!! But, seriously, the black market does flourish, particularly miserably in the 'tipping' system. Giving presents to the tradespeople for favours seems as ugly as blackmail and involves everyone!

Even my 'writing-hating' mama has taken to writing to the press and fellow members of the Housewives Leagues! Examples of the injustices they fight are the allowance of only three sheets to newly married people (and none available for other families) at the reasonable utility price of 26 shillings a pair, while the stores are stocked with sheets at 9 guineas, not always even of better quality, and completely unrationed! Expensive curtaining and linen is unrationed, too, while reasonably priced household material and necessary towels and so on are on personal coupons now.

Then there are grapes, melons and peaches at exorbitant prices, but no controlled-price fruit is imported.

There seem to be ample materials and labour for the luxury trade, and quantities of unrationed food are imported for rich people and for banquets! Meat and eggs from Australia and needed goods from Czechoslovakia are refused because the country cannot afford them. This is making more socialists (or communists!) than the government bargains for.

Good night now.

My love and love to you,

Joan xxxxxxx

## 15 MARCH 1946

Joan, my darling,

Tomorrow I plan to be very, very lazy. I shall make a big effort and finish all my work in the morning and then sit in an easy chair on the lawn in the sunshine all the afternoon!!

With the approval of the AOC I have started an 'Iraq Command Personnel Bulletin'. Very many of the men grumble about things but never ask for them to be put right, so I have instructed all stations in the Command to provide a letterbox in which people can put written questions. All questions are forwarded to me, and I answer them myself or send them to the department concerned. The questions and answers are then published in the bulletin for general information. It means a little more work, but if it keeps the men contented and morale high it is well worth it.

I am so very, very grateful to you, dearest. You have been so wonderfully patient, waiting all this time, and so very kind to me. I shall never be able really to thank you.

Goodbye and God bless you, dear heart. I will try to tell you soon how much I love you.

With all my dreams and thoughts,

Tony xxxxxx

## 20 MARCH 1946

Joan darling,

Please don't write about me, darling. You see, I could go if I really pressed the point, but it would be letting the AOC and the whole Command down; they depend on the SPSO to post them home on release and at the end of their overseas tours. My entire staff consists of a newly promoted flight lieutenant and a newly commissioned pilot officer, and they are both very young and inexperienced. If I handed over to them and left it would turn the Command into complete chaos.

Oh, it is so difficult to explain, but the Personnel Branch covers so very many subjects and, unless it is fairly efficient, morale of the men falls rapidly. So far Iraq Command has had no strikes or mutinies, and I would feel very guilty if I left and the inefficiency of 'P' staff caused discontent. I have no intention, though, of remaining to save Air Ministry. They know now that I'm due to go, and the AOC has warned them. If no one comes I shall insist on my rights and leave with a clear conscience. But when release was accelerated and I suddenly became due to go it was rather different. Please say you understand, dearest; I feel so badly about it for your sake. I am almost certain anyway to be home in about a month.

Goodbye, dear heart. How many things there are to tell each other and, oh, how I long to see you again and hold you in my arms. Now that our reunion is so close I am impatient even of the minutes apart.

All my love and every thought,
Tony xxxxxx

## 23 MARCH 1946

My dearest Joan,

Yesterday evening I met the members of the Palestine Commission. They were quite interesting. They had been given some wonderful gifts by King Ibn Saud of Saudi Arabia: jewelled daggers, a chiming gold watch, lovely robes and golden headdress. I think I, too, must become a member of a roving Middle East Commission!

Air Commodore Runciman also visited us on his way home to England. He, too, is being released – he was Air Attaché at Tehran. I told him that I would not be very far behind him!

The journey home should not take very long, dearest. I shall try to fly back, but if that is not possible the sea trip takes only ten days or so.

My office has almost completely collapsed now. I should have a squadron leader and a flight lieutenant; instead I have a flight lieutenant and a newly commissioned pilot officer, neither of whom know anything about administration. I had an experienced warrant officer as my chief clerk. He has been posted, and, instead of having one warrant officer, one flight sergeant, four sergeants, five corporals and eight airmen, I have one sergeant, two corporals and six airmen, only two of whom can type. Instead of the work decreasing, it is multiplying every day. Although I don't normally despair of things very easily, I feel like giving up now – I shall be very, very pleased to leave. It is like trying to build a house of cards in a strong wind on a shaking table.

I spent this morning writing very strong letters to HQ RAF MED/ME telling them about the position. I don't suppose they will bother to do anything.

Forgive me if I write about my work and troubles, darling, but they seem to be almost the only things I can think about nowadays, except of seeing you again.

With all my love and dreams,

Tony xxxxxxxx

## 26 MARCH 1946

Joan, my dearest,

The days are being struck off my calendar in quick succession, and the time of parting grows shorter and shorter. Oh, how good it is to be alive and to have so much to look forward to. I almost welcome all the work, since there is no time to think and wonder how many more days – but I would like a little time off; there are so many things I have to do.

The AOC invited me over to his house the other evening. His wife is staying with him at the moment, and it seemed like being home again. They are both really charming. Mrs Strafford – the AOC is Air Vice Marshal Strafford – has just come back from a holiday in Turkey, which she enjoyed very much.

That conjures up thoughts of our own holidays. As long as you are there and happy, I do not mind where we go. It is really your holiday: you have had to put up with so much monotony and dull work. I have been lucky in travelling about.

Goodbye and God keep you always, dear heart.

With all my love and eager, happy dreams,

Tony xxxxxxx

## 31 MARCH 1946

Joan, my darling,

Please forgive me if this is rather a sleepy letter, but I have had a very busy day.

I managed to bring my work almost up to date and added quite a lot to my personnel bulletin. I asked the AOC to write a foreword to it, and he agreed but asked me to write it and said he would sign it! I hope to show you a copy when it is printed.

Goodbye and God keep you safe, my darling.

All my happy, eager thoughts,

Tony xxxxxx

## 1 APRIL 1946

Darling Joan,

Today was a very good start to my last month in Iraq. An officer arrived for P1 duties!! Although it does not free me altogether, it will be a great help, and I shall have quite a lot less work to do. Unfortunately, the AOC has ruled that he does not consider him capable of taking over as SPSO, which I feel is rather a double-edged compliment to me!

I shall let my new P1 have four of my trays and several of my weighty volumes. My desk will then begin to look like the AOC's, which is always beautifully neat with very few papers on it. If anything is sent to him he summons the head of the appropriate branch and asks for an appreciation of the position. Then, when all is laid before him, he announces his decision. I wonder if I shall be able to get my officers to do the same!

I hope to go up to Cairo with the AOC next week and will try to force an answer from HQ MED/ME. I hope to persuade them to let me fly home.

All my thoughts and lovely dreams,

Tony xxxxxx

## 7 APRIL 1946

My darling Joan,

I went swimming again this morning, and once more the water was very pleasant. Soon it will begin to get hot. All around the sides of the pool are fine sprays, and in the summer these play ceaselessly on to the surface of the water to keep it cool enough for swimming. How very different from English open-air pools!

I am flying to Cairo in the AOC's aircraft but have been asked to navigate some Venturas back here. It will be a pleasant change to do some serious flying again!

All my love and eager dreams.

Tony xxxxxx

## 10 April 1946

Tony darling,

I have been thinking of you specially today, disturbingly in fact. It seems almost that there must be a reason: were you doing anything unusual today, Tony?

Do two sweethearts present *such* a problem, dearest? It is well you are not a sailor!!

I took over my new section today, and I think I shall be quite happy. The girls are nice enough, but not very industrious! The 'Mansions' is a rambling old building inside, although it appears so dignified from the street, and, since the lift breaks down frequently, it is not a great advantage to be on the fifth floor! Our staff is even more depleted than yours, Tony: of ten there are only two and a half (a part-timer) in my section! It just isn't any use worrying; there seem no office workers left in the land, for the cry is nationwide.

Good night now, Tony.

Your so tired,

Joan xxxxxx

## 12 April 1946

Joan dearest,

Strangely enough – or is it really strange? – HQ MED/ME are in an even greater muddle than we are! I despair of ever getting any real sense from them.

With all my love and happy dreams,

Tony xxxxxxx

## 14 APRIL 1946

My dearest Joan,

When I was in Cairo I saw a very odd sight: a train of flat, horse-drawn trucks going along the street with a camel lashed to the top of each truck. The camels had their usual sardonic look so it was quite impossible to tell whether or not they were enjoying their ride!

Tomorrow I shall write to HQ RAF MED/ME and remind them that I shall be leaving by the end of the month and that in their own interest they had better find a relief for me immediately.

Goodbye and God bless, my darling. I grow more and more impatient each moment!

Your eager, hopeful,

Tony xxxxxx

## 19 APRIL 1946

My darling Joan,

We shall be working tomorrow after all. It is such very, very varied work. For example, today I had the following things to do: select four crews to fly aircraft to England; advise the AOC on the possible political repercussions if he issues a new order concerning civilian employees; lay down a policy for re-engagement of civilians when they have been called up for a period of service with the Iraqi army; write a letter to Air Ministry explaining the facts of a theft of ammunition; request Air Ministry authority to write off equipment valued at £1,500 which was destroyed in a fire.

The SPSO is responsible for all civilian labour in the command and has to liaise with the embassy to make sure that his regulations do not clash with the laws. He has to decide rates of pay and is the only person who can authorise an increase in pay. At present we have over 15,000 civilians alone, so it is quite a busy job – quite apart from the service side! I must confess I shall be very glad to hand it over and relax for a while.

A very Happy Easter to you and all my love and dreamy thoughts,

Tony xxxxxx

## 20 APRIL 1946

Joan darling

A Happy, Happy Easter to you. I have just received a lovely Easter egg: a signal which said 'Wing Commander A.C. Stewart arriving 23 April as relief for SPSO'!! Of course, I shall not believe it until I see him, but anyway I have his name.

In the meantime I have been busily working to clear up all outstanding files and action so that there will be no delay in handing over to him. If all goes well I should be away by the 30th. I fear that I cannot travel by air all the way but will come by sea from Port Said. Still, the journey only takes about ten days.

Forgive me, dearest. I am far too excited to write. I can only think that I shall be seeing you, oh, so soon.

Goodbye and God bless.

All love of your happy, very excited,

Tony xxxxxx

## 23 APRIL 1946

Joan, my darling,

My relief arrived today! I propose to start handing over to him tomorrow and should be away by the 30th.

Oh, I cannot really believe that it is time. I have conditioned myself so much against disappointment that I shall not realise I am on my way home and to you until I set foot in England.

I am growing more and more excited, and I greatly fear that my last few letters will be very scrappy. Still, I will make up for it when I see you.

All my love and excited jumbled thoughts,

Tony xxxxxx

## 26 APRIL 1946

Joan darling,

Another rather hasty letter. I am well in the process of handing over to my relief and hope to leave on Tuesday. He is not very happy about the work, but after all, he is a regular officer who commanded a station in England, and he should be suitable for staff work. The AOC is rather doubtful whether he will manage or not, but I am most certainly not going to stay on any longer!

Oh, I can hardly believe it is really true at last.

Goodbye and God bless you, dear heart.

All the love and thoughts of your bewildered, but happy,

Tony xxxxxx

## 6 MAY 1946

Darling Joan,

I should have set out for the embarkation centre yesterday, but the plane was delayed; I am leaving tomorrow.

I have been given a priority by HQ RAF MED/ME, so hope to see you very soon.

Goodbye and all my love, my darling.

Your very excited,

Tony xxxxxx

## MV DUNNOTTAR CASTLE

Joan darling,

We shall be calling in at Malta tomorrow morning for a few hours and have been told that we can post letters.

So far the journey has been very good. We had a rather trying train journey to Alexandria, during which one engine broke down and had to be replaced and the new one had to stop every half-hour to be oiled!

We boarded the ship at midday and sailed at five o'clock. If all goes well we should reach Toulon on Sunday morning and be at Calais or Dieppe on Tuesday evening. We have to go to Hednesford, near Stafford, for release, and with luck everything will be completed by Friday and I should be with you on Saturday. Oh how lovely it is to think that parting will soon be forgotten.

I will try to phone you as soon as I get to Hednesford and tell you what is happening.

Goodbye and God bless, my darling.

All my eager love,

Tony xxxxxx

# 9

# DREAMS THAT REALLY
# DID COME TRUE

We had parted in 1943 as good friends. We had kissed only once. We now met, for the first time in nearly three years, as an engaged couple, planning to be married within a month. We had no home, no furniture and no plans for our honeymoon!

One thing was certain: we knew that we were destined to spend our lives together.

We needed to make up our minds fairly quickly about our work. If we married, Joan could no longer continue as a permanent civil servant; there was a Civil Service ban on married women. I could take up a place at Cambridge to read History, but not if I was married.

Having waited so long we decided that, for both of us, marriage was most important. I would go back to Shell, where I had worked before the war, and Joan would make a home.

Friends and relations rallied round with odd items of furniture, cooking equipment and china. We were given coupons to buy three sheets and two blankets! By this time, we were so confused that it was only on the eve of our wedding that we realised we had not bought a ring.

We found a delightful small hotel, The Old Manor at Witley in Surrey, where we could stay for three weeks for our honeymoon.

We had been very fortunate. We had both survived the Second World War, and it had brought us together. We were both young enough to be relatively unscathed by it. We had been separated for nearly three years but had written over 670 letters between us. These letters were the most important factor in determining our future life.

Our wartime letters were now safely packed away and forgotten, but the deep feelings and love which had prompted them remained and guided the development of the rest of our lives. It was only when I was re-reading them, 60 years later, that I realised we had made nearly all of the dreams in them come true.

Times were difficult for the first few years, but from the beginning we had our own house. This was a small end of terrace with a dilapidated kitchen and an old gas stove thick with grease. It had a long garden overgrown with brambles. Joan had always wanted to be an architect, and this was a challenge for her. She changed the interior layout, and we completely redecorated the house to make a comfortable home.

By 1949 Joan was expecting a baby, and this, combined with our war service, gave us sufficient 'points' to apply for permission to build a house for ourselves. We found a corner plot on Epsom Downs, in Joan's beloved Surrey.

We compiled lists of all the things we wanted in our ideal home, and Joan drew up endless plans and budgets. We even made an accurate cardboard model. We found a very good builder, and the house was completed soon after our son, Christopher, was born. It included all the things Joan had dreamed of, including central heating, not very common in those days.

All was not work. We found time to go to an Arabian Nights Ball at the Dorchester in the presence of the King of Jordan – where I met friends from Iraq – and to a candlelit reception at the Tate organised by the Contemporary Art Society, of which we were members. Through the Society Joan met many artists, including Henry Moore and John Piper.

Four years later, I was seconded to East Africa for 12 months. This, at that time, included Kenya, Uganda and Tanganyika, and Joan began, as she had wished, to see the countries of the world at close quarters and not merely as a tourist.

On our return she made contact with a number of artists and very good craftsmen and established the East Sussex Arts and Crafts Society, which met at our house.

We frequently took holidays in Europe, usually finishing in Paris where Joan loved to sit and draw in the Place des Vosges, on the banks of the Seine or in restaurants, where she made quick sketches of the entertainers. She visited art galleries and bought the elegant clothes she liked so much.

She had always wanted to see the spring flowers breaking through the snow in the Alps, and, long before the tunnel had been constructed, we drove across the Great St Bernard Pass and down to Aosta.

It was with regret that I now left Shell to work for a large American management consultancy. I was assigned to Algiers to advise the government on the organisation of the oil industry. Whenever possible, Joan joined me there.

A year in apartheid South Africa followed, and Joan made friends in all communities: British, Boer, Indian, Coloured and Bantu. She volunteered to teach art in a Bantu training college. She provided all the materials and imbued the girls with her own enthusiasm. They loved her and continued to write to her long after we had left the country.

My next assignment was in Kuwait, and Joan joined me for an extended stay in the Sheraton. She soon made many friends in the local and international communities and went off to parties with her young Kuwaiti, Egyptian, Lebanese and American friends. She still found time to design a poster for the local theatre, advise on the restoration of the oldest house in Kuwait, redesign two flats for an American company and talk to the American Women's Guild on the conservation of old houses.

Returning to England, we bought a large stone house in the Golden Valley in Hereford, looking over the Dore and Wye Valleys to the Malverns. A mile or so away was an ancient village church. It might have been the country house of our dreams in 1944.

Joan now combined her love of art with her charitable work. She organised a large and very successful art exhibition in our house in aid of Sue Ryder and personally selected and arranged all the exhibits. The artists included four Royal Academicians who lent work that they subsequently exhibited at the Royal Academy.

She had, in the meantime, been proudly following the progress of our son as he was successively awarded an Exhibition in Mechanical Sciences by Emmanuel College, Cambridge University, an MA (Biological Sciences) by Oxford University and an MSc (Computing Science) by Newcastle University.

The house in Hereford was rather remote if I was away and Joan alone. We therefore bought a Voysey-style house in Sussex. Here, Joan created a large herb garden and formed the East Sussex Herb Society, of which she was President. It soon had a membership of 70. She also gave talks on herbs on Radio Brighton.

The Balkans war was now on, and Joan organised collections of clothes for Bosnian refugees. Every Christmas, she pressured supermarkets to donate clothes and food to a local women's shelter.

Following assignments in India and Gabon, we decided to settle down and bought a mellow hamstone house in Dorset, set in seven acres of untidy grounds.

This was Joan's favourite home, and she lovingly restored and redecorated it. She planted rose and herb gardens and surrounded the house with flower beds. She designed a solid maple dining table cleverly combined with an elegant ceramic hob, so that she could cook while talking to her friends.

Joan always had great enthusiasm for art, design, flowers, the countryside, cooking, theatre, clothes, poetry and, above all, friendships. Frequent travel prevented serious painting, but she loved sketching wherever she went. Her beautiful drawings hang around me as I write.

I am very grateful that she was able to realise so many of her dreams.

In 2001, Joan became ill, and no one could find the cause. I took her to see doctors all over the country and consulted doctors on the Internet as far afield as the west coast of America, all with no result.

Eventually, she decided she would like to be near our son, who was living in France. We bought a small house in a very peaceful location and with wonderful views.

For the last two years of her life, I was able to be with her all the time, including several stays in French hospitals, where I could sleep on a bed in her room. The French health service sent in-home nurses morning and night to ensure that she was comfortable. I read her favourite poetry to her every night until she fell asleep.

I was beside her in hospital when she died quietly in bed, still talking to me. It was 3 September 2006, her 86th birthday and the 67th anniversary of the outbreak of war.

She lies in a simple grave, carved from the white stone of the Lot. The tiny cemetery is set on a small hill overlooking one of the most beautiful villages in France. All around are wooded valleys and hills, and the silence is broken only by the song of birds.

The home of our much-loved son is on another hill, just a mile away.

# IO

# A LAST LETTER

My dearest Joan,

It is now three years since you left me, and the pain and loneliness are still as sharp as ever.

Writing this last letter to you brings back so many happy memories and so many regrets. It is strangely familiar: turning over in my mind the things I want to say to you, as I have done so many hundreds of times in the past.

When we were young the words and dreams flowed naturally. In very different circumstances, I must now consider carefully all the thoughts I would share with you.

When we were apart you often wrote of your wonderings: where was I, what was I doing, what was I planning for us?

Wonderings are now all I have to bring you back to me again. Where are you? Are you still aware of me? Do you forgive me my shortcomings? And, most of all, shall we ever meet again?

I once had clear beliefs in an afterlife, but, across the years, my certainty has diminished, until now I am lost between the hope of eternity and the fear that there may be nothing after death.

And, if we meet again, will you gently reproach me for the things in which I failed you?

Yet, as I look back over the many years we were together, I am happy that so many of our youthful dreams did come true.

We must have had our differences, but these were so insignificant that, try as hard as I can, I cannot remember what any of them were about.

But, in truth, none of this weighing and balancing is necessary. The simple and wonderful fact is that we were drawn to each other from our first meeting and that our love developed and strengthened in the crucible of our parting, until it became the most important thing in both our lives.

I am so very grateful that in your last few days you still felt able to say 'I *do* love you' and 'Thank you for looking after me'.

Thank you from my heart for all you meant to me, both during the war and in the more than 60 years that followed.

With all my love now and forever,

Tony xxxxxx